Darkness Visible

W. R. JOHNSON

❀❀

Darkness Visible

A Study of Vergil's
Aeneid

UNIVERSITY OF CALIFORNIA PRESS
BERKELEY   LOS ANGELES   LONDON

University of California Press
Berkeley and Los Angeles, California

University of California Press, Ltd.
London, England

Copyright © 1976, by
The Regents of the University of California

First Paperback Printing 1979
ISBN: 0-520-03848-7

Library of Congress Catalog Card Number: 74-30523
Printed in the United States of America

1 2 3 4 5 6 7 8 9 0

> ... yet from those flames
> No light, but rather darkness visible
> Serv'd only to discover sights of woe,
> Regions of sorrow, doleful shades, where peace
> And rest can never dwell. . . .
>   MILTON

> ... usque adeo taetra nimborum nocte coorta
> impendent atrae formidinis ora superne . . .
>   LUCRETIUS

CONTENTS

PREFACE

In writing these essays on the *Aeneid*, I have not aimed much at originality, and I have tried to avoid argumentation. What I have to say about the surfaces of Vergil's poem, about its narrative and stylistic modes, has been said or adumbrated by Pöschl, Otis, Clausen, Quinn, Anderson, Putnam, and other contemporary readers of Vergil who have worked hard and well to recover aspects of Vergil's poetic that have been lost or obscured both in the recent and in the not so recent past. I see this aspect of my work, then, as essentially concerned with the qualifying and modifying of emphasis of recent formulations of Vergil's poetic.

When I turn from the poem's narrative and stylistic modes to what the poem means, I naturally lose my equanimity from time to time: each reader feels that each of his favorite poems somehow belongs to him and therefore resents any intrusions into his private and special gardens. Even here, however, what I am mostly trying to do is to synthesize and mediate rather than to define and to prescribe. I am keenly aware that the *Aeneid* means all kinds of things, and I am also aware that the meaning or meanings that I find in it—though I am sure that they are present in it—are in some sense my own meanings, not because I have created them but because I, like other readers, select and emphasize them in a personal (but not subjective) way. What I am specially engaged in when I discuss the meanings of the *Aeneid* is to mediate between varieties of pessimism and optimism, and here too I am mostly elaborating the mediations and syntheses of Perret and MacKay.

The Greek texts for Homer are from the Cambridge editions of Arthur Platt (*Iliad*, 1894; *Odyssey*, 1892); for Apollonius the text is that of R. C. Seaton (Oxford, 1900). I am very happy to be allowed to reprint sections from Allen Mandelbaum's superb rendering of the *Aeneid*. (Berkeley and Los Angeles, 1971). I am very grateful to the Oxford University Press for its kind permission to use passages from T. E. Shaw's rendering of the *Odyssey* (1932). The versions of the *Iliad*, the *Argonautica*, and Longinus are my own.

It is a great pleasure to record my debt to T. G. Rosenmeyer, August Frugé, Frederick Williams, my wife Sabina, and my anonymous reader for their careful and kind criticisms. For the errors and infelicities that spurned their warnings and remain, they are not, of course, in any way responsible. I should also like to thank Elizabeth Block for her help in preparing some of the manuscript, Lois A. Benson for her extraordinary care in editing it, and all of my students in Comparative Literature at Berkeley for their grand enthusiasms and their fresh, bright minds.

Finally, I call attention to two books that I wish I had seen before my book was completed: J. W. Hunt's *Forms of Glory* (Carbondale, 1973), which offers excellent descriptions of Vergil's "unique fusion of triumph and regret," and Jean Pépin's *Mythe et Allégorie* (Aubier, 1958), which provides splendid descriptions of the nature of ancient allegory and is particularly rich in its meditations on multiple allegories.

ABBREVIATIONS
USED IN NOTES

AJP	American Journal of Philology
CJ	Classical Journal
CR	Classical Review
CSCA	California Studies in Classical Antiquity
CW	Classical Weekly
GR	Greece and Rome
GRBS	Greek, Roman and Byzantine Studies
HSCP	Harvard Studies in Classical Philology
JRS	Journal of Roman Studies
REL	Revue des Études Latines
TAPA	Transactions of the American Philological Association
YCS	Yale Classical Studies

I

ELIOT'S MYTH AND
VERGIL'S FICTIONS

. . . as every half-truth at length produces the contra-
diction of itself in the opposite half-truth.

D. H. LAWRENCE

Myth operates within the diagrams of ritual, which
presupposes total and adequate explanations of things
as they are and were; it is a sequence of radically un-
changeable gestures. Fictions are for finding things out,
and they change as the needs of sense-making change.
Myths are the agents of stability, fictions are the agents
of change. Myths call for absolute, fictions for condi-
tional assent. Myths make sense in terms of a lost order
of time, illud tempus as Eliade calls it; fictions, if suc-
cessful, make sense of the here and now, hoc tempus.[1]

It may seem an injustice that Eliot should be made to serve as the
instigator of a wild-goose chase that, in a sense, he only strayed
into and out of accidentally. But he cast himself as the defender
of the grand orthodoxies. He glories in that role, and so it is not
wholly unfair that he should be taken as a representative figure
when we examine the major approaches to Vergil that developed
during the age of Eliot, that period between the two wars (and a
little before and a little after) when Western civilization was lost
and reviled and recovered and sentimentalized with all the passion and imprecision that the millennistic sensibility is capable
of. My object in this essay is to sketch the fortunes of Vergil's reputation in the last century and a half with a view to showing that
the *Aeneid*, having been reduced from a poem to a myth, was first

rejected as a bad myth and then exalted as the good European (Western) myth, and that the habit of reading the poem as a political and cultural allegory (however much the debate over the meaning of the allegory alters its direction) persists to the present day, obscuring the quality of the poetry and limiting, disastrously, the range and depths of the poem. Having briefly surveyed the general outlines of this reductive allegorical approach to the poem and having described and assessed the results of this approach in its most recent flowering, I shall attempt to show how and why the *Aeneid*, in all the complexity and rich configuration of its multiple allegories and its dialectical movement, will not allow its living fictions to be transformed into a dead myth—into Eliot's *Aeneid*, the emblem of a vanishing, vanished world whose death the young Eliot announced and whose rebirth the middle-aged and elder Eliot, not to his discredit, undertook to fabricate. What follows may seem tendentious, frivolous, unfair. I can only plead that, having come to find that the myth of Vergil is as dangerous as it is unreal, I grow ever more certain that the fictions of Vergil remain as potent and as useful as they were when, out of the courage of his despair, he struggled to imagine them.

1

The history of how the *Aeneid*—or, to be more precise, the history of how the first six books of the *Aeneid*—became essentially a high-school textbook in the nineteenth century and in the first half of the twentieth century is a droll and complicated affair. The broad outlines of this story are fairly well known, but the significance of the story, for a variety of reasons, is generally ignored. Parts of its meaning are amusingly discussed by Ogilvie and brilliantly defined by R. D. Williams,[2] but so far as I know there is no methodical study of the entire story, perhaps because it is not only funny and complex but also faintly depressing. In the interests of brevity and at the risk of oversimplification, I suggest that the major reasons for the demotion of the *Aeneid* from a great living epic to the role of co-drudge with Xenophon, Nepos, and the *Gallic Wars* were Homer *redivivus* (again) and the Romantics, poets and professors alike (it was once the fashion for young living professors to read the work of recently dead poets). Vergil's main problem after the French Revolution was that he was clearly the darling of the neoclassical establishment. The late eighteenth-century Homer, on the other hand, a dim adumbration of our free-spirited Yugoslavian minstrels, did not have the misfortune of being literate, and he was not intimately connected with Roman Europe. This Homer, however he changed in the course of the Romantic generations, was here to stay; and Vergil, standard-bearer of the hated old order, had to go.

The French and the Italians (and, because of cultural lag, the Americans) remained tepidly loyal to Vergil, but the English and the Germans had no vested interest in the myth of *Roma aeterna* and, delighted by the final failure of the Latin Middle Ages (the vernacular Middle Ages were rediscovered along with the un-latinized Homer), they shifted their gaze from the exhausted and oppressive rubble of Rome and the ruins of Aquinas' Paris to the old, new glories of the Acropolis. There is a fresh dry irony in the fact that the teen-age Nietzsche was just about to enter high school as Matthew Arnold was giving his inaugural address, "The Modern Element in Literature," from the Chair of Poetry at Oxford; for different as these two poets were in temperament, achievement, and destiny, it tingles one's spine to hear the words, though not of course the music, of Nietzsche's Hellenic revelations in the staid accents of the Scholar-Gypsy on his best behavior:

> Now, the peculiar characteristic of the highest literature—the poetry—of the fifth century in Greece before the Christian era, is its *adequacy*; the peculiar characteristic of the poetry of Sophocles is its consummate, its unrivalled *adequacy*; that it represents the highly developed human nature of that age—human nature developed in a number of directions, politically, socially, religiously, morally developed—in its completest and most harmonious development in all these directions; while there is shed over this poetry the charm of that noble serenity which always accompanies true insight. If in the body of the Athenians of that time there was, as we have said, the utmost energy of mature manhood, public and private; the most entire freedom, the most unprejudiced and intelligent observation of human affairs—in Sophocles there is the same energy, the same maturity, the same freedom, the same intelligent observation; but all of these idealized and glorified by the grace and light shed over them from the noblest poetical feeling. And therefore I have ventured to say of Sophocles that he 'saw life steadily, and saw it whole.' Well may we understand how Pericles —how the great statesman whose aim it was, it has been said, 'to realize in Athens the idea which he had conceived of human greatness' and who partly succeeded in his aim—should have been drawn to the poet whose works are the noblest reflection of his success.

Some of what Arnold is saying here is that Pericles could qualify as Victoria's prime minister, and that he and Sophocles and lots of their contemporaries could wear the school tie without dishonoring it, mingle without indecorum with other old boys. "Adequacy" is obviously a key word in this passage, as it is throughout Arnold's lecture, and to "adequacy" we shall turn in a moment; other key words are "energy," "maturity" (a word that we shall see on prominent display in Eliot's lecture on Vergil), "freedom," and "intelligence." Nietzsche will be focusing on the same concepts some fifteen years later, and he will be pinning his argument about the insuperable greatness of the pre-Socratic Greeks on the same texts—Aeschylus, Sophocles, and Thucydides —the last of whom Arnold deems the perfect historian for Pericles and his achievement, even as he finds Sophocles the perfect poetic celebrant of Periclean grandeur. But the sickly German recluse will see more clearly than the muscular English Christian what "the utmost energy of manhood" meant in fifth-century Athens. In his cultivated self-deception, Arnold worshipped the will to power under the illusion that he was merely paying homage to the ideals and the realities of "human greatness." Whatever illusions Nietzsche labored under—and when he was at his best (which was astonishingly often) they were few—the realities of the imperial sensibility did not moisten his eyes when the trumpets and the drums played *dulce et decorum.* Nietzsche did not read his Thucydides sentimentally, and he, like Milton (though obviously for very different reasons), knew that alliances between pagan and Christian culture were few, delicate, and uncertain. But Arnold, who is pagan *malgré-lui* and unawares, is as busy as Nietzsche in welcoming the modern, that is to say, the post-Christian and neo-pagan era. For this new world Arnold, like Nietzsche, finds abundant models in Periclean Athens; unlike Nietzsche, who liked Rome only for Horace and for Sallust (who furnished the equipment for French epigrammatic style), Arnold is willing to admit that the Rome of Cicero and Augustus is very modern indeed, is perhaps even more modern than fifth-century Athens: it shows vividly "the utmost energy of mature manhood" in combination with "cultivation of mind and intelligence"; it qualifies, that is to say, as a successful empire. But the literature of Rome, unlike the literature of Periclean Athens, is inadequate to its modern greatness. Lucretius, for instance, frequently manifests "depression and ennui" (is he thinking of the dreadful things that are being written, across the Channel, in Paris?), and so he is modern, but in a wrong, negative way. "Yes, Lucretius is modern;

but is he adequate? And how can a man adequately interpret the activity of his age when he is not in sympathy with it? Think of the varied, the abundant, the wide spectacle of Roman life in his day; think of the fulness of occupation, its energy of effort." Yes; read Lily Ross Taylor; then think of the spectacle; then reread Lucretius. But let us pass from Arnold's scoutmasterly condemnation of the Lucretian exhortation to *lathe biōsas* to his evaluation of the adequacy of Vergil:

> Over the whole of the great poem of Virgil, over the whole *Aeneid*, there rests an ineffable melancholy; not a rigid, a moody gloom, like the melancholy of Lucretius: no, a sweet, a touching sadness, but still a sadness; a melancholy which is at once a source of charm in the poem, and a testimony of its incompleteness. Virgil, as Niebuhr has well said, expressed no affected self-disparagement, but the haunting, the irresistible, self-dissatisfaction of his heart, when he desired on his death-bed that his poem might be destroyed. A man of the most delicate genius, the most rich learning, but of weak health, of the most sensitive nature, in a great and overwhelming world; conscious, at heart, of his inadequacy for the thorough spiritual mastery of that world and its interpretation in a work of art; conscious of this inadequacy—the one inadequacy, the one weak place in the mighty Roman nature! This suffering, this graceful-minded, this finely gifted man is the most beautiful, the most attractive figure in literary history; but he is not the adequate interpretor of the great period of Rome.

This is, of course, the kiss of death. I do not mean that Arnold is singly responsible for the decline of Vergil's reputation, nor do I think that his diagnosis of Vergil's "weakness" is altogether incorrect, since in my final chapter I shall be saying rather similar things, though for quite different reasons. Nor should we take occasion to wax merry over the follies of British imperialism; it is hardly the place of an American to castigate another nation's dreams of glory, since if Americans can read "The Modern Element in Literature" and see what Arnold's comparisons between Periclean Athens and Victorian England really mean, and are chilled by what they read, it is only because we too are the people our parents warned us about.

I emphasize Arnold's lecture for two reasons. First, Arnold clearly frames an attitude toward the *Aeneid* that was popular for more than a century, and he is representative of a majority opinion that, though it was seldom voiced so elegantly or so shrewdly, was not effectively countered by voices from the minority until

Klingner, Büchner, Pöschl, and Otis.[3] Second, if Arnold is wrong here, he has nevertheless seen, however dimly, the heart of the matter. In its negative way, his judgment on, and description of, Vergil's poem foreshadows the findings of a major contemporary school of Vergilian criticism. Members of this school, to whose views I shall presently turn, also find Vergil's epic essentially melancholy and his world overwhelming, but they nevertheless find Vergil, because of his special gifts and special limitations, as adequate to his world as any poet can be.

Since Arnold had found Vergil inadequate to the task of expressing the greatness of the Roman Empire, Eliot, who both loved and resented the sage whose mantle he spent most of his adult life snatching and donning, naturally found that Vergil was adequate not only to expressing the greatness of the Roman Empire but also to defining the greatness of Western civilization. In other words, both in "What Is a Classic?" and in "Vergil and the Christian World," Eliot restores Vergil to the position from which Arnold had carefully exiled him. These two essays are not samples of Eliot's most inspired criticism (I at least can find nothing in them that is not more passionately and more precisely said by Haecker in his *Vergil, Vater des Abendlands*, a book which Eliot conspicuously praises in the second of these essays[4]), but they were delivered and published at a time when Eliot's reputation was at its zenith and when his audience was as captivated as it was enormous. His fans in the forties, old and new alike, were doubtless more interested in the man who had written *The Wasteland* and *A Cooking Egg* than they were in the prophet who recalled them to kneel at the Mantuan's shrine, but German critics were more than merely polite in their reception of Eliot's remarks on Vergil. Here was the Urwastelander himself, proudly displaying some of the fragments he had come upon in his retreat from modernism, lifting up the *Aeneid* on his shoulders as he struggled onward toward the twenty-first century. This was something to write home to the learned journals about. This was a catch. Büchner and Pöschl, both of whom were at this time engaged in serious and fruitful reevaluations of the *Aeneid,* record Vergil's readmission into the ranks of the blessed with solemn thanksgiving.[5] Büchner and Pöschl had not learned anything new from Eliot; they found nothing useful in him that they could not have found in Haecker. So they ignore the fantastic fudge that makes up most of what he has to say about Vergil ("A classic can only occur when a civilization is mature; when a language and a literature are mature; and it must be the work of a mature mind," etc.) and concentrate their attention on the conclusions rather than the proofs: "Virgil acquires the centrality of the unique classic; he is at the centre of European civilization, in a position which no other poet can share or usurp. The Roman Empire and the Latin language were not any empire and language but an empire and a language with a unique destiny in relation to ourselves; and the poet in whom that Empire and that language came to consciousness and expression is a poet of unique destiny." Home run with the bases loaded! This is what Büchner and Pöschl needed: a living and authentic *Weltdichter* vouching for the authenticity of a dead, and in recent times dubious, *Weltdichter*. Homer, Sophocles, and Pericles, it turned out, had not ushered us into the twentieth century. Maybe our grandfathers had got it wrong. Maybe we should read about *labor* and *pietas* for ourselves.

Down, malice, down! Even if we grant that this is Eliot not at his best, the instinct of the German critics in focusing on Eliot's re-affirmation was both natural and correct, nor was Eliot's act of homage foolish. In his remarks on Vergil he addresses himself to a problem that inevitably engrossed the attention of Western intellectuals (and particularly European, as opposed to American and Soviet, intellectuals) after the end of World War II. How was Europe to become reunified in the aftermath of what seemed, and very probably was, the most massive disintegration it had suffered in many centuries? The center had not held—had, in fact, failed to hold disastrously. Where was a new center to be found? The question is not really a literary one, and Eliot obscures the question by giving it a literary answer (that obscuring is essentially the subject of my essay since by obscuring the political question he obscures the poem), but Eliot was, after all, a literary man and literary answers were what he had to give. Vergil had guided Dante; Dante, through the late twenties, through the thirties, and into the forties had guided Eliot. So, in the hour of supreme crisis, it is not strange to find Eliot announcing that it is Vergil who stands at the center of European civilization, and it is not strange to find, so wild are the changes, the super Englishman reaffirming the primacy of the Roman Empire and the Latin language. It is clear that politicians and financiers were not much interested in what Eliot had to say about Vergil; even the younger generation of modernists (Sartre, for example, and even the young Auden—but the case of Auden would soon begin to change) seem not to have paid attention to Eliot's call for unity. But for European classicists—and particularly for German classicists—Eliot's recommitment to Vergil, his reassertion of Vergil's central place in the image of Europe's essential and unending unity was a heartening and necessary event. Thus, though Eliot's lectures on Vergil may seem dated to us now, though they fail of the boldness and the precision that articulate his major critical essays, it is worth our remembering that when these fine German critics set about the task of reevaluating Vergil, it was Eliot's authority that they offered as an earnest of their own aims and methods because Eliot, at the height of his prestige, had said not merely to classicists but to the literate world that the greatness of Vergil's poetry was to be measured by the truth of his vision of *Roma aeterna*.

2

It is the nature of that vision, its truth or falsity, that has tended to engross the attention of Vergil's critics since the forties. This is, of course, an old concern for readers of the *Aeneid*, but the urgency of Eliot and his most sympathetic listeners seems new in the intensity of its almost audible question, What is Vergil also saying about the unity and the salvation of *our* civilization?[6] Many generations flatter themselves that they are the apocalyptic generation, and other generations who have found or thought that they have found the barbarians at their gates most likely read the *Aeneid* as Eliot and his listeners have been reading it. But the events of this century constrain admirers of *Roma aeterna* to temper their enthusiasm for *imperium sine fine dedi*, to pay more attention to the blessings of peace and to the *anima naturaliter Christiana* than to the grandeur of empire. In this reformulation of what *Roma aeterna* means, victory (and of course conquest) yields to "love of order" in a way that most Romans and even Gibbon himself might find somewhat maudlin. But beyond this softening, this christening, of the concept of Rome and her empire, this magnification of Vergil's own compassions and charities, the events of this century have caused some readers of the *Aeneid* to redefine Vergil's attitude to *imperium* in a quite radical way: what these readers have understood is that the problem is not so much that the barbarians are at the gates or even within the gates, but rather that we are ourselves the barbarians. Both those who trust in the concept of *imperium* and those who distrust and dread it even in its softer aspects have been forced to review the Roman Empire and Vergil's epic from a dizzy and frightening vantage point, from this planet in this century.

There are, then, at present two quite distinct schools of Vergilian criticism that seek to explain and to justify the *Aeneid* by constructing for it two radically opposed political allegories. The major achievement of the essentially optimistic European school has been to show that what had been taken as Vergil's chief defects might better be seen as his particular virtues. What had been named a slavish or incompetent dependence on Homer becomes in their hands a brilliant recreation, a thorough and fresh rethinking of Homeric problems and Homeric solutions. For them, the genre of epic is not so much artificially resuscitated by Vergil as it is reinvented. If, for instance, a constant complaint throughout the nineteenth and much of the twentieth century had been that Aeneas is a poor excuse for a hero, the European school counters that it is not a question of Aeneas' failing as a hero but a question of Vergil's rethinking the concept of heroism which was a process that entailed a distillation of post-Socratic ethical speculation and that implied some criticism of the Homeric concept of heroism. In Aeneas we do not have some paltry Hellenistic epigone, clumsy and frightened and embarrassed as he bumbles about in armor too heavy and too huge for him; rather, we have an authentic Stoic (or perhaps Epicurean, or Academic, or Pythagorean—the sect hardly matters) who struggles from the old, primitive code and the mindless, amoral jungle into the clear sunshine of the Augustan enlightenment: *humanitas, pietas, ratio, salus.* Not the old shame-culture or even the old guilt-culture; rather the world where conscience, compassion, reason, and free will matter. The tendency to emphasize the growth of Aeneas' resolve and character had begun at the turn of the century, but the achievement of demonstrating not only Stoic resolve but also pre-Christian sensitivity and compassion is (in modern times) a fairly recent one; this demonstration required, above all else, that the last six books of the *Aeneid* be read as carefully as the first six books had been read. When these later books began being scrutinized, Aeneas became less priggish, less stupid, more complex and his real dilemmas and his real inner conflicts came into sharp focus. In short, with the readings of this school we begin to glimpse profound tensions between the brutal nasty world Aeneas moves in and the virtues and ideals, which are as complex as they are strong and dramatic, that his character expresses; these virtues and ideals shine ever brighter as the darkness of the chaos that menaces him and what he stands for increases in the accelerated and violent tempos of the last six books of the poem. This gentle power that survives the onslaughts of darkness and disaster is a fit vehicle for the kind of empire that, in these readings of the poem, the *Aeneid* exists to celebrate. Thus, for Pöschl and the

9

school to which he belongs, Aeneas and his *muthos* are capable of signifying not merely a temporal equilibrium, a historical triumph of virtue over unreason, but also, in a way that all myths of empire require, a transcendental cosmic order; for in this reading of the poem, the political allegory is sanctioned by Homer's vision of the unity of nature as well as by Cicero's vision of the unity of the *civitas*.[7]

This philosophical epic, then, becomes a kind of compendium of all that is best in the poetry, history, philosophy, and theology of the Graeco-Roman world (a notion that is more elaborately defined by Knauer[8]), and in this way it becomes, as Eliot had hinted, the *Weltgedicht* without rival before or since. If Aeneas is less vital, less single-minded than Achilles, Hector, or Odysseus, well, that is because the concept of heroism changes constantly, and perhaps the concept that Vergil formulated poetically a few decades before the birth of Christ was more civilized than any concept that Homer could possibly have shaped (the Homer-Vergil debate sometimes rears its head in this reading of the poem, though usually in a rather oblique way[9]). If Vergil's style is less unified than Homer's, more charged with lyrical wavering, more prone to indeterminate clarities, well, that is perhaps because the world that Vergil has to express and wants to express is a more complicated and more subtle world than the world that was available to Homer. Finally, even if we grant that Vergil's poem is less dramatic than Homer's on its surface, that Aeneas and the other figures in the poem seem somewhat dim, somewhat overwhelmed by the vastness of the fate which moves them and toward which they move, well, that is perhaps because Vergil himself was fated to live and work in a crucial moment in Western history when History itself, the birth and death of nations, the concept of national destiny, and, finally, the high price of civilization, were questions that could at last be fashioned with a fair amount of precision. Such questions as these, at least in the forms that Vergil encountered them, could not be asked until a Thucydides or a Polybius had hammered them out of the harsh, intractable experience of Greek and Roman history, and, indeed, they are not questions that Homer would be likely to take an interest in, even if they could be explained to him. For Homer human action is not a progression in time and space but an aspect of things as they are in eternity, a vibrant *coincidentia oppositorum* that catches the light and holds it.

The studies of Vergil's inner and outer forms which reaffirm both the unique greatness of his poem and his role as a maker of the myth of Europe evidence precision and vigor of imagination that are almost unparalleled in contemporary Latin studies. This school of Vergilian criticism has ventured on a tremendously difficult task and has performed it with extraordinary success, so it is with real diffidence that I turn from the strengths of this school to its weaknesses. Those weaknesses can best be described by their being contrasted with the strengths of the somewhat pessimistic Harvard school.[10] In this reading of the poem the superior virtues and the high ideals of Aeneas are sometimes grudgingly allowed him, but he is in the wrong poem. His being in the wrong poem furnishes it with a kind of tragic greatness that calls into question not only the heroisms of Homer's poems but also Augustan heroism and indeed any herosim. The presence of the Stoic or the Epicurean sage on the Homeric battlefield creates a *concordia discors* that is clearly wrong for a celebration of *Roma aeterna* and evades any possible kind of good resolution to the conflicts the poem mirrors. The historical and the metaphysical stakes in this race between order and disorder are too high, and the hero, the order, and the disorder are all gathered up into, and at last devoured by, an implacable and unintelligible nihilism. It is worth noting that this reading of the poem seems to begin its real history at just about the time that Pöschl, Klingner, and Büchner were producing their important reevaluations of the *Aeneid*, but Brooks and, later, Adam Parry seem not to be listening to Eliot but rather to the news from the Left Bank or to Auden's *The Age of Anxiety*, that wild and scandalously neglected masterpiece which captures its era and outlives it. As politically sensitive as the critics of the rival school, these critics had read their Syme and their Taylor as closely as they read the front pages of their newspapers, and for them the value, much less the grandeur, of the Roman Empire was not taken for granted. For them Pöschl's version of the "Augustan idea of Rome," whether inside or outside Vergil's poem, was utterly problematic. What did Vergil think of Augustus? What did he think of the Roman Empire? Is he not, at the very least, ambivalent in his attitude toward the Augustan peace? Is the poem not considerably darker than Eliot and Pöschl had suggested?

This school's difficulties with the *Aeneid* as political allegory that celebrates not only Rome, but the Graeco-Roman concept of Cosmos as well, are nourished by a deep sensitivity to what Arnold had experienced profoundly but had misidentified and misnamed:

Vergil's "melancholy," his "sweet, touching sadness." Brooks, Parry, Clausen, and Putnam have all written telling descriptions of Vergil's infatuation with twilight moods, with blurred images, with haunted, half-enacted interviews and confrontations that disintegrate before our eyes just as we begin to perceive them. Again and again, and often on the edge of a sharply etched dramatic moment, clarity and conflict are sacrificed to *Stimmungskunst*, and the actors, now iridescent phantoms that dwindle into unrealities, dramatize only the fact of illusion. In place of Homer's clarities of scene and articulations of action, in place of "the healing centrality"[11] toward which those clarities and articulations flow, Vergil offers images and actions that promise completions and harmonies but that seldom deliver them. And the vanishing surface of the poem, the light and outlines that fail, the actions and the confrontations that end unachieved, faithfully reflect not only the political but also the metaphysical depths of the poem. For Pöschl and Otis and other critics of the European school, the order, the stability, and the goodness of the empire that Vergil imagines in the *Aeneid* are reflections of a Homeric, a Platonic, a Ciceronian cosmos wherein evil and the disorders that Juno sets in motion and of which she is symbolic are seen finally as part of a larger pattern, are seen, that is to say, not as evils or disorders at all. Pöschl and Knauer seem to think that an educated Roman of Vergil's time, having Homer, the tragedians, Plato, and Aristotle at his fingertips, will find strength and comfort in the great syntheses of the heroic age, the tragic age, and the final age of the Greek enlightenment. That is a possible way of looking at the meaning of classical humanism in Vergil's age, but the poised rationalism of Cicero's *De republica* needs to be balanced against the more pressed, more tentative, more uncertain tone of the late philosophical works. And we want to remember, too, how E. R. Dodds characterizes the last century B.C. in the final chapter of his *The Greeks and the Irrational*:

Many students of this subject [he is talking about astrology] have seen in the first century B.C. the decisive period of *Weltwende*, the period when the tide of rationalism, which for the past hundred years had flowed ever more sluggishly, had finally expended its force and begins to retreat. There is no doubt that all the philosophical schools save the Epicurean took a new direction at this time. The old religious dualism of mind and matter, God and Nature, the soul and appetite, which rationalists had striven to overcome, reasserts itself in fresh forms with fresh vigor. In the new unorthodox

Stoicism of Posidonius this dualism appears as a tension of opposites within the unified cosmos and the unified nature of the old Stoa.[12]

In respect of intellectual climate, then, it is possible to see in Vergil's time not an age of faith but the beginning of the age of anxiety that Dodds went on to describe. It is against these intuitions of a terrible dualism that the *Aeneid* should be viewed. Few readers of the *Iliad* today would seriously maintain that Homer's world is one of primeval simplicity, but the complexities of his powerful and dynamic world are gathered into an adumbration of the great affirmations of unity and intelligibility that we encounter in the classical moment of Greek philosophy. Vergil's world, on the other hand, prefigures (it does not affirm) a world where matter and reason and unity *may* be only illusions, where madness and discord *may* be the only realities, here below, in space and time.

It is with this aspect of the *Aeneid* that the European school has the most difficulty, toward which it shows the least sensitivity. If Aeneas is not only symbolic of classical rational freedom but is also himself, in his *muthos*, possessed of rational freedom, why do we last view him as a victim of the very anger and madness that he has so gallantly opposed throughout the poem? Has the champion of Western civilization triumphed? Over his foes, yes; over the immediate evils that Juno has designed, yes. But over what Juno is and wants and stands for? I think the general design and in particular the closure of the poem argue against Aeneas' victory over those evils.[13]

Buchheit, who has written what seems to me one of the finest works that the European school has produced, correctly sees that Juno cannot be written off as a minor aberrancy in an otherwise perfect universe and demonstrates that she is the central figure in the poem's structure, but he is nevertheless satisfied with her reconciliation with Jupiter and to Fate.[14] But that reconciliation, as I shall try to demonstrate in my third chapter, is fraught with difficulties, some of which I sketch briefly here. The curse that Dido puts on Rome will be fulfilled with a vengeance long after she and Aeneas are dead, and there is a special irony in Jupiter's prophecy of the Punic Wars in Book 10 (11–15):

> adveniet iustum pugnae (ne arcessite) tempus,
> cum fera Karthago Romanis arcibus olim
> exitium magnum atque Alpes immittet apertas:
> tum certare odiis, tum res rapuisse licebit.
> nunc sinite et placitum laeti componite foedus.

> The fitting time for battle will yet come
> (and soon enough without your hurrying)
> when savage Carthage will unleash its hate
> and ruin on the towers of Rome, unlock
> the Alps against them: then it will be right
> to rage and fight and ravage everything.
> Now it is time to stop, to give your glad
> assent to what I want: a league of peace.

For the cunning, malevolent fiend of the *Aeneid* has no connection but their common type-scene with the silly, charming, sensual lady of the *Iliad*. Hera's capitulation is real enough because her anger, or rather her petulance, is skin deep; but the anger of Juno, which is close to being the central theme of the *Aeneid*, is in her heart and in her blood; it cannot be altered even by the ritual of *evocatio* that Jupiter himself performs and that reads like a grim parody of Athena's transfiguration of the Furies in Aeschylus. No less sinister in this regard is the appearance of the Dira whom Jupiter sends against Turnus. The figure of Allecto, a kind of outdoing of Lyssa in Euripides' *Herakles*, is bad enough: the satanic in the service of the divine. But in Book 12, the satanic Dira at the throne of Jupiter is herself somehow divine, and this connection between the Dira and Jupiter lends to the closing scenes of the epic a peculiarly desperate horror—it is almost as if Jupiter himself had come under the spell of Juno. And feeling the horror of this perversion of justice and the savagery of the Dira's attack on Turnus, one looks back a few hundred lines to what had then seemed an innocently formulaic and rhetorical statement of *aporia* in the invocation to Jupiter:

> quis mihi nunc tot acerba deus, quis carmine caedes
> diversas obitumque ducum, quos aequore toto
> inque vicem nunc Turnus agit, nunc Troius heros,
> expediat? tanton placuit concurrere motu,
> Iuppiter, aeterna gentis in pace futuras?
>
> (12.500–504)

> What god can now unfold for me in song
> all of the bitterness and butchery
> and deaths of chieftains—driven now by Turnus,
> now by the Trojan hero, each in turn
> throughout that field? O Jupiter, was it
> your will that nations destined to eternal
> peace should have clashed in such tremendous
>   turmoil?

The question posed here neatly echoes the desperate question, the cry of anguish, with which the poem had begun: *tantane animis caelestibus irae?* There was no answer then; there is none now. Until the coming of the Dira, this question, like the first question, might seem merely rhetorical, and the universe of the *Aeneid* might seem the enlightened, free, and intelligible universe that a Plato or a Zeno bore witness to; after the coming of the Dira, these questions continue to sound and they will not cease: they reverberate with an endless disintegration of reality, with the dull despairing silence that haunts Turnus as he flees from sure destruction. And so the poem ends, with a taste of ashes and death, and one hopes that life is only a nightmare that we wake from, and we pray only that reality is at last unreal. This is not to say that Aeneas is not heroic in precisely the way that his champions claim him to be: he is a deeply humane and profoundly good man; he is also fearless and courageous, as powerful and as energetic as he is compassionate and gentle. But what this poem says is that, in a universe where Juno holds sway, even these qualities are not enough. It is a terrifying poem.

The major weakness of the Harvard school is, as I see it, that it is obviously rooted in our peculiarly contemporary brand of pessimism. It is hard to imagine how this reading of the poem could exist without the support of our agnostic and atheistic existentialisms. And it is therefore only too possible that such readings of the poem project back upon Vergil a taste for the cult of failure and for the sense of the absurd and the meaningless that ancients, even the ancients that Dodds characterizes so well, would have found all but incomprehensible. Furthermore, it is clearly impossible to ignore Vergil's very real (if qualified) admiration for Augustus, his hope for political salvation, his desire to believe in cosmic order, and, failing a strong faith in human nature, his reverence for human dignity.

So the debate stands—a sober, cautious celebration of human beings and the cosmos they inhabit countered by a deeply pessimistic lamentation for the human condition. I confess that I favor the second reading, chiefly because it tries to deal with the world in which Vergil shaped his fictions and does not project the symbolic world in the poem back onto the difficult world that he lived and wrote in. And I also admit that I am grateful for and deeply influenced by the first reading and am troubled by what I am sure are the uncertainties of the second. The question then is: Are we now trapped into choosing one over the other? Until recently I have thought so but am now increasingly tempted to say, A plague on both your houses. What triggers my skepticism about both positions and continues to nourish that skepticism has been precisely set forth by Jaspers:

> Visions of universal harmony can function as ciphers. Their beauty appeals to us at certain moments, but soon we come to question their truth. At all times two ciphers have been current. One is expressed in the philosophical view that the world and all things in it are governed by a fundamental harmony; the other, in the view that the world originated in deviltry and that its existence is a fraud. Both must be rejected. They are only to be taken as symbolic expression or as ciphers of a passing experience; apart from this they have no validity.[15]

I wonder if critics of both schools of Vergilian criticism that I have described have not been essentially engaged in attempting to fix and order their own moods about disorder and order by freezing the dialectical rhythms of this poem in the static shape of one or the other of Jaspers' ciphers. The question, Can our civilization be saved? is, I suppose, valid enough, and one can often understand why we are prompted to ask it with urgency and sometimes with more than urgency. But it is both unreasonable and unfair to Vergil to ask him to answer this question for us, and that, I submit, is what readers of the *Aeneid*, particularly in the last few decades, have been asking him to do. It is an unreasonable question to ask Vergil because Vergil does not know any more about the answer than we do; furthermore, when we ask this question of Vergil, we usually, by the manner in which we frame our question, predetermine the answer he will give us in an outrageously subjective way. Poets, of course, are not less vain than professors or men and women in the streets, and not a few poets, therefore, have succumbed to the temptation of giving their opinions on current events, thereby degenerating from poets into *vates* and bards. Dante certainly felt this temptation from time to time; Milton was not above it; nor was Goethe, nor Arnold, nor Eliot, nor even Ginsberg. Vergil was clearly tempted, yielded a bit too much, and then finally yielded no more; he defused the splendid, silly, dangerous myth and used what was left of the myth to make his somber and nourishing fictions.

3

ad evidentiam itaque dicendorum sciendum est, quod
istius operis non est simplex sensus, immo dici
potest polysemum, hoc est plurium sensuum; nam

alius sensus est qui habetur per literam, alius
est qui habetur per significata per literam.
                                    (Dante to Can Grande, 8)

For a clear understanding of what I am saying here, therefore,
you should know that this poem yields no single meaning;
rather, it might best be described as being *polysemous*, that
is, as being possessed of several meanings. For in its
literal aspect it offers one kind of meaning, but in its
metaphorical aspects (allegorical, moral, anagogical) it
offers another kind of meaning, which is manifested through
the literal aspect.

Littera gesta docet, quod credas allegoria,
moralis quod agas, quo tendas anagogia.
                                    (Nicholas of Lyra)

The literal portion tells the sequence of fictional or historical events; the allegorical tells what you should believe
to be true about the nature of reality; the moral tells what
you should do (and not do) in living your life; the anagogical
tells what the purpose of your earthly life is, the goal of
your pilgrimage through this world.

Few contemporary readers of the *Aeneid* would deny that the poem
is in some sense *polysemous*, but it is our habit, if not in fact our
nature, to make myths out of poems as we make myths out of
other realities—because it is easier and usually more comforting
to make myths than to think thoughts and to feel feelings accurately. Even when we are willing or eager to admit the complexities of *allegoria*, we want always to say, But, of course, the
real meaning of the poem is . . . .[16] It is this lust for the real
meaning, the real solution (as if a poem were a problem or even
a crime) that persuades us to forget that most great poems are
polysematic to an extraordinary degree and that whenever we ignore this fact we are probably about to turn a fiction (that is to
say, a polysematic configuration) into a convenient and probably
an intensely private cipher. In so transforming fiction into myth,
and into private myth at that, we all but make certain that we will
not, cannot hear much of what the poet is trying to show us or
tell us, or, beyond the showing and telling, prepare us for. I am
not arguing here against the truth or the uses of myth, but I am
insisting that myths, which are as dangerous as they are necessary
for the private religious life, belong to the chapel, the launching-
pad, the vegetable garden, the football field, the beauty contest—
in short, to the public and social religious life where the truths
that shape our existence can be recovered, believed, and lived in
order that members of the community can gain the patterns of

confidence necessary for the continuation and enrichment of human life in the society. Myths have no place in poems except as a part of the raw materials out of which the poetry is imagined by the poet. The use of poetic fictions is to exercise our spirits, to make us think and feel more precisely and more abundantly than we normally think and feel by reminding us vividly of the beauties and the hazards of our existence. When we reduce living fictions to dead, fake myths, we are perverting the nature of both myth and poetry, and we are cheating ourselves of the real blessings that myth and poetry, in their separate and very different ways, can confer on us. If we need myth in our lives (and we do, and one way or another we find it), we should go off to the mass, or the dance floor, or the playing field, or the county fair, or the Thanksgiving Day dinner table, or the golf course, or the stock market (in short, to the myth or myths of our choice), wherever myths are alive and well and beneficial. If we want the solace and the strength of religion, I suppose we learn to go into our secret names and learn to pray. If we want poetry we rush into the delights and dangers that the great poets have furnished us as pure gifts. But if we persist in trying to convert poetry into religion and myth, our sustenance will be ersatz ritual, ersatz theology, ersatz ethics, and ersatz politics. And we shall perish of real hunger from illusory food.

My partial remedy to the ailment I diagnose may seem feeble and inappropriate, but what I offer is the jingle by Nicholas of Lyra that I quote above. It is an easy matter to dismiss this doggerel as another example of scholasticizing drivel, but in fact the verses condense and adequately contain the wisdom of more than a thousand years of some of the best work in literary criticism that the West has known—I mean the allegorical schools from the Stoicizing Homerists through Philo and the church fathers, through the School of Chartres and Dante down to—whom? Spenser? When did the habit of enjoying polysematic richness get lost? When did readers (and writers) of poetry stop being beholders of the ineffable configurations and become mere detectives, sniffing and squinting, determined to puzzle out the riddle? In positing Nicholas' couplet as our stratagem against monochromatic solutions to the *Aeneid*, I am not, of course, suggesting that it or the views and methods that it condenses are right about literature or reality or life. Nor, of course, am I suggesting that Vergil could have intended or planned a fourfold pattern for his poem. But I am insisting that the benefits of the fourfold methods of interpretation offer an elegance, an economy of effort that accords with recurrent features of literary artifice and that provides a good defense against the reductive mythmaking that I complain of. But in recasting the contents of Nicholas' couplet, I am aware that I am trying to shape a tool for a particular purpose; I am not trying to reestablish a dead dogma to whose measure all fictions everywhere and anytime must fit, nor am I suggesting that this fourfold method explains the *Aeneid*. What it may do is to allow us to see this poem with a certain kind of accuracy. And when we have seen it from the perspective this method offers, we are free (must and should be free) to take what we have seen with us and reexamine it according to other categories and in other ways. All that the principle of multiple allegory ensures is that we will have considerable complexity to begin our work with, or, to put it another way, that multiple allegory, if we truly insist on the multiplicity, will not permit us to rest satisfied with false and reductive unity. With these qualifications in mind, then, I offer the following list of possible allegorical aspects for the *Aeneid*; the list is intended to be illustrative, not exhaustive, definitive, or prescriptive.

1. *Littera—Gesta*
    a. Aeneas' flight from Troy
    b. His wanderings
    c. His struggles to secure a new homeland in Italy
2. *Allegoria—Quod Credas*
    a. Origin and Development of Roman Republic and Roman Empire
    b. Renovatio Augusti
    c. Bella Civilia
3. *Moralis—Quod Agas*
    a. Progress of the Soul to Virtue
    b. Paradigm of Vergilian Heroism—Pietas, Fortitudo, Humanitas
    c. The Moral Dangers of Pietas
    d. The Effect of Ira on the Human Personality and on Communities
4. *Anagogia—Quo Tendas*
    a. Election of Rome by Jupiter and Fate
    b. Terror of History (here a metaphysical principle)
    c. Possibility of Dualism; Prevalence of Evil in Hoc Tempore; Illusion of Time, Space, and History

In the chapters that follow this one, I shall be concentrating on aspects of the *Aeneid* that show the strength and the resonance of 2c, 3c and 3d, and 4b and 4c, and I shall be tempted to speak, as an ally of the Harvard school, as though these themes were somehow blended into a single theme and as though that theme were quintessential to the poem. But if I were merely to do this, I should be attempting to dissolve the fictions of the poem into another myth, one that ignored the strength and resonance of themes 2a and 2b, 3a and 3b, and 4a. I accentuate the darkness of Vergil's fictions because the myth of light that is attributed to him is still so prevalent that his unique equilibrium of light and darkness, without which his poem becomes superior propaganda or remarkable melodrama, is destroyed. I am, then, chiefly concerned to redress a balance and have no desire to invent a myth of darkness and call that fabrication the *Aeneid*. And my hope is that the conspectus of multiple and interdependent allegories that I sketch will keep reminding me and the reader: that in the shifting patterns of polysematic fictions the separate themes illumine one another in new and different ways as now one and now another theme achieves a special prominence and as the various themes keep entering into new configurations with one another; that these fluctuations of emphasis and revolving views will not allow us to come to rest with optimism or with pessimism.

The *Aeneid* moves constantly in the dialectic of its polysematic configurations between these two poles. Unlike the *Iliad*, for example, it is not designed to achieve a synthesis from its countermotions, and it therefore moves out beyond the limits of its own arguments to a place where neither glad tidings nor dreadful news have any meaning for individuals or for nations or for humankind. Vergil's poem, then, is polysematic in two ways. First, at any given moment, one of its three allegorical aspects—or two or three aspects simultaneously—operates in shaping the literal aspect of the *muthos*, and much of the poem's resonance, as well as much of its peculiar elusiveness, is due to the constant variations and modulations of the patterns the allegorical aspects enter into. Second, within any given allegorical aspect, both its positive and its negative forms may be present at the same time. For example: in the scene in which Aeneas kills Lausus, both a postive (*a*) and the negative (*c*) connotation of 2 are present and interact with each other and with positive and negative connotations of 3 (*b* and *c*). This kind of thematic conflict and harmony is, of course, characteristic of much great poetry (any page of middle and late Shakespeare may show it, though most pages of other Elizabethan and Jacobean dramatists will not), but in Vergil's poetry this impartial interplay of opposites (it is not really a matter of mere ambiguity, irony, tension, double vision, or what have you) became central in the *Aeneid* (it is adumbrated in the pastorals and reaches a limited but formal perfection in the *Georgics*), and it is this final experiment with the strengths and limits of polysematics that gives us much of our pleasure in, and much of our difficulty with, this poem.[17]

The *Aeneid* is, as has been seen through the ages, a political allegory, but it is not merely positive in its political connotations, and it is no less a metaphysical and also a moral allegory. Not three allegories moving parallel, separate and independently, but three allegories moving interdependently, at once harmonious and dissonant, shaping iridescent fictions that force us to ponder for ourselves the shapes they configure. *Tis aēthēs krasis*, some extraordinary mixture—the phrase is by another master of allegory, Plato, describing another mystery that defies language that will not submit to the disciplines of multiple and interdependent allegory (*Phaedo* 59A).

> ... There is a dark
> Inscrutable workmanship that reconciles
> Discordant elements, makes them cling together
> In one society.

But as Wordsworth sometimes (inevitably) forgot, the "society" so formed remains unnamable and invisible and unknowable apart from the intricate reconciliation in which, and by virtue of which, it exists. If we call the "society" of the *Aeneid* a political allegory (or, what is the same thing, if we call it a symbolic poem about Rome and Augustus), we have not mere prose (there is no such thing as mere prose), but bad prose (which the *Aeneid* is not). The free and powerful fictions of Vergil's poem do not explain to us or resolve for us the problems of man's fantasies about bondage in time or his fantasies about freedom from time, but they bring the existence of those fantasies and the danger of those fantasies into clear focus. So far from existing for the sake of myths, which pretend to give us explanations of the human condition, the fictions of the *Aeneid* use myths to discredit myth's unwarranted and hazardous claims. It is ironic that a poem that has among its aims the banishing of myth should gain and hold much of its esteem because it is mistaken for a myth; but poetry has always been misused in one way or another and has survived, its integrity undiminished and its proper powers unbroken, and the *Aeneid* has survived and will survive the irony of being confused with its opposite. The unique interplay between courage and despair that enforms this poem is proof against all efforts to hear in its tempos and cadences only our own good luck or bad luck, to imprint upon the poem our personal guess about what reality is or means. The bold justice and the unpersuadable honesty of these fictions require that we learn to suspend our beliefs, to put aside our craving for final answers, and to learn, by experiencing and absorbing the exact impartiality of these fictions, to live with, to live richly with, our weakness and our ignorance.

What Vergil offers in this poem that other poets do not is a passionate, grieving, but uncommitted meditation on man's nature and on the possibilities and impossibilities of his fate. It is the free and open dialectic of Vergil's polysematic fictions that makes possible this kind of meditation, and we misread the poem and refuse the wisdom (it is not knowledge) that Vergil makes possible for us (he cannot bestow it on us) when we reduce his many allegories to one allegory and pervert his good fictions to bad myths.

II

LESSING, AUERBACH, GOMBRICH: THE NORM OF REALITY AND THE SPECTRUM OF DECORUM

1

Clearly, the more a painting or a statue mirrors natural appearances, the fewer principles of order and symmetry will it automatically exhibit. Conversely, the more ordered a configuration, the less will it be likely to reproduce nature. . . . An increase in naturalism means a decrease in order. It is clear, I think, that most artistic value rests among other things on the exact reconciliation of these conflicting demands. Primitive art, on the whole, is an art of rigid symmetries sacrificing plausibility to a wonderful sense of pattern, while the art of the impressionists went so far in its search for visual truth as to appear almost to discard the principle of order altogether.[18]

E. H. GOMBRICH

"The art," says Hofmannsthal somewhere, "is hidden on the surface." So it is the surface of Vergil's epic that must concern us before we try to figure out what Vergil's art is for or what it means. Yet it is clear enough that it is the surface that is somehow, of all the aspects of Vergil's poetry, the least easy for us to get at. It stares us in the face. We feel emotions rising from it toward us. We know ideas issuing from it into our minds. Yet the surface of the *Aeneid* is more invisible to us than the surfaces of Vergil's pastorals or his didactic poem. Syntax, sound patterns, imagery, sentence structure, figures of speech and thought, the personae that enact the poet's *muthos* and *praxis*[19]—all show a brilliance, a resonance, and, in general, an extraordinary significance that are at once utterly apparent, and, parodoxically, utterly impalpable. The sounds and images are so familiar to us because

they are—however transformed they may be at any given time—
so frequent in the later masterworks of European poetry, and it is
in part this pervasiveness of the *Aeneid*, the ubiquitous presence
of Vergil in his last perfection, that makes it so difficult for us to
go back to the initial surface and to see it with fresh eyes. For the
perfection of those reflections inevitably blurs the perfection of
their inspiration. So, in a similar way, now that Homer has been
gradually restored to us, we must address ourselves to the echoes
and the reflections of Homer in Vergil, the sights and sounds in
Vergil's recreation of Homer, and in doing so we must be careful
to perceive the differences and the similarities of echo and image as
precisely as possible.

This may seem very obvious, but I think it is not generally emphasized enough that we often risk reading Homer on the one
hand and Dante or Milton on the other into our Vergil when we
are in the act of reading Vergil. For, like any other major poem
which happens to be in a major tradition, Vergil's *Aeneid* is as
much in danger from what came before it and what came after it
as it is enhanced and magnified by its ancestors and its progeny.
The *Aeneid* is, for better and for worse, not only the artifact that
Vergil made but also, in part, the artifacts that Homer, Dante,
and Milton made, and this problem confronts us each time we
read this poem.

What concerns me in this essay, then, is to attempt to search
out and to define as accurately as I can such criteria as may help
in distinguishing the surface of the *Aeneid* from the surface of
Homer's poems. If we can do that more carefully than it has
usually been done in the past, we may have some hope of avoiding
the mistakes of reading Vergil as though he were somehow essentially an extension of Homer or of reading him as though he were
obsessed with the desperate, futile desire of wanting to be Homer,
or wanting to rival him, or surpass him. And if we could avoid
these mistakes, systematically, we might secure the benefit of al-
lowing the beauties of both poems to illumine and clarify each
other, without feeling called upon to enjoy one poem at the expense of the other.

One of the most difficult problems that a critic of the *Aeneid*
must face is that Homer's poems, in particular the *Iliad*, not only
seem to set norms for the epic genre but also perfect a particular
mimetic style that appears to be especially appropriate to the epic
genre.[20] Different ages see this norm and this style in different
ways, of course, and they value and name them in different ways.
Since the middle of the eighteenth century, there has been a steady

tendency to see and to prize the style of Homer's narrative and language as realistic. The reasons for this developing perception of Homeric verisimilitude are numerous and complex; for my purposes, I emphasize only the gradual rejection of neoclassical ideals and the rise of the long prose narrative and its eventual triumph as the favorite and the most significant of modern literary forms. In times and places where the most fruitful and exciting literary form is the novel, a poem like the *Aeneid* must inevitably come to seem artificial, rhetorical, or fantastic in exact proportion as the *Iliad* and the *Odyssey* (in different ways) come to seem natural, spontaneous, and true to life. Seem so, that is, to readers who have grown up with, and become accustomed to, the successful norms and conventions of the realistic prose novel (by "successful" I mean several things: I mean that many novels —good, bad, and indifferent—have given great pleasure to many kinds of readers; that many discerning readers approve of the aesthetic solutions the novelists devise for their novels; that novelists themselves can use these conventions for finding interesting problems and interesting solutions to those problems). Nor is the reader of Tolstoy or Scott who feels at home with the *Iliad* but not especially at home with the *Aeneid* mistaken in his feelings (or even in his judgments about his feelings), nor is the reader of Stendhal or Austen who feels at home with the *Odyssey* but not with the *Aeneid* mistaken either. For such readers the artifice, rhetoric, and fantasy of Homer—ubiquitous and powerful as they are; different as they are from the artifice, rhetoric, and fantasy of the great modern masters of realistic fiction—disappear because the modes of vision and the concern with plausible representation of Homeric poetry seem familiar to them, right and natural to them. Tolstoy and Scott, Stendhal and Austen have, of course, their own artifices, since no enjoyable work of literature can exist without some degree of linguistic dexterity and extraordinary imagination. But in these moderns, as in Homer, verbal magic and fantasy are adequately subordinated to (and, when necessary, utterly sacrificed to) designs that effect an illusion of "normal" space and time and that offer interesting and convincing collections of ordinary minute particulars selected from our daily existence; yet these plausible designs do not frustrate either our desire for unusual sensuous and emotional stimulation or our desire for an extraordinary degree of clarity and harmony in the arrangement both of universals and particulars.

In recent times it has been usual to call this kind of design "realistic," but in earlier times such a design was sometimes called "classical." When neoclassical writers, who were perhaps uncertain of themselves, began calling everything classical that was ancient—a singularly unclassical failure of taste and judgment—the word could no longer really connote this kind of design. Let us, for the moment say that Homer, Raphael, and Beethoven are classical. This does not mean that any or all of their contemporaries are classical. Or that the "period" they belong to or the synchronic language at their disposal is classical.[21] Periods and language cannot be classical because a classical work only comes into existence when a specific artist chooses to shape his design in such a way as to combine the maximum clarity and unity with the maximum iridescence and complexity. This does not happen very often in the history of any kind of art or of any nation. For some reason there is, indeed, a tendency for several individuals who live close to one another in time and space to decide to shape such designs, but we do not understand the reason for this kind of concurrent decision.[22] At certain periods there may be a feeling that this kind of art (this kind of design) is the most perfect kind of art, but at other periods there is no such feeling, and other kinds of art are found to be more satisfying to the people living in these periods.

We do not understand the reasons for these alterations in taste. In part they come about because human beings are given to frivolity and boredom. They like stability, but they can also learn to dislike stability, and they like to have ways of rationalizing their brief yet intense passion for change. One fairly plausible rationalization for changes in matters of artistic taste (it will not, I think, do quite so well for alterations in hairstyle or cut and color of what we wear or the look of what we live in or sit in) has to do with the notion of reality.[23] What kind of art does in fact render life as it is (or as human beings perceive it) most carefully? Does any "ism" fail to claim that it approaches the really real more nearly than its rivals; in other words, is not "truth" the spoken or unspoken formative principle of every artistic group or movement or school, even if they deny it? Can we imagine an artistic school that said, Our claim is to tell you lies, unless it added, Because reality is a lie? No, there is a constant tendency in poetry and painting (and it is so constant that one is tempted to call it a law) to want to, to try to, imitate or record or explain or reexplain reality. It is simply that what men decide is really real changes from time to time and from man to man and indeed sometimes in a single man. And as men alter their notions of what constitutes the real, they naturally learn to alter their ways of perceiving what there is to perceive. And so, when they seek to imitate or somehow record what they perceive, whether to help them to understand it better, to see it more clearly,[24] or to enjoy it more, they experiment tirelessly with different (not always new, sometimes old) ways of recording their perceptions in order to make their records accord as nearly as possible with their perceptions. This much we have some notion of. But we have no adequate understanding of what causes ideas and perceptions to change, and we can no more predict future changes than we can explain past ones.[25] What we know is that men want truth and beauty as much as they want food and sleep. How they get any of these things depends mostly on who and where and when they are—the variables are impossible to imagine, much less isolate and define. In terms of art or poetry, we can say that sometimes, for reasons we seldom know, human beings want their images to be extremely plausible and extremely clear, and sometimes they prefer that their images be, in some way or other, unclear, because they have come to think and feel that unclarity is more nearly capable than clarity is of representing what is true and beautiful. But when they desire stick figures or scumbled blurs they still want truth and beauty, are still trying to get truth and beauty.

Or to put it another way, sometimes Vergil is less popular than Homer; sometimes Vergil and Homer are more or less equally popular; sometimes Vergil is more popular than Homer. This does not necessarily say anything about whether Vergil's images and sounds are less or more significant than Homer's. It merely reminds us that we are very much ignorant of something that we would very much like to understand and perhaps never will— namely, taste and alterations in taste. And maybe it can help us to speculate on the possibility that Homer represents in European poetry a norm for plausible representation that Vergil used— was forced to use—in creating his own designs.

2

Homer does not paint the shield finished, but in the process of creation. Here again he has made use of the happy device of substituting progression for coexistence, and thus converted the tiresome description of an object into a graphic picture of an action. We see not the shield, but the divine master-workman employed on it. Hammer and tongs in hand he approaches the anvil; and, after having forged the plates from the rough metal, he makes the pictures designed for its decoration rise from the brass, one by one, under his finer blows. At last it is done; and we wonder at the work, but with the believing wonder of an eye-witness who has seen it a-making. . . . The same cannot be said of the shield of Aeneas in

Vergil. The Roman poet either failed to see the fineness of his model, or the things which he wished to represent upon his shield seemed to him not of such a kind as to allow of their being executed before our eyes. They were prophecies, which the god certainly could not with propriety have uttered in our presence as distinctly as the poet explains them in his work. Prophecies, as such, require a darker speech, in which the names of persons to come, whose fortunes are predicted, cannot be well spoken. In these actual names, however, lay, it would seem, the chief point of interest to the poet and the courtier. But this, though it excuses him, does not do away with the disagreeable effect of his departure from the Homeric method, as all readers of taste will admit.[26]

LESSING, *Laocoon* 18

I do not quote this passage from *Laocoon* at such length in order to mock it. If Vergil gets short shrift here, it is because Lessing is justifiably tired of watching the epigones of Scaliger revel in their total failure to understand what Homer is about.[27] Furthermore, not only in its originality but also in its zest and precision, this passage may be taken as proof, if proof were needed, that Lessing remains one of Homer's most imaginative and acute critics. And finally, as is often the case with fine critics, Lessing's misses are as useful as his hits. What he hits here, exactly, are the extraordinary action, the clarity of articulations, and the narrative unities—in short, the moving image of this passage in Homer. What he misses, but not quite, is the essential surface of the corresponding passage in Vergil, for, though he is properly aware of "the disagreeable effect of his departure from the Homeric method," and though he also senses the "darker speech" of what he not unreasonably terms "the prophecies," he does not sufficiently consider the possibility that the departure is intentional and the darkness calculated for ends other than those that engaged the imagination of Homer. Rather, Lessing assumes that the courtier has been forced to depart from the Homeric method because his highest priorities are not beauty, truth, and accurate mimesis but chauvinism and servility. To do him justice, Lessing does not see the evidence differently from some of Vergil's stoutest champions; it is simply that he interprets the evidence differently than they do and so is not tempted to prefer the claims of patriotism and history to those of good poetic craftsmanship. He does not, that is to say, make the mistake of supposing that the passage must be somehow possessed of beauty because its patriotism is sincere, or that it is good, even if it fails of adequate beauty, because it is patriotic.

Lessing's great achievement as a critic of Homer owes not a

little to his having absorbed the essential lesson of Longinus about the *Iliad*. It is not, of course, strange to find that Longinus is being enthusiastically and accurately read on the eve of a new manifestation and triumph of realistic method, but it is a pleasure to see the splendid insights of Longinus on the *Iliad* shining through the splendors of Lessing:

> when he wrote the *Iliad*, at the height of his powers, he produced a work that was, from start to finish, dramatic and energetic, while the *Odyssey* shows throughout a leisured and descriptive narrative style that is proper to a work of mellowed old age. Thus we may compare the Homer of the *Odyssey* to a sunset: though the grandeur remains, the power has vanished. For Homer does not have in his *Odyssey* the same forceful tension that is characteristic of the *Iliad*, nor the sublimities that never level off or dwindle to a stale steadiness, nor a deluge of constantly changing passions, the quick and varied tempo, the naturalism, nor the canvas crowded with, burgeoning with pictures of things as we see them and know them.
>
> Longinus 9.13

Longinus' list of the virtues of the *Iliad* sputters with rapture, sparkles, and is gone. The greatest literary critic who has survived from Graeco-Roman antiquity was not taken with his own impressions, had no time to squander on uncertain proofs and boring conclusions. His beast was in view again, and he was off again in hot pursuit of it. But Lessing loiters where this truth had been glimpsed, and many of the brightest and best passages of the *Laocoon* are the result of Lessing's patient siftings of the intuitions that Longinus had not the time or the temperament to scrutinize, and Lessing succeeds in establishing—to my mind beyond doubt —the complete veracity of those intuitions. Gloriously right, then, about the surface of Homer and his depths, but inevitably wrong, because of the way he phrased his questions, about most of Vergil's surface and all of his depths. But he moves near the central questions about Vergil's poetic in the *Aeneid* when he speaks of the darkness of the prophecies and the departures from the Homeric method. For Vergil does not offer, at his most crucial moments, purity of dramatic action (*to dramatikon kai enagōnion*), and he does not therefore use a method that centers on *tais ek tēs alētheias phantasiais katapepuknomenon* (crowded with images of things as they are). The center of Vergil's method and of his power is elsewhere, far from the actions and the clarities that Lessing understood so perfectly.

We have compared these two texts {the scar of Odysseus and the sacrifice of Isaac}, and, with them, the two kinds of style they embody, in order to reach a starting point for an investigation into the literary representation of reality in European culture. The two styles, in their opposition, represent basic types: on the one hand fully externalized description, uniform illumination, uninterrupted connection, free expression, all events in the foreground, displaying unmistakable meanings, few elements of historical development and of psychological perspective; on the other hand, certain parts brought into high relief, others left obscure, abruptness, suggestive influence of the unexpressed, 'background' quality, multiplicity of meanings, and the need for interpretation, universal-historical claims, development of the concept of historically becoming, and preoccupation with the problematic.[28]   AUERBACH, *Mimesis 1*

Some of the essential features of Homeric poetry that we find pinpointed by Longinus and carefully elaborated by Lessing are brilliantly reformulated by Auerbach in the passage that is quoted above where the clarities and the exact articulations are foiled by what Auerbach takes to be the countermodes of the Old Testament narrative. In Auerbach the analysis and the vindication of realism, as against neoclassical concerns for intellectual precision and rhetorical decorum, reaches its logical perfection. Since Auerbach's interest, unlike Lessing's and Longinus', is explicitly stated as being with realistic pictures and narrative articulations, we need not concern ourselves with the fact that it is the *Odyssey* rather than the *Iliad* that engages his attention, nor need we worry that Auerbach is not concerned with Longinus' "dramatic action." What we first notice in Auerbach's descriptions of Homeric methods is that the emphasis on realism that we find in Longinus and Lessing is now viewed as a central, if not the central, factor in Homeric poetic. What concerns us next about Auerbach's criteria for the Homeric mode as against the mode of the Old Testament is that the countermode of the Old Testament, as it is presented both in Auerbach's description of the sacrifice of Isaac and in his list of its defining criteria, suggests at many points a poetic and a list of defining criteria for that poetic that could as well be constructed, and that I shall attempt to construct in my third chapter, to define Vergil's poetic in the *Aeneid*.

I admit, of course, that Auerbach might complain that in suggesting certain analogies between his descriptions of Old Testament style and Vergilian style I am distorting the significance of his formulations. But as I see it, what I am attempting to do is not to condemn or to distort Auerbach's basic perceptions of

Homeric poetic and the Old Testament poetic that it contrasts with, but rather to modify and to qualify those perceptions in such a way as to correct what seems to me an erroneous conclusion that Auerbach draws from his examination of the two passages in question. It is incorrect to say, for instance, that "the basic tendencies of the Homeric style . . . remained effective down into late antiquity."[29] At least some of the basic tendencies of that style were ignored—if not in fact vigorously opposed—by Hesiod, and many of the major classical poets from Hesiod to the end of antiquity continue to ignore or reject the central methods of Homeric style, not for the reasons that Auerbach suggests when he admits that ancient poetry after Homer shows differing degrees of variation from the Homeric realistic style,[30] but for reasons that are so different and so complex that, even when we can make plausible inferences about them, we cannot gather them into a significant pattern. Hesiod and Euripides, Vergil and Lucan— widely as they differ in how they see reality and how they try to picture realities—are united in their apparent indifference to the supremacy of Homeric realism. Furthermore, though none of these poets has read the Old Testament, all of them use different combinations of mimetic techniques that Auerbach finds characteristic of Old Testament narrative technique. Finally, each of these poets, again in different ways, shows a marked preference for addressing himself to what is "dark and incomplete"[31] in the *muthos* that he has selected and because of such a preference enters into the labyrinth of historical narrative which Auerbach describes so well, a formulation to which we shall be returning frequently in our examination of Vergil's poetic problems and his solutions to those problems.[32] This concern for what is "dark and incomplete" inevitably renders narrative techniques that offer clarity and realism less useful than the techniques that Auerbach lists as characteristic of Old Testament narrative, where mimesis does not illumine for us what we ourselves see in our daily lives or shape and sharpen the focus of our vision or "bewitch us" or "make us forget our own reality for a few hours," but rather forces us to reexamine, indeed to criticize, "our own reality" which "it seeks to overcome."[33] The problems, then, that Hesiod and Vergil choose to try to solve and the solutions that they shape for these problems are closer to Auerbach's reading of the sacrifice of Isaac than they are to his reading of Homer, and for this reason Auerbach's attempts to make Homeric realism not only the norm but also the conventional practice for ancient mimesis are unsuccessful.

But there is another way of stating the problems that Auerbach is dealing with. Suppose that Hesiod and Vergil cannot always reach the Homeric norm. Suppose that the kind and quality of plausible representation that Homer achieves is sometimes impossible for these un-Homeric poets, not only because they are interested in emphasizing problems that do not interest Homer but also because they do not have the degree of mastery in realistic technique that Homer happens to have in such abundance. Suppose, that is to say, that Homer's realism is in fact a norm for the ancient world, but is a norm that few, if any, of the other Greek and Roman writers were able to achieve whenever they wished. In this sense, what Auerbach calls Homer's "simply narrated reality"[34] would turn out to be anything but simple, would turn out to be the product of the most elaborate and rigorous artistic discipline imaginable. If we take this position as the axis of inquiry, we no longer pit Homeric simplicities against Vergilian elaborations when comparing the two poets.[35] Rather we examine two different kinds of elaboration: Homer's, which issues in the perfection of realism that Longinus, Lessing, and Auerbach have, in their different ways, defined; and Vergil's, which, as I hope to show in my third chapter, tends often to exclude the methods of realism even when it might have employed them successfully. But it must be emphasized that it is not clear that Vergil (either because of the material he chose or because of his temperament or his talent) was always capable of realism. Let us now turn to two passages in Vergil, compare them with their Homeric parallels, and see how the means and ends of both poets—as evidenced in these passages—look when we juxtapose them and what light this mutual illumination can throw on the problem of Homeric "simplicity," which I shall take as an instance of Gombrich's norm of realism, and Vergilian "complexity," which I shall take as an instance of conscious deviation from that norm.

4

ἀλλ' ὅτε δὴ σχεδὸν ἦα κιὼν νεὸς ἀμφιελίσσης,
καὶ τότε τίς με θεῶν ὀλοφύρατο μοῦνον ἐόντα,
ὅς ῥά μοι ὑψίκερων ἔλαφον μέγαν εἰς ὁδὸν αὐτὴν
ἦκεν· ὁ μὲν ποταμόνδε κατήιεν ἐκ νομοῦ ὕλης
πιόμενος· δὴ γάρ μιν ἔχεν μένος ἠελίοιο.
τὸν δ' ἐγὼ ἐκβαίνοντα κατ' ἄκνηστιν μέσα νῶτα
πλῆξα, τὸ δ' ἀντικρὺ δόρυ χάλκεον ἐξεπέρησε·
κὰδ δ' ἔπεσ' ἐν κονίῃσι μακών, ἀπὸ δ' ἔπτατο θυμός.

τῷ δ' ἐγὼ ἐμβαίνων δόρυ χάλκεον ἐξ ὠτειλῆς
εἰρυσάμην· τὸ μὲν αὖθι κατακλίνας ἐπὶ γαίῃ
εἴασ'· αὐτὰρ ἐγὼ σπασάμην ῥῶπάς τε λύγους τε,
πεῖσμα δ', ὅσον τ' ὄργυιαν, ἐϋστρεφὲς ἀμφοτέρωθε
πλεξάμενος συνέδησα πόδας δεινοῖο πελώρου.
βῆν δὲ καταλοφάδεια φέρων ἐπὶ νῆα μέλαιναν
ἔγχεϊ ἐρειδόμενος, ἐπεὶ οὔ πως ἦεν ἐπ' ὤμου
χειρὶ φέρειν ἑτέρῃ· μάλα γὰρ μέγα θηρίον ἦεν.
κὰδ δ' ἔβαλον προπάροιθε νεός, ἀνέγειρα δ' ἑταίρους
μειλιχίοισι ϝέπεσσι παρασταδὸν ἄνδρα ϝέκαστον. . . .
ἐκ δὲ καλυψάμενοι παρὰ θῖν' ἁλὸς ἀτρυγέτοιο
θηήσαντ' ἔλαφον· μάλα γὰρ μέγα θηρίον ἦεν.
αὐτὰρ ἐπεὶ τάρπησαν ὁρώμενοι ὀφθαλμοῖσι,
χεῖρας νιψάμενοι τεύχοντ' ἐρικυδέα δαῖτα.
ὣς τότε μὲν πρόπαν ἦμαρ ἐς ἠέλιον καταδύντα
ἥμεθα δαινύμενοι κρέα τ' ἄσπετα καὶ μέθυ ϝηδύ·

(*Odyssey* 10.156–173, 179–184)

I was going down and was already near the ship when surely some
God took compassion on my forlorn state by sending a great stag
with branching horns across my very path. The sun's heat had
driven the beast from the grove where he had been feeding, down
to the stream to drink. He was coming up from the water when I
hit him in the spine, half-way along the back. My copper weapon
went clean through, and with no more than a sob he fell in the
dust and died. I put one foot on the carcass and drew my point from
the wound. Then I laid the shaft on the ground near-by while I
broke off and twined twigs and withies into a rope some six feet
long, well-laid throughout. With this I bound together the four feet
of my noble kill, passed my head through, and went staggering
under the load and staying myself on the shaft of my spear, down
to the ship. The burden was far too great for me to heave it to my
shoulder and balance it there with the disengaged hand as usual,
the beast being hugely grown. I dropped it on the shore before my
vessel and summoned each individual man with honeyed words.
. . . All heads came out from the cloaks; upon the edge of the sea
they stood to admire the stag, my wonderful great trophy. After
they had looked their fill they cleansed their hands and prepared a
glorious feast over which we sat till sundown eating the abundant
venison and drinking the wine.

Aeneas scopulum interea conscendit et omnem
prospectum late pelago petit, Anthea si quem

33

iactatum vento videat Phrygiasque biremis
aut Capyn aut celsis in puppibus arma Caici.
navem in conspectu nullam, tris litore cervos
prospicit errantis; hos tota armenta sequuntur
a tergo et longum per vallis pascitur agmen.
constitit hic arcumque manu celerisque sagittas
corripuit, fidus quae tela gerebat Achates,
ductoresque ipsos primum, capita alta ferentis
cornibus arboreis, sternit, tum volgus et omnem
miscet agens telis nemora inter frondea turbam;
nec prius absistit, quam septem ingentia victor
corpora fundat humo et numerum cum navibus aequet.
hinc portum petit et socios partitur in omnis.
vina bonus quae deinde cadis onerarat Acestes
litore Trinacrio dederatque abeuntibus heros,
dividit et dictis maerentia pectora mulcet. . . .

(*Aeneid* 1.180–197)

Meanwhile Aeneas climbs a crag to seek
a prospect far and wide across the deep,
if he can only make out anything
of Antheus and his Phrygian galleys, or
of Capys, or the armor of Caicus
on his high stern. There is no ship in sight;
all he can see are three stags wandering
along the shore, with whole herds following
behind, a long line grazing through the valley.
He halted, snatched his bow and racing arrows,
the weapons carried by the true Achates.
And first he lays the leaders low, their heads
held high with tree-like antlers; then he drives
the herds headlong into the leafy groves;
they panic, like a rabble, at his arrows.
He does not stay his hand until he stretches,
victoriously, seven giant bodies
along the ground, in number like his galleys.
This done, he seeks the harbor and divides
the meat among his comrades. And he shares
the wine that had been stowed by kind Acestes
in casks along the shores of Sicily:
the wine that, like a hero, the Sicilian
had given to the Trojans when they left.
Aeneas soothes their melancholy hearts:

Behind the customary modesty of Odysseus' reminiscences there lies the customary and irresistible swagger that, if it excludes him from the ranks of Achilles and Hector and therefore perhaps excludes his poem from the epic genre, makes him the model for high picaresque and high romance. Odysseus has done something moderately difficult—he has seen to the welfare of his men—and they are an appreciative audience for their leader's exploit. The realism of his braggadocio and his fake modesty enhance the realism of this carefully shaped picture of how he kills the deer, gets it ready for transportation, carries it back to his companions, and plops it down at their feet. One may wonder if Odysseus does not exaggerate the size of his kill, which he carefully emphasizes by repeating *mala gar mega thērion ēen* and by noting the re-action of his companions (*ek de kalupsamenoi . . . thēēsant' elaphon*), but if it is exaggeration, he renders it plausible by the skillful attention to the details of his story and their articulation. We take pleasure in his marksmanship, ingenuity, strength, and stamina even as we take pleasure in his sly boasting and droll humility because the picture he paints of his exploit is suffused with zestful verisimilitude. The story—whether it actually oc-curred as he claims it did, whether it was or was not as difficult to transport the stag as Odysseus says it was—exists to spotlight Odysseus the stalwart, inventive, considerate captain of men, and whether it is God's truth, cunning exaggeration, or pure invention makes no difference; it is a good story, very well told, and we believe it—that is to say, we feel it and see it, even as we see and enjoy Odysseus' self-esteem and guile and ironic self-effacement as he relates it. The passage, in short, for all its simplicity, is a marvel of elaborate naturalism and imaginative, subtle, psycho-logical description.

The corresponding passage in the *Aeneid* is a very different matter. That the slaying of the deer is narrated not by the actor himself but by the omniscient narrator makes very little difference, for when Aeneas himself narrates his story in Books 2 and 3 he shows no more interest in consecutive plausibilities than he shows in self-aggrandizement. Our main question about this passage is, How did Aeneas and Achates get the seven deer back to the ship, particularly since in the model, Odysseus had such trouble with one deer? Were the deer very small? Did Aeneas carry three and Achates four? Or vice versa? Did they summon help?[36] Readers who have been bred up strictly in the sublime may find these questions boorish, philistine, and frivolous. Yet the Homeric model is before us, and one wants to ask these questions because even sublimities and high seriousness are not exempt from common sense if their poet does not take the trouble to suspend common sense by issuing formal notice that it has been suspended (the Odysseus poet, by the way, is very good at giving such notice of suspension[37]). One answer to these questions—and I think that it is the correct one here and often elsewhere in the poem—is that Vergil is not as interested in plausibilities as he is in mood and background.[38] There must be a landscape for the figures to move in, and there must be a pretext for what is to come, a vacancy, so to speak, in which *o passi graviora* and *forsan et haec olim meminisse iuvabit* can achieve their fullest resonance. Homer's scene may be, indeed doubtless is, a typical stag-hunting scene composed of oral formulae, but the abstract types and formulae avoid an abstract and conceptual formalism and are brilliantly fleshed out with exact particulars in such a way that, as is usually the case with successfully controlled realism, we experience the universal through the particulars and our sense of the particular is heightened by our sense of the presence of the universal. In a highly stylized way, Vergil abstracts as many particulars as he possibly can from the typical scene and leaves us with its barest outline. The verses that picture this scene are elegant and austere, distilled to a bare essence that magnifies, for there is nothing to distract us from, the gravity and magnificent pathos of Aeneas' *sententiae*. Vergil has imagined an elemental moment of despair and recovery from despair with extraordinary economy and power by excluding Homeric clarities and actualities in favor of an ideal and abstract design that can frame an ideal and abstract emotion. It would be incorrect to say that this segment of narrative exists only for the sake of the emotions that are expressed in Aeneas' speech to his men, but it would be more correct to say this than to say that the emotions exist for the sake of the story or for imitation of realities. It is probably not too much to say that in Homer everything tends to exist for the sake of the story, for the sake of the visible *muthos* through which we see the else invisible *praxis*; and it is probably not too much to say that in Vergil the *muthos* frequently exists for the sake of something beneath its surfaces and beyond its limits. But such speculations take us from our present concerns. What interests us about Aeneas as hunter is that Vergil designs the scene by excluding[39] *to politikon, to dramatikon*, and *to enagōnion* as completely as this is possible for ancient narrative poetry.[40]

But Vergil has another way of evading realism when he does

not want or need it (or cannot achieve it), when realism would jeopardize the representation he is trying to achieve. Instead of giving us not enough in the way of physical detail or psychological motivation, he gives us rather too much of them. Let us look now at how Homer and Vergil handle the mimesis of erotic compulsion: Helen in Book 3 of the *Iliad* and Dido in Book 1 of the *Aeneid*. The closest model for what Vergil does with Dido is to be found in Apollonius, *Argonautica* 3, but what Vergil has done with the Dido passage and how he handled the Apollonian model can best be appreciated, I think, after we have clearly in mind the Homeric norm.

Aphrodite snatches up Paris from the battlefield, deposits him safely in his house in Troy, then goes to fetch Helen for him. Disguised as an old woman, a weaver, she approaches Helen and summons her, in Paris' name, to her Trojan husband.

> ὡς φάτο, τῇ δ' ἄρα θυμὸν ἐνὶ στήθεσσιν ὄρινε.
> καί ῥ' ὡς οὖν ἐνόησε θεᾶς περικαλλέα δειρὴν
> στήθεά θ' ἱμερόεντα καὶ ὄμματα μαρμαίροντα,
> θάμβησέν τ' ἄρ' ἔπειτα ϝέπος τ' ἔφατ' ἔκ τ' ὀνόμαζε·
> δαιμονίη, τί με ταῦτα λιλαίεαι ἠπεροπεύειν;

$$(3.395–399)$$

Thus she spoke, and her words made the heart in Helen's breast tremble. And when Helen perceived the goddess' matchless throat, her delightful breasts, and her glistering eyes, she was astonished and spoke out, calling upon her: Fantastic Being, why do you so crave to delude me?

Helen then proceeds to remonstrate with Aphrodite for her foolish suggestion and to suggest that the goddess herself become Paris' playmate. In short, she angrily refuses to comply with the goddess' demand.

> τὴν δὲ χολωσαμένη προσεφώνεε δῖ' Ἀφροδίτη·
> "μή μ' ἔρεθε, σχετλίη, μὴ χωσαμένη σε μεθήω,
> τὼς δέ σ' ἀπεχθήρω ὡς νῦν ἔκπαγλ' ἐφίλησα,
> μέσσῳ δ' ἀμφοτέρων μητίσομαι ἔχθεα λυγρά,
> Τρώων καὶ Δαναῶν, σὺ δέ κεν κακὸν οἶτον ὄληαι."
> ὡς ἔφατ' ἔδϝεισεν δ' Ἑλένη, Διὸς ἐκγεγαυῖα,
> βῆ δὲ κατασχομένη ϝεανῷ ἀργῆτι φαεινῷ,
> σιγῇ, πάσας δὲ Τρῳὰς λάθεν· ἦρχε δὲ δαίμων.
> αἱ δ' ὅτ' Ἀλεξάνδροιο δόμον περικαλλέ' ἵκοντο,
> ἀμφίπολοι μὲν ἔπειτα θοῶς ἐπὶ ϝέργα τράποντο,
> ἡ δ' εἰς ὑψόροφον θάλαμον κίε δῖα γυναικῶν.

τῇ δ' ἄρα δίφρον ἑλοῦσα φιλομμειδὴς Ἀφροδίτη
ἀντί' Ἀλεξάνδροιο θεὰ κατέθηκε φέρουσα·
ἔνθα καθῖζ' Ἑλένη, κούρη Διὸς αἰγιόχοιο,
ὄσσε πάλιν κλίνασα, πόσιν δ' ἠνίπαπε μύθῳ·

(3.413–427)

And bright Aphrodite cried out to Helen in fury: "Do not try my patience, you miserable fool, or I shall lose my temper with you and abandon you, shall come to loathe you as much as now I cherish you, shall design dreadful hatred for you, and you be crushed horribly in the collision of Greeks and Trojans." Thus she spoke, and Helen, daughter of Zeus, was terrified, and, wrapping herself in her white gleaming cloak, she moved forth in silence, unseen by the women of Troy, and the divine and sinister being guided her going. And when they came to the exquisite mansion of Alexander, the serving women went quickly to their tasks, but Helen, bright among women, moved to the lofty bedchamber, and Aphrodite, she who delights in laughter, took up a chair, goddess though she was, and brought it forward and placed it opposite Alexander. And on the chair sat Helen, daughter of Zeus of the Shield, and she would not look at her husband, and she began to rebuke him.

She begins in derision; challenges him to go forth and fight with Menelaus; then bethinks herself:

ἀλλά σ' ἐγώ γε
παύεσθαι κέλομαι, μηδὲ ξανθῷ Μενελάῳ
ἀντίβιον πόλεμον πολεμιζέμεν ἠδὲ μάχεσθαι
ἀφραδέως, μή πως τάχ' ὑπ' αὐτοῦ δουρὶ δαμήῃς.

(3.432–436)

But no, no, I beg you to desist, beg you not to fight with fair-haired Menelaus, nor contend with him foolishly, for I fear you might soon be mastered by his spear.

Paris answers her briefly with a plausible excuse for his behavior, expresses his amorous intent with suitable gallantry and guile, and takes her to his bed.

at Cytherea novas artes, nova pectore versat
consilia, ut faciem mutatus et ora Cupido
pro dulci Ascanio veniat donisque furentem
incendat reginam atque ossibus implicet ignem.

(1.657–660)

At Venus Ascanio placidam per membra quietem
inrigat et fotum gremio dea tollit in altos

38

Idaliae lucos, ubi mollis amaracus illum
floribus et dulci adspirans complectitur umbra.

(1.691–694)

mirantur dona Aeneae, mirantur Iulum
flagrantisque dei vultus simulataque verba
pallamque et pictum croceo velamen acantho.
praecipue infelix, pesti devota futurae,
expleri mentem nequit ardescitque tuendo
Phoenissa et pariter puero donisque movetur.
ille ubi complexu Aeneae colloque pependit
et magnum falsi implevit genitoris ə morem,
reginam petit. Haec oculis, haec pectore toto
haeret et interdum gremio fovet, inscia Dido,
insidat quantus miserae deus. At memor ille
matris Acidaliae paulatim abolere Sychaeum
incipit et vivo temptat praevertere amore
iam pridem resides animos desuetaque corda.

(1.709–722)

nec non et vario noctem sermone trahebat
infelix Dido longumque bibebat amorem. . . .

(1.748–749)

But in her breast the Cytherean ponders
new stratagems, new guile: that Cupid, changed
in form and feature, come instead of sweet
Ascanius and, with his gifts, inflame
the queen to madness and insinuate
a fire in Dido's very bones.

But Venus pours upon Ascanius
a gentle rest. She takes him to her breast
caressingly; and as a goddess can,
she carries him to her Idalium
where, in high groves, mild marjoram enfolds him
in flowers and the breath of its sweet shade.

They marvel at Aeneas' gifts, at Iülus—
the god's bright face and his fictitious words—
and at the cloak, the veil adorned with saffron
acanthus borders. And above all, luckless
Dido—doomed to face catastrophe—
can't sate her soul, inflamed by what she sees;
the boy, the gifts excite her equally.

And he pretends to satisfy a father's
great love by hanging on Aeneas' neck
in an embrace. Then he seeks out the queen.
Her eyes cling fast to him, and all her heart;
at times she fondles him upon her lap—
for Dido does not know how great a god
is taking hold of her poor self. But Cupid,
remembering his mother, Venus, slowly
begins to mist the memory of Sychaeus
and with a living love tries to surprise
her longings gone to sleep, her unused heart.

So the luckless Dido
drew out the night with varied talk. She drank
long love. . . .

These passages are admittedly very different in function and in
tone, but what I want to emphasize in juxtaposing them is the
dramatic, externalized representation of erotic compulsion in
Homer's passage as against the blurred uncertainties in Vergil's
passages. The beauty of Homer's invention lies in the argument
between Aphrodite and Helen, which ends with the angry goddess
leading the terrified woman back to the lover she does not want
or thinks she does not want. The scene of confrontation ends with
a hushed and sinister rallentando: out of all the complexity and
vehemence of the emotions comes a superb solution—radiant,
haunting, and terrible: *hos ephat' . . . ērche de daimōn.* The beauty
of Helen melts with the beauty of the goddess, and the utter silence
of their going and the radiance of the clothing are gathered into
the fateful word, *daimōn*, the unanthropomorphic terrible divine.
But no less beautiful and no less clear and intelligible are the
economy and realism of our final view of the goddess in this scene,
when she pushes forward the chair for her victim to sit in. It is
the sudden presence of the chair, delicately expressing the mocking solicitude of the awful deity for her victim, that leavens the
whole passage, naturalizes it, completes its growing plausibility.
The supernatural interference has been modulated into a familiar
commonplace setting (*to politikon*). In this setting, the conver-
sation between Helen, unpersuaded but obedient, and Paris, apol-
ogetic but lustful, can complete this imagination of erotic compulsion. The action has been sinister, dramatic, vaguely touched
with mystery but has been gathered finally into the common light
of day. Despite the complexities of Helen's feelings, what she is
doing and why she is doing it become fairly clear to us because

her action and her motives have been unfolded before us in realistic speech, in economical and graceful pictures, and the divine intervention, fearful as it may be, is no less intelligible than the human action that it influences. Even the irreconcilable feelings of Helen toward Paris, which are as deep as they are violent and conflicting, even that complexity is illumined for a moment, when her angry taunt—No, don't fight him; you're weaker than he by far; he'll kill you—dies on her lips, because her ironic mocking concern for his safety becomes, as her submission shows, unironic. The woman hates and loves, and this is what Homer's picture, mostly because of the divine intervention, is able to show. Something complicated has been rendered intelligible without being simplified. Exact selection of detail and precision of emphasis combine to help us imagine the divine without diluting its grandeur and power and to imagine the effect of that grandeur and power on human action without destroying our sense of the human, that is to say, our sense of a realistic moment in time. The goddess smiles, shoves a chair forward, and the action, once and for all, is made actual. That so complicated and fantastic an event can be presented without confusion or bewildering multiplicity of impression or overstatement stands as yet another proof of Homer's extraordinary tact and precision in narrative method, of his immense skill in handling the immense resources that make possible his simplicities and his realism.

Vergil's exact model in the passage before us is in Apollonius, not in Homer, and though the relevant passages in Apollonius show neither much tact nor much power, they have a superb realistic veneer. In its articulations and picturing of events, its selection of details, visual, psychological, and verbal, the passage abounds in the playful, mannered yet relaxed naturalism that is Apollonius' glory. But the sinister and complex aspects of the problem, which Homer handled with seeming effortlessness, have been reduced to pure ornament:

Τόφρα δ' Ἔρως πολιοῖο δι' ἠέρος ἷξεν ἄφαντος,
τετρηχώς, οἷόν τε νέαις ἐπὶ φορβάσιν οἶστρος
τέλλεται, ὅν τε μύωπα βοῶν κλείουσι νομῆες.
ὦκα δ' ὑπὸ φλιὴν προδόμῳ ἔνι τόξα τανύσσας
ἰοδόκης ἀβλῆτα πολύστονον ἐξέλετ' ἰόν.
ἐκ δ' ὅγε καρπαλίμοισι λαθὼν ποσὶν οὐδὸν ἄμειψεν
ὀξέα δενδίλλων· αὐτῷ δ' ὑπὸ βαιὸς ἐλυσθεὶς
Αἰσονίδῃ γλυφίδας μέσσῃ ἐνικάτθετο νευρῇ,
ἰθὺς δ' ἀμφοτέρῃσι διασχόμενος παλάμῃσιν
ἧκ' ἐπὶ Μηδείῃ· τὴν δ' ἀμφασίη λάβε θυμόν.

αὐτὸς δ' ὑψορόφοιο παλιμπετὲς ἐκ μεγάροιο
καγχαλόων ἤιξε· βέλος δ' ἐνεδαίετο κούρῃ
νέρθεν ὑπὸ κραδίῃ, φλογὶ εἴκελον· ἀντία δ' αἰεὶ
βάλλεν ὑπ' Αἰσονίδην ἀμαρύγματα, καί οἱ ἄηντο
στηθέων ἐκ πυκιναὶ καμάτῳ φρένες, οὐδέ τιν' ἄλλην
μνῆστιν ἔχεν, γλυκερῇ δὲ κατείβετο θυμὸν ἀνίῃ.
ὡς δὲ γυνὴ μαλερῷ περὶ κάρφεα χεύατο δαλῷ
χερνῆτις, τῇπερ ταλασήια ἔργα μέμηλεν,
ὥς κεν ὑπωρόφιον νύκτωρ σέλας ἐντύναιτο,
ἄγχι μάλ' ἐγρομένη· τὸ δ' ἀθέσφατον ἐξ ὀλίγοιο
δαλοῦ ἀνεγρόμενον σὺν κάρφεα πάντ' ἀμαθύνει·
τοῖος ὑπὸ κραδίῃ εἰλυμένος αἴθετο λάθρῃ
οὖλος Ἔρως· ἀπαλὰς δὲ μετετρωπᾶτο παρειὰς
ἐς χλόον, ἄλλοτ' ἔρευθος, ἀκηδείῃσι νόοιο.

(3.275–298)

Meantime through the gray fog, Eros, unseen, achieved his goal,
and brought such havoc there as gadflies make for heifers as they
graze (I mean the creatures that herdsmen call breeze flies). Now
standing in the doorway of the porch, he snaps his bowstring taut
and from his quiver takes a fresh arrow, anguish-laden. Then un-
perceived he passes over the sill, then, quick-eyed for hazards, he
crouches in front of Jason, centers the notch and flexes the bow between his hands, and shoots Medea. A mute amazement seized and
held her spirit, and Eros, with outrageous laughter, fled away from
the lofty hall, but the arrow stayed, burned deep in the girl's body,
burned like flames. Again and again on Jason the girl cast glistering
glances, and in her breast the heart shuddered incessantly, and she
could fix her mind on nothing but the man: her soul by such de-
licious sickness was distilled. And as a poor woman, spinner of
wool, piles brittle twigs upon a redhot brand to coax, against the
coming of the night, bright comfort for her shelter, rises early to
end this chore before her work begins, and from this small beginning, splendid fire utterly devours the twigs: so, wreathing round
and round Medea's heart, annihilating Love clandestine blazed, and
on her delicate cheeks the color shifted, now paled, now crim-
soned, in her reason's ruin.

oulos Erōs. It is as charming and as fantastic as the wavering
iridescence of the ivory and crimson on Medea's cheeks. And as
lacking in resonance, and properly so, for resonance is precisely
what this passage (and indeed this poem) neither needs nor seeks.
Apollonius' Eros is a brilliant evasion of Homeric seriousness and
an equally brilliant imitation (but he is not more than an imita-

tion) of Homeric clarity. Like the figures in the opening of Book 3—Athena, Hera, and Aphrodite—whose deliberations set him in motion, like the figure of Ganymede, with whom he plays at dice when Aphrodite comes to bribe him to wound Medea, Eros is a figure not so much of high comedy as of light opera. He exists in the fabric of the narrative in his own right[41] and is therefore not merely a projection of Medea's psyche; though his weapon is physical, the wound he inflicts is wholly psychological, and this juxtaposition of physical weapon and psychological wound mimics realism even as it delicately smiles at the substance of anguished love, its causes, its dangers, and its nature. The divine intrusions, then, show a charming frivolity and the simplicities of the narrative and the easy unity of mood and feeling are mirrored by the easy unity of sight and sound, of the pictures of what happens in space and time. There is not, and need not be, the tough and subtle tension that exists in Homer between the complexities of the reality and the simplicity that imitates those complexities when Homer carefully orders their connections and precisely emphasizes their central aspect. The passage is Viennese: "the scenery real and the actors cardboard," and it is superb. But it is not Homer, and it is not Vergil either.

In Vergil Dido is, like Medea, at first unaware of what she is experiencing, of what has caused her love and her pain (indeed, she never really knows what has caused them), and in this she is utterly unlike Helen, who knows perfectly well the cause of her compulsion because she has met the goddess who compels her face to face in a highly dramatic confrontation. But Dido and Medea, for all the obliquity they share in the presentation of their falling in love, are presented in very dissimilar ways in respect to how they receive their compulsions and how they react to them. In Apollonius, as we have seen, the bow and arrow are real, but the wound is (naturally) psychological; and the effect of the wound is instantaneous as befits this perversion or caricature of realistic method. In other words, the action in Apollonius is graphically rendered and takes place, in Auerbach's terms, in the foreground. In Vergil, both the immediate source of Dido's compulsion and the compulsion itself are essentially psychological, despite the suggestions of physical infection (namely, the touch of Amor); and the reaction of Dido, unlike that of Medea, is hidden, retarded, foreshadowed. It will not be until Book 4 that we see the effects of what Venus has, through the agency of Cupid, accomplished. Homer shows the action, as usual, in a dramatic mode with dialogue and debate that are heightened by

43

Helen's attempt to defy Aphrodite, by her grief in yielding *before our eyes*, and finally by her bitter recriminations to Paris which suggest—but only faintly suggest—the contrary emotions she feels towards him and which explain, together with the action we have seen before, her final submission to him.

There is no drama in Apollonius' rendering of the action, but the action is visually plausible and it is portrayed in a way that is intelligible because we can see what has happened, even if the defeat and therefore the vulnerability of Medea's will are obscured, indeed ignored, by the brilliant plausibilities of the surface of the action. In a sense, the rendering of Dido's infatuation is naturalistic because it is Ascanius' resemblance to his father, combined with his display of physical affection to her, that causes the infatuation. But this naturalism is weakened not only because Ascanius is in fact Amor but also because, in a way that we are not *shown*, in a way that remains mysterious and is sinister and almost macabre, Amor *does* poison and wound Dido. The mystery (and its horror) exists in exact proportion as the infection of Dido is not or cannot be rendered by plausible images. And where Apollonius in the full brazen courage of his frivolity can leap the void between the physical and the psychological, Vergil chooses to create a baffling design in which the supernatural and the natural, the physical and the psychological, divine intervention and psychological realism are merged together implausibly—the pattern is baffling and disturbing because we see the action from without and from within at different times and sometimes at the same time. Fantastic, abstract, impressionistic, and realistic, Vergil's rendering of Dido's falling in love may be taken as a paradigm for one of his favorite narrative modes. The outside world is no longer sufficient to explain the inner world; indeed, what happens outside obscures our understanding of what happens in the inner world, though the confusions and the obscurities of the outer world can (must) help to picture, though they cannot explain, the confusions and the obscurities within.

In some ways Vergil's presentation of Dido's falling in love may seem to us more sophisticated than the corresponding presentations of Homer and Apollonius, but Vergil's representation is, in fact, essentially impressionistic rather than realistic, and impressionism is not necessarily more sophisticated or more subtle than realism. The multitude of conflicting images and signals may betoken the complexity of the situation (Dido's nature, her dangerous circumstances, her ignorance, the elaborate machinations

44

of Venus, the countermachinations of Juno, the uncertainty of just how Amor succeeds in infecting her, poisoning her, with love), and in this way the richness of the design and the blur of impressions may accurately represent what is being imagined; but such a representation is not realistic, because it is (however artfully, however satisfyingly imagined) essentially confused as a picture, and because it fails to—indeed refuses to—explain precisely what is happening and precisely how and why it is happening.[42] The representation suggests more than it states or shows, and the impressions, nuances, colors, and intuitions are not gathered into a design that clarifies all or even most of its parts. But Helen knows what is going on, exactly, and because she knows it, we know it. In Apollonius the clarity of the design (borrowed mostly from Homer) is still very much in evidence, but the figures in the design have no trace left of the elemental, typical, abstract precision that belongs to Homeric epic and that highlights, indeed makes possible, the particular quality of Homeric realism.[43] The figures of Apollonius have become heavily individualized, have become almost idiosyncratic, to such a point that the *praxis* they represent and the *muthos* they enact, for all their surface clarity, lose any significance they might have. In Vergil, though we tend to lose clarity of design, the richness and multiplicity of impressions and interior detail (detail not clearly represented) suggest mythical significance in another way, in what is for epic a new way.

Vergil's Dido is, as has often been noticed, a figure from Greek tragedy,[44] but she is as much presented in terms of tragic stasima as in terms of tragic episodeia. The scene of her falling in love gives the impression of moving forwards and backwards in time —we do not have the continuity of a single process, a clear and present nowness. Rather, we experience the dramatic moment suffused with and finally vanished into reminiscences and presentiments. Subjective, evocative, impressionistic—the style of the passage shows all these qualities, but what it shows in special abundance is a careful exclusion of its models, both the powerful and exact realism of the Homeric model and the lighter, delicately comic, somewhat sentimental realism of its particular Apollonian model. Realism has little place in this scene, and what the scene stands most in need of Vergil supplies perfectly—a faithfulness to the imperceptible stirrings of emotions and the impalpable and unintelligible griefs that gradually dissolve the basic order, reason and clarity that high realism proffers.

5

We have a right to talk in Aristotelian terms when we discuss what Aristotle called 'final causes,' that is, human aims and human instruments. As long as painting is conceived of as serving a human purpose, one has a right to discuss the means in relation to these ends. There are indeed quite objective criteria for their assessment. The idea of an 'economy of means,' even the idea of perfection, makes complete, rational sense in such a context. One can say objectively whether a certain form serves a certain norm. It would not be too difficult I believe to translate the traditional eulogies of such classical artists as Raphael into a terminology of a great purpose perfectly fulfilled. I have mentioned before that to my mind both the correctness of drawing and the achievement of a balanced composition can be judged by objective criteria, both singly and in their interaction. I would go further and venture to think that even the achievement of a lucid narrative and the presentation of physical beauty are norms that have a permanent meaning. At least, it seems to me that relativism in these matters can be exaggerated. I know quite well that ideals of beauty vary from country to country and age to age, but I still think we know what we mean when we call Raphael's Madonnas more beautiful than Rembrandt's, even though we may like Rembrandt's better.[45]

In recapitulating my discussion about the nature of Vergil's narrative style, I enlist the aid of Gombrich again, for his imaginative and precise demonstration of the norm of realism as well as his real tolerance for and understanding of variations from that norm have particular significance for our reading of Vergil in respect to Homer's poems. It cannot be too strongly or too often emphasized that Homer's essential triumph in realism ("the plausible evocation of a sacred or at least significant story in all its naturalistic and psychological detail, the means and mastery of representation"[46]) was for Vergil, and in large measure remains for us, the norm of poetic fiction. But because we know this so well, however we may happen to phrase our knowledge of this fact, emphasizing now this aspect of it, now that, because Homer's victory in plausible representation influences and will probably continue to influence how Western writers make narratives and how we judge them in fundamental and in often imperceptible ways, we are liable to shape questions about Vergil's art with varying degrees of inaccuracy. Did Vergil do what Homer did as well as Homer did it, or better, or worse? None of these questions is asked much these days perhaps quite so baldly as I pose them here. But these questions have been posed, very much as I pose them, very frequently in the past, and they have received the kinds of answers that their shapes permitted or required. It may seem clear enough today that Vergil was attempting to do something quite different from what Homer had done and that he succeeded magnificently in reaching his own goals. But if we are correct in seeing Vergil's problems and solutions in this way, we are nevertheless left to confront the fact that Homer's art represents a very special norm for poetic fiction; we must, therefore, try to determine how Vergil deviated from that norm and how we are to approach that deviation, how we are to assess its significance both in respect of Vergil's achievement and in respect of Vergil's influence on later poetry.

One answer to this question is that Vergil and Homer belong to different orders of being. In their aesthetic and intellectual perfections both Homer's problems and his solutions hold a rare, inexplicable, all but unique position on the spectrum for literary mimesis. In Gombrich's spectrum, whose poles are abstract primitivism on the one hand and radical impressionism on the other, Homer, alone among ancient poets, finds the exact equilibrium between extreme abstract conceptualization (which sacrifices minute particulars and accidents to universals and substances) and extreme undifferentiated perception (which sacrifices the simple universal and the substance for the accidents and qualities of the moment, in all its rich confusions and intensities). Seen in the light of Gombrich's scheme, Vergil does not exclude order and design from his narratives or from his imagined worlds; but he does sacrifice a maximum of clarity and harmony in order to accommodate the priorities that interest him most—the complexities of history, the secret springs of human behavior and human destiny. What Vergil has to imagine is, essentially, unknown and probably unknowable. This means that the Homeric norm and the forms that it calls into being, though Vergil can and does make use of them frequently, must often be sacrificed in favor of both of the extreme modes that they mediate between: in favor of the exalted reifications of history and fate which Homer would not understand and which he would doubtless scorn if he could understand them; and in favor of a rich yet radically disordered complexity of impression, evocation, wild emotion, and incantation. Vergil's poetic vacillates between these two extremes in an extraordinary way, and it is this essential instability that most nearly characterizes his position on the spectrum, though perhaps if one had to choose one extreme over the other as being more closely connected with the Vergilian tendency, it would be toward impressionism that one turned, both because of the aesthetic modes that he chose and because of the intellectual predilections that he deliberately fostered.[47] If we should try to rate him on Gombrich's scale, Vergil's score for realism would be considerably lower than that of most other poets of the first rank. If the choice is between emotional complexity combined with visual uncertainty on the one hand and clarity combined with plausibility on the other, not always, but at many crucial moments in his poem, Vergil opts for "unknown modes of being" and for the beautiful filtered light that reveals realities only to hide them again.

We take nothing from Vergil if, insisting on the preeminence of Homer's art, which represents a configuration of perfect solutions to all but impossible problems, we suggest that Vergil would have been, so far as we can tell, incapable of this kind and this degree of plausibility, even if it had interested him—and it did not and it could not. Nor, of course, do we take anything from Homer if, emphasizing the special complexities and anxieties that Vergil closed with and affirming his courage and ingenuity in grappling with them, we wonder if he was temperamentally suited to look at, let alone to combat, the problem of evil in the form that it presented itself to Vergil. These are idle questions because they tend to construct unreal polarities where there is rather only a spectrum of decorum with Homer constantly moving toward its center from both its extremes while Vergil moves always from its center toward both its extremes. Furthermore, though these questions help save us from the banality of making Vergil Homer's equal, in asking them we still involve ourselves in the dreary, useless, and arrogant make-believe of bestowing prizes on the very great. But it is not our business to hand out gold watches and certificates of service to our betters. It is our business to learn to see the spectrum of decorum in its varieties and immensities and to learn to watch how its poets move, each in his way (*individuum est ineffabile*) in the patterns of their making.

III

VARIA CONFUSUS IMAGINE RERUM:
DEPTHS AND SURFACES

*The inner image of the verse is inseparable from the
numberless changes of expression which flit across
the face of the teller of tales as he talks excitedly.*
MANDELSTAM[48]

*In reading Virgil, I often cry: "Out hyperbolical fiend!
How vexest thou this man!"*
HOUSMAN *to Mackail (1920)*

novae cacozeliae repertor   *Vita Donati*

After sketching a quick, sure portrait of the melancholy Victorian Vergil, R. D. Williams issues this shrewd and timely warning: "The twentieth-century critic, immersed in this pool of tears,
may well look longingly for a dose of the hard and robust Dryden,
asking to be allowed to disinvolve himself, to be permitted a
little distance. And this surely is what Virgil gives him, provided that he does not substitute for the *Aeneid* an anthology of
the most intense parts of the second, fourth, sixth, and twelfth
books."[49] As I look over the passages chosen for discussion in
this chapter and the way I have organized those passages, I realize,
with some chagrin, that I have been busily constructing the for-
bidden anthology. But the portrait that emerges from the following pages bears no resemblance to the portrait that Williams
correctly designs from the Victorian (and later) readings of this
kind. In examining Vergil's style and narrative structure in these
"intense parts" of the books in question, in looking at Vergil's

concern with *nescius, vacuus, umbra, imago, res,* I have found strong traces of—and have chosen to emphasize—the harsher aspects of Vergilian "unreality" and "deliberate confusedness,"[50] a bitterness in the famous lyricism that borders on despair—in other words, the muscle beneath the "softer emotional mode"[51] that is strained almost beyond its limit in a fateful and unequal struggle against madness, anger, profound ignorance, vulnerability, and malevolent darkness. In choosing to emphasize these qualities of Vergilian poetic I am not denying the existence or the importance of wistful lyricism or melancholy lustre or tender humanism; still less am I seeking to pretend that the tough and dynamic aspects of Vergil's art which Williams stresses so strongly and brilliantly do not exist. What I want to investigate here are the dark places of Vergil's impressionism and the mordancy of the stiff, almost expressionistic gestures of his language and narrative, for these parts of Vergil's poetic have not yet, I think, received the attention they merit. And until we have a clear notion of the forms these poetic modes may take, we are apt to mistake them for modes that are deceptively similar to them. Specifically, what interests me most in this chapter is what I call the negative image: what it is, what it looks like, how Vergil goes about shaping it, and, finally, the kinds of things it tends to signify.

I. THE OPENING OF BOOK 12

> *at regina nova pugnae conterrita sorte,*
> *flebat, et ardentem generum moritura tenebat,*
> *"Turne, per has ego te lacrimas, per si quis Amatae*
> *tangit honos animum, spes tu nunc una, senectae*
> *tu requies miserae; decus imperiumque Latini*
> *te penes; in te omnis domus inclinata recumbit:*
> *unum oro: desiste manum committere Teucris.*
> *qui te cumque manent isto certamine casus,*
> *et me, Turne, manent; simul haec invisa relinquam*
> *lumina, nec generum Aenean captiva videbo."*
> *accepit vocem lacrimis Lavinia matris*
> *flagrantes perfusa genas, cui plurimus ignem*
> *subiecit rubor, et calefacta per ora cucurrit.*
> *Indum sanguineo veluti violaverit ostro*
> *si quis ebur, aut mixta rubent ubi lilia multa*
> *alba rosa: tales virgo dabat ore colores.*
> *illum turbat amor, figitque in virgine vultus:*
> *ardet in arma magis paucisque adfatur Amatam. . . .*
>
> (12.54–71)

But frightened by the terms of this new duel,
the queen, weeping, prepared to die, held fast

her raging son-in-law: "Turnus, by these
tears and by any reverence you still
feel for Amata—you, the only hope
and quiet left my sad last years: the honor
and power of Latinus is with you,
this house in peril stands or falls with you;
I beg one thing: you must not meet the Trojans.
For in this duel that you so wish to enter,
whatever waits for you waits for me, too;
together with you, I shall leave this hated
light; for I will not be a captive, see
Aeneas as my son-in-law." Lavinia's
hot cheeks were bathed in tears; she heard her mother's
words; and her blush, a kindled fire, crossed
her burning face. And just as when a craftsman
stains Indian ivory with blood-red purple,
or when white lilies, mixed with many roses,
blush: even such, the colors of the virgin.
His love drives Turnus wild; he stares at his
Lavinia; even keener now for battle,
he answers Queen Amata with few words....

At the opening of Book 12 Turnus confronts Latinus and reaffirms his decision to fight Aeneas in single combat. Latinus, torn
by bad conscience since he knows what Fate has commanded and
knows, too, that he has been impotent to fulfill those commands,
begs Turnus to desist from his plan and to submit to the will of
Heaven, both for the good of the Latins and for his own good.
Latinus' passionate plea fades with a skillful compressed echo of
Iliad 22.38–76, Priam's shrewd appeal to filial love:

> *miserere parentis*
> *longaevi, quem nunc maestum patria Ardea longe*
> *dividit.*
>
> (12.43–45)

Pity your aged father: even now his native
Ardea holds him far from us, in sadness.

So, far from convincing Turnus to yield to the inevitable, Latinus'
common sense and his concern serve only to inflame Turnus the
more:

> *haudquaquam dictis violentia Turni*
> *flectitur; exsuperat magis aegrescitque medendo.*
>
> (12.45–46)

Words cannot check the violence of Turnus:
the healing only aggravates his sickness;
his fury flares.

51

The oxymoron ("he sickens because of the cure") emphasizes Turnus' irrationality (this is the second use of *violentia* in this scene: *haud secus accenso gliscit Turno* [9]) even as it illumines much of what is strange about the opening scene as a whole. If *aegrescitque medendo* corresponds to anything in its Homeric model in *Iliad* 22, it can only be to the two occurrences of *oud' Hektori thumon epeithon* (78 and 91). The spare precision of Homer's phrase gains force with repetition (neither Priam nor Hecuba can change Hector's *thumos* with their separate pleas), and its lack of imagery brings into clear focus the heightened imagery of sickness with which Vergil chooses to complete the confrontation of Turnus and Latinus. It is not enough to say that Vergil desires to show by his oxymoron the wide difference between Turnus' state of mind and that of Hector (Turnus' unbridled passion as against Hector's controlled excitement and resolve: *amoton memaōs Achilēi machesthai* [36]) in order to emphasize, by this artful contrast, the full force of Turnus' *violentia.* The chief function of the oxymoronic metaphor is to dissolve the outlines of a scene that never quite gets under way. As we move from Turnus' second outburst to Amata's outburst, to Lavinia's blush, and, finally, to Turnus' third and last speech, we sense that Latinus' gesture is, like all of his gestures, futile: not because it is in itself unreasonable, but because Turnus suffers from an irrational sickness that is beyond this help or any help.

In the case of Hector, the fact that both Priam and Hecuba fail to persuade their son to desist from his resolve does not mean that persuasion could not possibly work in this instance; it means only that it happens not to work in this instance because both Fate and Hector's own character are more powerful even than the cunning, honest, and elemental rhetoric of his parents. Homer's world in this scene, as in his other scenes, is the common world where health and rational discourse are the norm from which sickness and irrationality deviate. In this world the outlines of events and the motives of the human beings who participate in those events are generally extremely clear. Priam and Hecuba know what they are doing, and what they are doing is reasonable. Hector knows what he is doing, and his choices and behavior are at once utterly rational and utterly honorable. But the motives, the behavior, and even the dilemmas of Turnus are far less clear than are those of Hector.

Vergil cannot present them with the clear outlines and exact articulations that Homer uses for his scene because Turnus is sick, as Vergil emphasizes with his powerful oxymoron, and because the causes of this sickness (and indeed the fact of the sickness itself) are unknown to Turnus himself, to Latinus, to Amata, and even, in a way, to Vergil and to us. The sickness that destroys Turnus, that is in some ways the central concern of Book 12 and therefore in some ways the central concern of the epic as a whole, is not susceptible to rational analysis and is therefore not susceptible to firm design and the sequential clarity that are the hallmarks of Homer's mode of beholding. Vergil will not, or, as I propose, cannot show us what Turnus suffers and does in this scene. Rather, what he does is to suggest the emotions that Turnus unconsciously suffers while under the illusion that he is performing a conscious, rational act. In saying this I do not mean to suggest that what Vergil offers us here is a psychological analysis of Turnus; that he is, to use another metaphor, being subjective rather than objective; or, to alter the same metaphor slightly, that he is turning from the outward appearance to the inward reality.

What Vergil offers here are clusters (not a series or groups) of blurred images that suggest but do not and cannot try to define the fluctuations and uncertainties of Turnus' distorted perceptions; what Vergil offers are not inner realities, but illusions. The fact that these perceptions are distorted from the outset (from, say, the moment when Allecto's magic firebrand becomes a real torment that really drives Turnus mad) means that they can never crystallize for him and for us into a true conception of who he is or what he is up against. Thus, whereas Hector has a fairly good understanding of the fate he moves toward inevitably and of why he confronts it, why he must confront it, Turnus gropes in blind frenzy to a death that is finally terrible and unredeemed (Hector's, as I shall try to show, is, essentially, redeemed) in exact proportion as it is finally hellish and incomprehensible. Both for Turnus' "point of view" in this scene, then, and for Vergil's own mode of beholding at crucial moments throughout his epic, the image of sickness as madness is, perhaps paradoxically, exact, and it shows "a clearness of the unclear"[52] that is, to my mind, a prime characteristic of Vergil's art. But for our present purposes, I wish to emphasize that the oxymoron stresses, by its twisted graphic antithesis, the essential futility of the interview between Turnus and Latinus: the diseased irrationality that is *violentia* has grown to such proportions that its virulence feeds on what should cure it. In its striving to suggest the nature and degree of Turnus' *violentia*, the oxymoron signals that there can be no further dramatization of Turnus' inner conflicts, and it dissolves such drama and reality as have been faintly sketched just before it. At this point we realize that Turnus, now so fully identified with his madness as to be indistinguishable from it, can neither speak to the issue with Latinus nor can Latinus speak to him; he is, in a very real sense, a phantom wandering through the broken images that constitute his delusions, his consciousness.

In this regard, it is useful to contrast the general outline of the scene with its Homeric counterpart. Book 22 opens, as Book 21 has ended, with the routed Trojans trampling one another in their efforts to get inside the walls of the city. Apollo, who has disguised himself as Agenor and so led Achilles on a wild-goose chase, mocks his victim and meets with an angry, defiant response from him; then Achilles wheels around and rushes back to the city. He is immediately seen by Priam, who is on the ramparts and who immediately begins to beg Hector to retire inside the walls. The setting for the first main action of the book, the parents' entreaties to the doomed warrior, is sketched with quick and characteristic economy and clarity. The transition between Book 11 and 12 of the *Aeneid* is less directly handled than is that between Books 21 and 22 of the *Iliad*. The rout of the Latins and the subsequent confusion and terror at the gates are briefly reflected in Turnus' view of this event (*ut infractos adverso Marte Latinos, / defecisse videt*), but there is a time lapse, which could best be called vague, between the two books (*sua nunc promissa reposci, / se signari oculis*). The transition between the time when Turnus apparently feels forced to make good his promise to meet Aeneas in single combat (*ultro inplacabilis ardet, / attollitque animos* [3–4]) and the time when he announces his decision to Latinus is supplied by the simile of the wounded, defiant lion (4–9); but where Turnus comes from and where Turnus goes to meet Latinus are left to the readers' imaginations (we may supply, I suppose, a room in the palace). It is perhaps churlish to suggest that we must also imagine for ourselves the entrances or presences of Amata and Lavinia; we must allow, to continue the contrast with Homer, that in a sense Hecuba also arrives on the scene out of thin air. Yet in Homer's shaping of the scene, once Priam is clearly and naturally represented as standing anxiously on the ramparts, responding to the commotion at the gates, it is hardly difficult to imagine that Hecuba, also concerned by the sudden commotion and thereby worried about Hector, is by his side. The appearance of Latinus has been briefly (yet more or less adequately) prepared for by the sudden and effective appearance (at court?) of Turnus:

haud secus accenso gliscit violentia Turno:
tum sic adfatur regem, atque ita turbidus infit. . . .

(12.9–10)

just so did violence
urge on fanatic Turnus. Hectic, he
cries out to King Latinus with these words. . . .

But Amata, whose presence and speech correspond to the presence and speech of Hecuba in the Homeric model, bursts into the
scene without preparation; so, without preparation, the even more
shadowy Lavinia glides into it. The effect of these entrances or
sudden presences suggests less the theatrical (or dramatic) *appearance* that is typical of Homer than the incantatory evocation
of *personae* that one *hears*, say, in an ensemble reading of *The
Wasteland*. This is not to say, of course, that there is no visual
excellence in this scene; indeed, I shall soon argue that this particular scene shows a highly elaborate and highly effective visual
organization. Rather, I am suggesting that the conventions of
visualization that are common in Homer are emphatically flouted
by Vergil here, as happens frequently.

Here, the clarity of picture that logical and sequential articulation makes possible yields to a deliberate blurring. Vergil's queen
has a form and gestures as well as a voice and emotions and
thoughts, but picture and gesture—because of the lack of careful
articulation and because of stylization and compression of representation—do not mesh and are not meant to mesh. Here, not
only because of what Amata has to say but also because of the
manner in which Amata is rendered in her speaking, we are reminded of Greek tragedy and, strangely enough, of Seneca. When
our attention becomes fixed on Amata, we become aware that we
are now confronted with a distancing, a stylization, almost a con-
tempt for verisimilitude that are utterly foreign to Homer but
not at all alien to the stages of Athens or Milan. Hecuba may be
larger than life, but, since she is Homer's creature, she is also
full of life (the miracle of stylization *and*, almost, of naturalism
that we witness in "and loosening her garment, with one hand
she showed her breast" [22.80] defies imitation even as it defies
analysis); Amata, on the other hand, cannot hide the fact that
she is, whatever else she is, a mezzo-soprano: *flebat, et ardentem
generum moritura tenebat* (55). "Virgil's besetting sin," wrote
Housman to Mackail, "is the use of words too forcible for his
thoughts, and the *moritura* of *Aeneid* 12.55 makes me blush for

him whenever I think of it."[53] It is not recorded, that I know of, whether Ribbeck blushed also; but he did the next best thing. He emended. *Monitura tenebat.* She becomes, that is, a sensible woman. She does not rush upon him, throw herself in his way as he attempts to stride from the room, catch him, and cling to him as if her life depended on him (as it does). Rather, having sage advice to give him, she takes him by the arm. No, the scene as Vergil imagines it, with the madness of Turnus expanding at each moment, demands precisely the extravagance, the histrionics, that *moritura* confers. Whether the word connotes only an adumbration of her resolve to die if Turnus dies—which she is to announce momentarily—or, with more excess, foreshadows her actual death (603), or represents a sudden deathly pallor, or suggests to us that we are supposed to feel the pathos of her situation (the word is used once again of Amata [602]; four times of Dido;[54] once, brilliantly, of Lausus [10.811]), it is unrealistic if what is wanted is a precise imitation of the emotions and state of mind of a woman in Amata's situation. Housman blushed, I presume, because his sensibility was embarrassed by what it took to be a failure of mimetic decorum. But Vergil is not trying to proffer intelligible realities; he is, through the eyes of Turnus, trying to imagine the incomprehensibility of reality by the disintegration of images. *Moritura*, then, is not Vergil's way of describing what Amata looked like or how she felt at this particular moment; it is rather a way of indicating a penumbra of doom that Turnus vaguely senses and that we observe—for us, a dreadful flash of clarity. An omniscient, an Homeric, narrator might very well have described Amata as being overcome by excitement or hysteria or anxiety. That he would have described her as *moritura* is doubtful. But the sinister, jarringly unrealistic prescience of the word, its emotional editorialization, is suitable to the frame of mind or of madness that Turnus is in, and for the purpose of suggesting how Turnus misperceives reality the word is as exact as its extravagance is troubling.

And so with *violaverit.* Perhaps, unwittingly, Housman blushed because he remembered Lavinia's blush, which is, of course, unforgettable.[55] But why does she blush? What is it that her mother says that conjures up this manifestation of simple embarrassment or of delicate, shy, turbulent eroticism? *Ardentem generum / generum Aenean?* We know nothing whatever of Lavinia's conscious thoughts, much less of her private fantasies. Does she respond to the passion of Turnus? Has she toyed with notions of the glamorous Asiatic barbarian, a white sheik come to brighten

56

her humdrum existence? One may speculate, but Vergil has seen to it that such speculation is as fruitless as it is boring. We are given nothing but a fleeting, tantalizing vision of possible erotic excitement, but that vision is as incisive and as artistic as anything Vergil wrote. Yet it was not imagined in order that we might understand something about Lavinia; it was imagined in order that we might understand something about Turnus. We do not know if Latinus or Amata notice their daughter's manifestation of shyness or involuntary revelation of hidden desires. But Turnus notices and he thinks he knows what her blush means. Sexual jealousy causes his own romantic notions to kindle higher, and his eroticism adds fuel to the martial fires that are already blazing out of control—the *violentia* of this scene can increase no more.

My point here is that we see Lavinia blush through Turnus' eyes, and it is Turnus' passion and his point of view that cause Vergil to select *violaverit* in order to render and to distort in the rendering the Homeric *miēnēi* of *Iliad* 4.141. What might otherwise seem, then, another flagrant example of gratuitous mannerism or slakeless *cacozelia* turns out to be determined by Vergil's careful shaping of Turnus' point of view. *Violaverit* echoes the *violentia* of Turnus that dominates this scene, as do *ardor, rubor, rubent, rubebit* (77), *ardentem generum*.[56] But it is also a projection of Turnus' *violentia* onto Aeneas; it is also, possibly, a way of fantasizing punishment of Lavinia for her suspected impurity. It is erotic, sensuous, and violent, crystallizing the images of blood, anger, roses, the dawn of vengeance into a single, complex, ineffable feeling. The flawlessly mixed simile describes the confused manner in which Turnus see Lavinia's blush, and the way he sees the blush and reacts to it describes the confusion that has now taken full possession of him as this final book opens and that will keep possession of him for the remainder of the poem.

Again, a contrast with Homer is in order. In its relation to Menelaus (*Iliad* 4.141–147) the ivory dyed with crimson is emblematic both of the glory of his wound (*kosmos, kudos* [145]) and of his vitality and his health as warrior:

> ὡς δ' ὅτε τίς τ' ἐλέφαντα γυνὴ φοίνικι μιήνῃ
> Μηονὶς ἠὲ Κάειρα, παρήιον ἔμμεναι ἵππῳ·
> κεῖται δ' ἐν θαλάμῳ, πολέες τέ μιν ἠρήσαντο
> ἱππῆες φορέειν· βασιλῆι δὲ κεῖται ἄγαλμα,
> ἀμφότερον κόσμος θ' ἵππῳ ἐλατῆρί τε κῦδος·
> τοῖοί τοι, Μενέλαε, μιάνθην αἵματι μηροὶ
> εὐφυέες κνῆμαί τε ἰδὲ σφυρὰ κάλ' ὑπένερθε.

> (4.141–147)

When a woman from Maeonia or Caria stains with purple dye a piece of ivory that is destined for a bridle, it comes to be stored in the royal treasure and is coveted by many riders; but in the king's treasury it remains, at once an ornament for the horse and a special distinction for its rider. So, Menelaus, your thighs were stained blood-red, and your trim legs and your fine ankles.

Here the neat repetition, *mianthēn*, serves as an ironic foil to the brightness and health that are imagined in *euphuees* and *kala*: blood from the wound might be thought to defile Menelaus' health and beauty, but in fact it only accentuates them. In Vergil's simile, on the other hand, however lovely Lavinia's blush is, however much it betokens her delicacy, there is a suggestion of possible corruption; as her beauty is momentarily spoiled by her tears (*lacrimis . . . flagrantes perfusa genas*), as the lilies are at once denatured and perversely beautified by their mingling with the red roses, so, in the mind of Turnus, the beauty of Lavinia and her innocence are jeopardized by what appears to be her equivocal response to her mother's speech. Without *violaverit* the mixed similes would be perfectly unexceptionable; with it, they take on an elusive but ineradicable tinge of corruption; they are, with this single word, gathered into the confusion, frenzy, and suspicion that grip Turnus' mind and heart.

An essential aspect of Homer's narrative art is his ability to achieve inimitable unity from multiplicity. If we compare Vergil's scene with Homer's in respect of point of view, we discover that Homer, using an omniscient narrator, moving from the throng at the gates; to Apollo and Achilles; then to Hector, Priam, and Hecuba; and, finally, to Hector alone, has been able to bring Hector and the tragedy and inevitability of his death into a steady, unshakable focus. In Vergil, on the other hand, the epic narrator merges imperceptibly with Turnus himself; we begin and end the scene by viewing Turnus from outside, but in the center of the scene we hear and see the other characters for the most part as Turnus hears and sees them, and, as a result of this shifting of focus and this absence of narrative distancing, we find ourselves in the situation that confronted us in Book 4 with Dido:[57] because we are, in some ways, too close to the narrator-protagonist, we are often unable to distinguish between what is taking place and what the hypersensitive narrator-protagonist believes is taking place, and we are at last unable to extricate ourselves from the illusions of a character whose words and actions we are supposed to be evaluating at some degree of distance. In the case of

Turnus, as in the case of Dido, we are necessarily by turns critical and sympathetic, yet we have finally no absolute index which enables us to distinguish truth from illusion; even though we understand that their perceptions are to some extent deranged, we do not know, cannot know, to what extent they are deranged, and, in any case, we must frequently depend on the information they offer us because no other information is available. In the case of Turnus, the shifting of narrative focus, the fluctuation of rhetorical emphasis, the hyperbole that is indicative of distortions that cannot quite be corrected, result in a baffling, disquieting uncertainty about who Turnus is, what he is doing, what is destroying him. This is not to suggest that Turnus is a complicated character and Hector a simple one. Hector shows pride, vanity, heroism, sense of responsibility and love, even as Turnus does, but in the scene in question the proof of Hector's final integrity is the desperate soliloquy in which he confronts and (unconsciously) masters his own uncertainties about himself. The measure of Turnus' final confusion about his motives and himself is the bluster and ranting that mark this scene's close. The crazed arrogance of Turnus' final speech in this scene compares unfavorably both with the vitality and candor of his speech against Drances in Book 11 and with Hector's self-scrutiny and essential humility in the soliloquy of Book 22. The vestiges of Turnus' earlier heroism dissolve before our eyes into the deceptive, destructive sweetness of the mixed similes. Soldier's honor, gallant patriotism, lover's passion are separated from one another at the very moment they ought to be united. Whereas Hector pulls himself together, is pulled together by the momentum of Homer's narrative, in Vergil's narrative Turnus in this scene is unmanned, and his image disintegrates under the pressure of the *violentia* which is reflected in oxymoron, hyperbole, blurred simile, and shifting point of view.[58] A deliberately violent and disordered poetics faithfully records a turbulent unintelligibility; this deliberate failure of images is a way of showing darkness.

2. DISSOLVING PATHOS

volvitur Euryalus leto, pulchrosque per artus
it cruor; inque umeros cervix collapsa recumbit:
purpureus veluti cum flos succisus aratro
languescit moriens, lassove papavera collo
demisere caput, pluvia cum forte gravantur.

(9.433–437)

He tumbles into death, the blood flows down
his handsome limbs; his neck, collapsing, leans
against his shoulder: even as a purple
flower, severed by the plow, falls slack in death;
or poppies as, with weary necks, they bow
their heads when weighted down by sudden rain.

ἦ ῥα, καὶ ἄλλον ὀϊστὸν ἀπὸ νευρῆφιν ἴαλλεν
Ἕκτορος ἀντικρύ, βαλέειν δέ ϝε ϝίετο θυμός.
καὶ τοῦ μέν ῥ' ἀφάμαρθ', ὁ δ' ἀμύμονα Γοργυθίωνα,
υἱὸν ἐῢν Πριάμοιο, κατὰ στῆθος βάλεν ἰῷ
τόν ῥ' ἐξ Αἰσύμηθεν ὀπυιομένη τέκε μήτηρ,
καλὴ Καστιάνειρα, δέμας ϝεϝικυῖα θεῇσι.
μήκων δ' ὡς ἑτέρωσε κάρη βάλεν, ἥ τ' ἐνὶ κήπῳ,
καρπῷ βριθομένη νοτίῃσί τε ϝειαρινῇσιν·
ὡς ἑτέρωσ' ἤμυσε κάρη πήληκι βαρυνθέν.

(Iliad 8.300–308)

He spoke and from his bowstring shot another arrow direct at
Hector, and his heart yearned to wound him. Hector he missed,
but Gorgythion, the fine son of Priam, his arrow struck, the
chest pierced. Him Castianeira bore, Priam's wife, a woman from
Aisyme—the beautiful Castianeira, like a goddess in form and
figure. As a poppy in a garden lolls its head to one side, heavy with
seed and spring rain, so, weighted with its casque, to one side
dangled his head.

δούπησεν δὲ πεσών, ἀράβησε δὲ τεύχε' ἐπ' αὐτῷ.
αἵματί ϝοι δεύοντο κόμαι Χαρίτεσσιν ὁμοῖαι
πλοχμοί θ', οἳ χρυσῷ τε καὶ ἀργύρῳ ἐσφήκωντο.
οἷον δὲ τρέφει ἔρνος ἀνὴρ ἐριθηλὲς ἐλαίης
χώρῳ ἐν οἰοπόλῳ, ὅθ' ϝάλις ἀναβέβροχεν ὕδωρ,
καλὸν τηλεθάον· τὸ δέ τε πνοιαὶ δονέουσι
παντοίων ἀνέμων, καί τε βρύει ἄνθεϊ λευκῷ·
ἐλθὼν δ' ἐξαπίνης ἄνεμος σὺν λαίλαπι πολλῇ
βόθρου τ' ἐξέστρεψε καὶ ἐξετάνυσσ' ἐπὶ γαίῃ·
τοῖον Πανθόου υἱὸν ἐϋμμελίην Εὔφορβον
Ἀτρείδης Μενέλαος ἐπεὶ κτάνε, τεύχε' ἐσύλα.

(Iliad 17.50–60)

And he fell with a dull clang, and his armor rattled about him as
he fell, and his hair, lovely as the hair of the Graces themselves,
and his braids, clasped with gold and silver, were soaked with his
blood. And like a flourishing young olive tree that someone tends
in a quiet place where fertile water gushes, a tree that flowers,

flowers in beauty, and it is shaken by every windy current, and it thrives in the whiteness of its blossoms—then a sudden wind with great whirling beats down and uproots it from its trench, flings it on the ground: even so was Euphorbus of the stout ashen spear, he, the son of Panthous, whom Menelaus, son of Atreus, killed and fell to despoiling.

> nec meum respectet, ut ante, amorem,
> qui illius culpa cecidit velut prati
> ultimi flos, praetereunte postquam
> tactus aratro est.
>
> (Catullus 11)
>
> ... nor let her regard, as she did before, my love—
> the love of him who, because of her sin, has fallen,
> like a blossom at the field's edge, when the passing
> plough has grazed it.

This grouping of passages suggests two things that we will want to keep in mind about the Vergilian simile in question: (1) for all the simplicity of its syntax and for all the brevity and clarity of its imagery, it is, *because* of its extreme compression, a highly elaborate and carefully organized *literary* contrivance that is as conspicuously artificial in its methods as it is in its ends; (2) Homer understood the artistic possibilities of pathos fully, but, because the essential nature of his art is tragic, he uses pathos sparingly, chiefly for purposes of ornament and relief. Vergil, whose art is essentially lyrical, uses pathos frequently, as is commonly known: it is the reason for, and the nature of, Vergilian pathos that I am trying to approach in this section of my examination of his poetics.

Two aspects of the Vergilian passage seem to me specially remarkable. First, the death of Euryalus is possessed of an extraordinary loveliness that is wholly appropriate to the tone and function of the Vergilian *Doloneia*, yet the beauty of these verses calls attention to itself in a way that impedes the progress of the narrative. In a certain way, they are too beautiful even for the climax of the dreamlike adventures of Euryalus and Nisus; they want almost to be excerpted from their surroundings, to be pondered over, repeated. Second, beneath their loveliness, the verses exhibit something that smacks of the grotesque, of *Liebestod*. Though Vergil is careful to understate the eroticism of the entire passage, he gives it vivid emphasis at the climax of this narrative: the physical beauty of Euryalus and a sudden vision of his unheroic fragility and helplessness are so stressed as to give emotional significance to the final act of the dying Nisus:

> tum super exanimum sese proiecit amicum
> confossus, placidaque ibi demum morte quievit.
>
> (9.444–445)

> Then, pierced, he cast himself upon his lifeless
> friend; there, at last, he found his rest in death.

The death of Nisus, in its grim violence (*exanimum amicum / proiecit /confossus*) and in its gentleness (*placida morte / quievit*), shows a sort of oxymoronic juxtaposition of opposites not dissimilar to the fused discrepancies of the Euryalus simile. The death of Euryalus is depicted as being pretty, not particularly noble; the death of Nisus, dissolving as it does into the previous images of blood and of blossoms broken and weary, attains a pose of nobility both by reason of his gesture of love and devotion and by reason of Vergil's patriotic apostrophe to the reckless, vainglorious lovers:

> fortunati ambo! si quid mea carmina possunt,
> nulla dies umquam memori vos eximet aevo.
>
> (446–447)

> Fortunate pair! If there be any power
> within my poetry, no day shall ever
> erase you from the memory of time. . . .

The story may affect us in several ways: We may feel sympathy for the young men, and we may admire their courage and reciprocal devotion, even though we cannot admire their intelligence; at another level we may feel that the Nisus-Euryalus episode functions chiefly as retardation of the central action (the arming of Aeneas) and as preparation for the *aristeia* of Turnus, which fills the rest of Book 9; or we may decide that Nisus and Euryalus have been deliberately sentimentalized and that the *Doloneia* has been carefully travestied in order to stress the nature of vainglory and to challenge the foundations of the epic sensibility. We may react in one or in all of these ways at different times, but one thing about the close of the narrative remains constant: the death of Euryalus—and, by extension, the death of Nisus—signals a retreat from Homeric mimesis by its mannered conflation of Homeric imagery and Catullan imagery, and it annihilates the possibility of our finding in these deaths a tragic statement about the necessity that governs human existence; we cannot say of these deaths, as we can say of so many deaths in the *Iliad*: "it was an actuality—stern, mournful, and fine."[59] Not because Vergil did not understand such actuality, not because Vergil did not understand what Homer had imagined; rather, because in the universe that Vergil imagines the knowledge that would make such an actuality intelligible is not available and because, therefore, such actualities are literally intolerable and are therefore minimized in a variety of ways. In a sense, the dissolving pathos of Vergil may seem a coward's stratagem to shield him and us from truths we cannot endure to see; in a deeper sense, the dissolving pathos functions ironically—it stresses both the immensity of what confronts human existence and our utter nakedness before that immensity. But to test these descriptions of Vergilian pathos, we must now turn to the Homeric originals that they at once imitate and transform.

The death of Gorgythion is the stuff pathos is made of, for he receives the arrow that Teucer had intended for Hector; so, at *Aeneid* 10.781 ff., the pathos of accidental death is represented in this fashion:

> sternitur infelix alieno vulnere, caelumque
> aspicit, et dulces moriens reminiscitur Argos.
> (10.781–782)

> Luckless, he has been laid low by a wound
> not meant for him; he looks up at the sky
> and, dying, calls to mind his gentle Argos.

Gorgythion, then, dies *alieno vulnere*. But where Vergil offers a compressed, almost dry catachresis to evoke a misfortune that would otherwise beggar language, Homer characteristically uses delicate and reserved modulation:

> Hector he missed, but Gorgythion, the fine son of Priam, his arrow struck, the chest pierced. Him Castianeira bore, Priam's wife, a woman from Aisyme—the beautiful Castianeira, like a goddess in form and figure.
>
> (8.302–305)

Teucer missed Hector and hit Gorgythion, who is *amumōn*, the son of Priam and Castianeria, *kalē, demas eikuia theëisi*. The familiar, limpid epithets are at once soothing and inevitable. The young man's death is an unfortunate accident, and he himself is almost incidental; he has strayed into the story and he strays out of it, a ripple on the bright violent stream. The pathos of his dying is restrained and tactful: his youth and vulnerability, the fact that he is, in a sense, merely a bystander, a victim of an inexplicable process that is beyond Homer's comprehension and ours—these things are balanced by his vigor and manliness. The poppy is beaten down by spring rains, but this possible suggestion of weakness is offset by *karpōi brithomenē*; Gorgythion is undone by circumstances, but he is healthy; indeed, it is his flourishing, his ripeness that have exposed him to the common hazards of existence and the special hazards of warfare that are symbolized by the rains. Furthermore, his head is bowed in death by the weight of his helmet: he dies a soldier's death, and the imagery that depicts that death is a handsome fusion of his vulnerability and his strength. In this sense, the pathos of the simile is subsumed, as is customary in the *Iliad*, into a larger vision of the nature of things. A wavering sense of inexplicable disaster, then grace and tenderness, then a brief sorrow, then the inevitable, *es muss sein.* He is young and full of life, yes. But he is also a soldier, he has accepted this role; such things happen to soldiers, he must accept this, does accept it, and so must we. I have belabored what Homer consummately understates in order to show that Homer uses pathos to transcend what would else be merely pitiful and thereby to attain, here as elsewhere, that strange tragic sense that is at once utterly ideal and utterly real. The pathos serves only to lead us beyond pathos to a sober, strangely comforting truth.

Compared with the dead Gorgythion (and it is well to bear in mind that Vergil not only invites but demands the comparison), Euryalus seems like a ruined mannequin. Where Homer had allowed us only to guess at Gorgythion's looks from his descriptions of Castianeira and from the indirect and terse imagery that evokes the poppy, Vergil emphatically asserts the beauty of Euryalus (*pulchros per artus*) and elaborates on it further by his handling of *purpureus flos* and *papavera.* This beauty is not merely vulnerable, it is utterly defenseless, and its pitiful demise is unrelieved by wider perspectives: we are locked into a sweet, tainted melancholy that the patriotic apostrophe, so far from exorcizing, can only foil with ironic indecorum. The echo of Catullus' self-mocking, pathetic lover, a dear little flower mangled by Vagina Dentata, merges (or, rather, fails to merge) with the echo of Homer's unfortunate young warrior. *Pēlēki barunthen* nudges us away from this mood back into the story. *Languescit moriens* and *lasso collo* create a stifling, mesmerizing stasis; their sentimentality side-steps the fact of disaster so that what is fearful about this death lingers—beautified, unresolved, and corrupt.

Lest it be thought that this comparison, though chosen by Vergil himself, is unfair because Gorgythion is a walk-on, let us glance briefly at the death simile of Euphorbus, a figure whom Homer develops at some length. Euphorbus, a not unlikable and a recognizable blend of audacity, swagger, vanity, and prudence, incapacitates Patroclus with a cast of his spear, thus putting the finishing touches to Apollo's work and getting him ready for Hector; after wounding his man, he ducks back in the crowd, emerging to look to his spoils only after Hector has killed Patroclus; then follows a shouting match with Menelaus, after which Menelaus kills him (*Iliad* 16.806–815; 17.1 ff.). It would be too much to say that, in this poem at least, Euphorbus' death is a matter of poetic justice; it is rather the natural outcome of who the man is and what he does and wants. He is vain about the luxuriance of his hair, a fact that amuses Homer and that he uses with delicate irony: the hair that reminded one of the Graces (reminded Euphorbus of the Graces, too) was once set off with gold and silver and is now adorned with his blood. It is a fact, not a judgment; it is noted down and let go. Otherwise he is a remarkably accomplished warrior for so young a man (16.808–811); he naturally challenges Menelaus and he naturally pays for it. Euphorbus is not an incidental character and his death is not accidental, but Homer touches it with a light pathos. The luxuriant hair and the ordinary youthful bluster are illumined by the splendid image of the olive tree, grown to near maturity, its white blossoms shaken by every wind (*pnoiai pantoiōn anemōn*), then suddenly set upon by a wind whose terrific force (*anemos sun lailapi pollēi*) it cannot withstand, by which it is uprooted and toppled to the ground. Sad? Yes. Intolerable? No. The zest and vigor are as admirable as the self-confidence and the naïveté are touching, but the nature of things is unalterable. With Euphorbus as with Gorgythion, it is the pathos itself that disappears, dissolved into a clarity that has no time for prolonged grief that may grow to unappeasable melancholy: *Atreidēs Menelaos epei ktane, teuche' esula.* The gaze is steady, but not dispassionate; the eyes pity but do not succumb to despair or terror. This is a far cry from the melting, languid rhythms and the soft equivocal images that Vergil uses to prevent us from seeing the death of Euryalus as it is. We can grieve for both Gorgythion and for Euphorbus because we can admire them and, in large measure, un-

derstand them; we admire and in part understand them because
we see them through the eyes of a tactful, helpful, and unobtru-
sive narrator who constantly persuades us that he is as omniscient
and as trustworthy as is necessary for our purposes and his. We
feel sorry for Euryalus, but that pity yields to an insoluble mysterious anxiety; we forget exactly who the beautiful lover was.
His lover embraces him in death and they are joined forever. The
glamorous broken doll and his lover are eternal patriots of Rome?
What have their deaths, their romance, their mindless, murderous
rampage to do with the destiny of Rome? We never find out. We
see the death of Euryalus through the eyes of a narrator whose
vision is colored by the terror and the passion of Nisus. When
Nisus dies, the picture disintegrates before our eyes. If what we
feel as a result of that disintegration is "doubt and carnal fear,"
that is what Vergil wants us to feel.

> tum Iuno omnipotens, longum miserata dolorem
> difficilesque obitus, Irim demisit Olympo,
> quae luctantem animam nexosque resolveret artus.
> nam, quia nec fato merita nec morte peribat,
> sed misera ante diem, subitoque accensa furore,
> necdum illi flavum Proserpina vertice crinem
> abstulerat, Stygioque caput damnaverat Orco.
> ergo Iris croceis per caelum roscida pennis,
> mille trahens varios adverso sole colores,
> devolat, et supra caput adstitit: "hunc ego Diti
> sacrum iussa fero, teque isto corpore solvo."
> sic ait, et dextra crinem secat. omnis et una
> dilapsus calor, atque in ventos vita recessit.
>
> (4.693–705)

But then all-able Juno pitied her
long sorrow and hard death and from Olympus
sent Iris down to free the struggling spirit
from her entwining limbs. For as she died
a death that was not merited or fated,
but miserable and before her time
and spurred by sudden frenzy, Proserpina
had not yet cut a gold lock from her crown,
not yet assigned her life to Stygian Orcus.
On saffron wings dew-glittering Iris glides
along the sky, drawing a thousand shifting
colors across the facing sun. She halted
above the head of Dido: "So commanded,

I take this lock as offering to Dis;
I free you from your body." So she speaks
and cuts the lock with her right hand; at once
the warmth was gone, the life passed to the winds.

In dealing with these verses, our special concern will be to examine the way in which Iris' epiphany, the shifting beauty of the rainbow that betokens her coming, distracts our attention from the fact of Dido's suffering and thereby blurs the significance of that suffering. But before we turn to this characteristic Vergilian *Kunstbegriff*, the scumbling of his outlines, we had best examine the question of point of view in this passage. At first glance one might suppose that we have only to do with an ordinary narrator who is reporting this event as he sees it. If we look more closely, however, and remember that, for the most part, the events of Book 4 unfold before us as Dido experiences them, we are confronted with several hard complexities. Is Dido aware that Iris has come? Does she hear the words that we hear? Is it possible that Dido sees the rainbow that we see and hears the death formula as we hear it? We know, at least, that the last time we see her clearly (*ter revoluta toro est, oculisque errantibus alto / quaesivit caelo lucem, ingemuitque reperta* [691–692]), her eyes are fixed on the light of the sky. *Ingemuitque reperta*, not admired by Racine alone, is justly celebrated, but it is so flawless as to defy translation, or paraphrase, or explanation. *Ingemuit* is, poetically speaking, *sui causa*–a perfectly accurate and perfectly simple metaphor for dying, looking one's last on the light of day. Yet she does not, or does not seem to, die at this moment. She dies when Iris, having descended in glory, has spoken the death formula and snipped off the gold lock of hair. My suggestion here is that the two moments that appear to be separated (*ingemuit, vita recessit*) are all but simultaneous: in short, we see Dido's death as Dido "sees" it, the fatal ritual utterance of Iris, the death blow (*crinem secat*), the groan. What Dido finds (*reperta*) as she anxiously searches the sky is the doom and the deliverance that Iris brings: the light is the shining fatal appearance of Juno's messenger. This baffling (and artistic) division of one instant into what seems to be two instants—indeed, into a succession of events—has the curious effect of removing us from Dido even while we remain with her. The division is accomplished by the unobstrusive intrusion of a voice that is, properly speaking, alien to what seems to be the tone and the function of this scene. *Tum Iuno omnipotens, longum miserata dolorem*. On one level, this

67

verse and those that directly follow it are spoken by the ordinary narrator, who is explaining what Juno does when she views Dido's agony and why she does it. But this level, which is one of direct, sequential narration, is rather deceptive here, as elsewhere in the poem. Is the regular narrator calling Juno *omnipotens*? If so, why? He must surely know that much of his poem is directed to showing that *omnipotens* is one thing that she is precisely not. Is it careless cliché that is essentially occasioned by metrical necessities or vague intuitions of oral composition? Not, probably, in this poem. Is it ironic? Perhaps, but if Vergil is merely being ironic, on this level, at Juno's expense (or Dido's), the irony is tasteless and cheap. And what of *miserata*? Juno's compassion is reminiscent of the compassion shown by Ovid's deities: it is utterly out of character, and, if we consider Juno's role in what has happened to Dido, a hypocritical, disgusting turn of the screw. The abruptness of Juno's appearance at this point in the narrative is as distracting from the business at hand as her omnipotence and her compassion. For a moment, our attention is focused on Juno and what she thinks she ought to feel about the event that is taking place; this focus prepares us for the brilliance of Iris' descent, which engages our attention for the rest of the close of Book 4, until the last sentence, when we return to the event proper. And this means that our attention has been averted from what is of central importance about Dido's death to peripheral details about the death; and in this process the gravity and the significance of Dido's death are lost from view. From *tum Iuno omnipotens* down to *damnaverat Orco* we have entered into the mind of Juno. It is she who describes herself as *omnipotens*, and it is she who describes herself as *miserata* and then goes on to give a clear and accurate account of Dido's tragedy and her innocence (*nam, quia nec fato . . .*). Readers who persist in thinking Dido guilty of wrongdoing have at least the excuse that the only clear vindication of her behavior is put in the mind of a character whom we know we cannot trust. Our natural distrust of Juno, coupled as it is here with the casual appearance of *omnipotens* and *miserata*, creates a bewildering admixture of illusion and truth and acts as a proper transition to the dazzling imagery that marks the epiphany of Iris, the death of Dido, and the finale of Book 4.

The use of color in the entire passage is at once notable and characteristic. The tawny gold of Dido's hair is foiled by gruesome darkness (*Stygio Orco*), then radiant yellows and fresh translucency (*croceis pennis, roscida*), and, finally, the splendid swirling indistinction of *mille trahens varios adverso sole colores*.

Varius, as we shall soon see in more detail,[60] is a favorite word with Vergil when he wishes to stress complexity and confusion. Here the word paradoxically at once presents a vision and annihilates that vision with excessive brightness. Hence, a delusive splendor throws a beautiful yet sinister screen between us and what we assumed we were meant to see. For us, as for Dido, it is precisely the moment when the light is at its fullest that the apprehension of darkness overtakes us. What was supposed to illuminate Dido's death obscures its significance in a frustrating, almost sinister way. Before the intrusion of Juno and Iris, Dido's imminent death—though painful and terrible—was affecting and not without its own courage and nobility. But with the appearance of Iris, Dido's autonomy fails; her death is gathered into a beauty that, colored as it is by *miserata* and *misera*, is almost sentimental; and yet, juxtaposed with that beauty—indeed, heightened by it —are the remorseless grimly supernatural words of Iris: *hunc ego Diti / sacrum iussa fero, teque isto corpore solvo.*[61] The effect of the brilliant imagery and the cold laconic speech differs considerably from the effect that Homer achieves in a passage where Athena descends at Zeus' behest to spur the Greeks on to get possession of Patroclus' body:

ἠΰτε πορφυρέην ἶριν θνητοῖσι τανύσσῃ
Ζεὺς ἐξ οὐρανόθεν, τέρας ἔμμεναι ἢ πολέμοιο
ἢ καὶ χειμῶνος δυσθαλπέος, ὅς ῥά τε ϝέργων
ἀνθρώπους ἀνέπαυσεν ἐπὶ χθονί, μῆλα δὲ κήδει,
ὡς ἡ πορφυρέῃ νεφέλῃ πυκάσασα ϝὲ αὐτὴν
δύσετ' Ἀχαιῶν ϝέθνος, ἔγειρε δὲ φῶτα ϝέκαστον.

(17.547–552)

When Zeus from the heavens unrolls the rainbow that glints darkling to be a signal of war or of uncomfortable winter, he forces mortal men to cease from their labors on the earth, and he troubles their flocks—even so, Athena, swathing herself in a darkly glinting cloud, entered into the crowds of Achaeans and goaded on each man.

Here the color word, *porphuros*, reverberates with a sinister, inhuman foreboding, but for all its menace, the word and the imagery that attends upon it nevertheless denote realistically a disruption of the *natural* order (*teras-wergōn anthropōus anepausen, mēla de kēdei*). Furthermore, the color word is not used here,[62] as the words of Vergil are used, to paint a pretty picture: the word is, beyond its realism, ominous, and its central function is to represent the superhumanity of Athena in her unpersuadable purpose. In Vergil the sweetness and light enchant and distract us at a moment of hazard; then, through conflicting dread and sensuous delight, we are propelled into a disintegration and a void where there is room for neither pleasure nor the original seriousness: *omnis et una / dilapsus calor, atque in ventos vita recessit.*

In this passage, then, the blurred imagery and wavering narrative focus combine to create an unexpected and, in respect to tragic canons, somewhat inappropriate pathos that first obscures and then nullifies the nature and the significance of Dido's death. Since we see her in Book 4 primarily through her own eyes, her courage, her magnanimity, and her honesty (*et nunc magna mei sub terras ibit imago*) are seen fitfully and are increasingly gathered into the confusions and misperceptions of her frenzies and agony. And if some of her essential nobility begins to be manifest itself in her death throes (*illa, graves oculos conata attollere, rursus / deficit*), that impulse to tragic sublimity and to dignity of death is immediately submerged in the petty hypocrisies of Juno and the beautified terror of the very close. Once again, a comparison with Homer may help us to focus on the quality of the Vergilian pathos. Just as Sarpedon is about to be killed by Patroclus, Zeus cries to Hera that he feels torn by conflicting desires (*dichtha de moi kradiē memone phresin hormainonti,* The heart in my breast is balanced between two ways as I ponder [16.435]) in his pity (*eleēse* [431]) for his son: he wants to submit to Fate, but he wants even more to save Sarpedon. Hera points out that it would be unwise of Zeus to do this, since other gods, who have loved ones among the mortals, would certainly want to imitate his action. Then she (and Homer) mitigates the full anguish of Sarpedon's death with some of the gentlest and most beautiful lines in the *Iliad*:

ἀλλ' εἴ τοι φίλος ἐστί, τεὸν δ' ὀλοφύρεται ἦτορ,
ἦ τοι μέν μιν ἔασον ἐνὶ κρατερῇ ὑσμίνῃ
χέρσ' ὕπο Πατρόκλοιο Μενοιτιάδαο δαμῆναι·
αὐτὰρ ἐπεὶ δὴ τόν γε λίπῃ ψυχή τε καὶ αἰών,
πέμπειν μιν Θάνατόν τε φέρειν καὶ ϝήδυμον Ὕπνον,
εἰς ὅ κε δὴ Λυκίης εὐρείης δῆμον ἵκωνται,
ἔνθα ϝε ταρχύσουσι κασίγνητοί τε ϝέται τε
τύμβῳ τε στήλῃ τε· τὸ γὰρ γέρας ἐστὶ θανόντων.

(*Iliad* 16.450–457)

But if he is dear to you and if your heart is grieved for him, nevertheless let him be mastered by the hands of Patroclus, son of

Menoetius, in harsh encounter; but when his soul and his lifetime
have abandoned him, charge Death and kind Sleep to bear him
off until they come to the land of wide Lycia where his brothers
and his friends will bury him with tomb and monument. For such
is the recompense of the dead.

The juxtaposition of death and sleep borders on oxymoron, for
though sleep is in a sense like death, sleep entails life and is thus
the opposite of death; there is, then, a *coincidentia oppositorum*,
a new unity that transcends mere euphemism and modulates softly
into the simple splendor of *to gar geras esti thanontōn*. This
blending of gentle solace and martial glory is enough:

> ὡς ἔφατ᾽, οὐδ᾽ ἀπίθησε πατὴρ ἀνδρῶν τε θεῶν τε.
> αἱματοέσσας δὲ ψιάδας κατέχευεν ἔραζε
> παῖδα φίλον τιμῶν, τόν ϝοι Πάτροκλος ἔμελλε
> φθίσειν ἐν Τροίῃ ἐριβώλακι, τηλόθι πάτρης.
>
> (16.458–461)

Thus she spoke, and the father of men and gods was not unpersuaded by her words. And tears of blood he wept upon the earth,
his dear son thus honoring—Sarpedon, whom Patroclus was about
to destroy, there on the fertile soil of Troy, far away from his own
country.

Zeus is persuaded and composed, the grief is pondered and let go
of. Then the inexorable movement to disaster begins again, and
Sarpedon dies with the magnificent ease and courage that befit a
son of Zeus. It is a spare pathos, enough to light up the depth
of feeling and the good sense of Zeus, enough to foil the heroism
of Sarpedon, not enough to ruin the bright firm outlines of their
dignity. In a way that we might be tempted to describe as Stoic,
feelings are allowed to function in their natural way, but they
are not allowed to overwhelm the characters or the audience and
thereby to deprive them of their ability to understand what they
are doing and what is happening.

In the Vergilian passage what first appears to be gentleness is
not balanced by anything, and the beauty gradually overwhelms
and dissolves the dignity of Dido's death and with it the meaning
of her life and the authenticity of her struggles. This sleight of
hand is accomplished with a very few words, which are carefully
set in a deceptively short and simple description of Dido's final
moments: *omnipotens, miserata, misera, nec merita morte, croceis,
pennis, roscida, mille varios colores trahens*. In the beauty of the
picture and in the heartsick loveliness of the cadences, we may

71

no longer remember that this frustrated and agonized woman is, by the testimony of the goddess herself, essentially the victim of the deity who proffers her a release from her torment. For this reason, there is a strangely disturbing fraudulence about this gentle demise. Part of this fraudulence is achieved by means of the ironic manipulations of pathos; part of it is achieved by a deliberate confusion of narrators: the view of Dido is superimposed on the view of the epic narrator, and on this delicate complexity there is further superimposed the view of Juno. In this composite image, the outlines of the final scene—and indeed of Book 4 as a whole —are blurred, and the action of this book and the significance of its leading character find no still center; the story of Dido drifts away from us, its momentum and conflicts are not gathered into a vanishing point, so they move off into Book 6 and beyond it to Book 12,[63] nor do they find unity or perspective anyplace in the poem.

> at vero ut vultum vidit morientis et ora,
> ora modis Anchisiades pallentia miris,
> ingemuit miserans graviter dextramque tetendit,
> et mentem patriae subiit pietatis imago.
>
> (10.821–824)
>
> But when he saw the look and face of dying
> Lausus—he was mysteriously pale—
> Anchises' son sighed heavily with pity
> and stretched out his right hand; the image of
> his love for his own father touched his mind.

These verses show a remarkable blending of simplicity of phrasing and syntax with rich elaborations and compressions of emotion. The first, third, and fourth verses are beautifully offset in their clarity and vigor by the aureate impressionism of the second verse, where the repetition of *ora*, the alternation of dactyls and spondees, and the patronymic, framed by caesuras, combine to fashion an unearthly, almost dreamlike languor. This quality of unreality is further augmented by Vergil's stress on Aeneas' intellectual response, apart from his compassion, to the death of Lausus: the young man's death becomes a kind of symbol or paradigm of filial devotion (*patriae pietatis imago*) that transcends this specific death. It is towards this paradigm of the virtue that Aeneas holds most dear that he responds with such emotion, and it is to this virtue that Aeneas addresses his great speech. The confrontation in this scene, then, is between Aeneas and himself, for, though the scene may in part remind us of the scene between Achilles and Lycaon in *Iliad* 21, there is no actual dramatic confrontation between Aeneas and Lausus. Lausus is dead when Aeneas speaks to him in a truly personal way; the initial cry, *quo moriture, ruis, maioraque viribus audes?* / *fallit te incautum pietas tua*, in its bitter irony, prepares us for the speech that follows, but it evokes no response from Lausus, and, characteristically, Vergil does not, in the Homeric manner, offer a dialogue wherein the opposing characters verbalize their conflicts as well as enact them. The conflict here, as in the scenes with Dido and the final scene with Turnus, is between the piety that is defined by patriotism and the larger, almost Epicurean piety that feels not only responsibility for persons of one's own family and *civitas* but also for persons whose humanity and suffering demand one's respect and help. In the dead Lausus Aeneas recognizes, unconsciously, himself, or rather, the part of himself that he most respects, that is most essentially his true self. And in his killing of this image of himself, Aeneas adumbrates the final scene of the poem where, in killing Turnus, he is forced to abandon compassion because he is finally caught in the fine web of *ira* and of patriotic obligations that are, in respect of the ideal compassion, rather narrow.[64] The scene, then, is emblematic of one of the great themes of the poem, *Anchisiades*: we remember the great scene between Priam and Neoptolemus in Book 2, and, more important, we remember the superlative moment between Achilles and Priam in *Iliad* 24:

ὣς φάτο, τῷ δ' ἄρα πατρὸς ὑφ' ἵμερον ὦρσε γόοιο·
ἁψάμενος δ' ἄρα χειρὸς ἀπώσατο ἦκα γέροντα.
τὼ δὲ μνησαμένω, ὁ μὲν Ἕκτορος ἀνδροφόνοιο
κλαῖ' ἀδινά, προπάροιθε ποδῶν Ἀχιλῆος ἐλυσθείς,
αὐτὰρ Ἀχιλλεὺς κλαῖεν ἑὸν πατέρ', ἄλλοτε δ' αὖτε
Πάτροκλον· τῶν δὲ στοναχὴ κατὰ δώματ' ὀρώρει.

(*Iliad* 24.507–512)

Thus Priam spoke and set Achilles craving to lament his own father. And Achilles clasped the old man's hand and gently he pushed him from him. So the two men pondered their dead in memory: Priam, hunched at the feet of Achilles, wept helplessly for Hector, killer of men, and Achilles now wept for his father, now for Patroclus. And the noise of their anguish streamed throughout the dwelling.

Here, for a brief inimitable moment, pitiless anger and bitterness are relieved by common grief. The impossibility of true reconciliation between these two will flare up again very soon (552–570) when Priam overplays his hand, but, if it is wishful thinking, indeed, misguided sentimentality, to speak of character change in Achilles, here or anywhere, we must nevertheless acknowledge that Achilles' sympathy for Priam and his willingness to suspend his bitterness temporarily shadow forth a profound and authentic humanity. But this vision of common suffering as compassion arises naturally out of the character of Achilles and the situation in which he finds himself. The compassion of Aeneas, though it is not—like the compassion of Juno in the previous passage—so inexplicable as to seem hypocritical, though it is utterly in character, takes us by surprise, for the epic battlefield is not the place for this kind of compassion. This seeming indecorum reminds us that, in a very real sense, the epic battlefield is not the place for Aeneas, that the hero of this poem is constantly forced to act against his instincts and his most cherished beliefs and ideals in a way that would be unthinkable for an Iliadic hero. This is not to say that Achilles is a pitiless monster. In *alla, philos, thane kai su* (*Iliad* 21.106 ff.) we glimpse beneath the cruel irony a stern pity that, as in the scene with Priam, issues from a restrained yet flawless intuition of universal suffering and common doom: *all' epi toi kai emoi thanatos kai moira krataiē* [Yet even I have also my death and my strong destiny] (21.110).

In this passage of Vergil such an exact and ruthless closing with tragic vision is not to be found. Vergil has discovered here the heart of his poem, the greatness of the human spirit (as it is reflected in *pietas*) ruined by murderous unreason (*violentia, ira*), but the fullness of this terrifying vision is shadowed with pathos and sentiment and is further obscured by Aeneas' own delusions: he still imagines that it will be possible for him to perform the role that destiny has thrust on him and to preserve the integrity of his personal sensitivity and decency.[65] But, again, the Epicurean saint has no place on the field of carnage, and there is something particularly horrifying in the Epicurean expressing this kind of sentiment just after he has killed his man. The final emphasis on this conflict and on the moral dangers of *pietas* Vergil properly reserves for the end of the poem. Here that ruin is adumbrated by Aeneas' unconscious recognition of the fact that he cannot quite be both the patriot and the sage. His compassion for the dead Lausus is itself pathetic because it is futile and reflects the hazard to his ideas. Yet the fact of this futility is too dark, too harsh, too intolerable. So, as is frequently the case, it is rendered opaquely.

With the words *moriture* (811), *tunicam, molli mater quam
neverat auro* (818), *ingemuit miserans* (823), *miserande puer*
(825), and *ipsum / sanguine turpantem comptos de more capil-
los* (831–832) we find ourselves once again screened, by a
delicate haze, a melancholy loveliness, from realities that are un-
bearable in exact proportion as they are unintelligible. But these
stratagems of solace are deliberately deceptive. In Vergil, the darkness does not serve to foil the light; rather, the light illumines
the quality and the extent of darkness. And as the brightness of
Vergil's images tends to dissolve so as to reveal an essential night,
so his tenderness and wistful regard illumine a universe in which
such feelings are futile, for in that universe the concepts of reason
and freedom, which are at the heart of the tragic classical vision,
are, probably, illusions; the reality is a massive, incomprehensible impersonality that manifests itself in the will of Juno.

3. BLURRED IMAGES

A. PERSONS

1.   οἱ δ' ὅτε δή ῥ' ἐς χῶρον ἕνα ξυνιόντες ἵκοντο,
σύν ῥ' ἔβαλον ῥινούς, σὺν δ' ἔγχεα καὶ μένε' ἀνδρῶν
χαλκεοθωρήκων· ἀτὰρ ἀσπίδες ὀμφαλόεσσαι
ἔπληντ' ἀλλήλῃσι, πολὺς δ' ὀρυμαγδὸς ὀρώρει.
ἔνθα δ' ἅμ' οἰμωγή τε καὶ εὐχωλὴ πέλεν ἀνδρῶν
ὀλλύντων τε καὶ ὀλλυμένων, ῥέε δ' αἵματι γαῖα.
ὡς δ' ὅτε χειμάρρῳ ποταμῷ κατ' ὄρεσφι ῥέοντε
ἐς μισγαγκέϊαν συμβάλλετον ὄβριμον ὕδωρ
κρουνῶν ἐκ μεγάλων, κοίλης ἔντοσθε χαράδρης·
τῶν δέ τε τηλόσε δοῦπον ἐν οὔρεσιν ἔκλυε ποιμήν·
ὡς τῶν μισγομένων γένετο ϝιϝαχή τε πόνος τε.
                     (*Iliad* 4.446–456)

And when the men who were moving towards each other had come
to the same spot, they clashed, shield on shield, spear on spear, in
bronze ferocity, and the studded bucklers collided and the great
rumble of battle gathered and spread. Then mingled the shrieks and
the cheers of killer and killed, and the earth streamed with blood.
As when winter rivers, flashing from their vast springs down the
mountains to a glen, clash their colossal waters in the hollow ra-
vine, and in mountains far distant a shepherd hears the tumult of
their meeting, such was the roar and clamor of the soldiers as they
met.

diverso interea miscentur moenia luctu
et magis atque magis, quamquam secreta parentis
Anchisae domus arboribusque obtecta recessit,
clarescunt sonitus armorumque ingruit horror.
excutior somno et summi fastigia tecti
ascensu supero atque arrectis auribus adsto:
in segetem veluti cum flamma furentibus austris
incidit aut rapidus montano flumine torrens
sternit agros, sternit sata laeta boumque labores
praecipitisque trahit silvas; stupet inscius alto
accipiens sonitum saxi de vertice pastor.

(Aeneid 2.298–308)

Meanwhile the howls of war confound the city.
And more and more—although my father's house
was far, withdrawn, and screened by trees—the roar
is sharper, the dread clash of battle grows.
I start from sleep and climb the sloping roof
above the house. I stand, alerted: just
as when, with furious south winds, a fire
has fallen on a wheat field, or a torrent
that hurtles from a mountain stream lays low
the meadows, low the happy crops, and low
the labor of the oxen, dragging forests
headlong—and even then, bewildered and
unknowing, perched upon a rock, the shepherd
will listen to the clamor.

    In dealing with these passages, it will not do us much good to
invoke Vergil's subtle artistry against Homer's naïve simplicities,
nor, on the other hand, to assert the sheer superiority of Homer's
drama and vigor as against Vergil's lyrical and wistful vagueness.
Homer excludes vagueness from his simile as surely as Vergil
emphasizes it in his; he seeks something *simplex et unum* because
that is what suits his purpose at this point in his poem. And Vergil
evades, indeed banishes, what is *simplex et unum* from this passage because unity and clarity of mood and image would be highly
unsuitable to what he is trying to imagine here.

    Homer's simile succeeds in defining the confusion and the
terror of this battle because Homer modulates the particular elements of the violence and disorder into an intelligible configuration which we experience because the shepherd in the simile is
able to experience something like it. The screaming and shouts of
triumph of the men who are killing and being killed (*olluntōn te*

kai ollumenōn), the magnitude of the tumult and the ineffable strain of the men as they close with one another (*tōn misgomenōn ...wiwachē te ponos te*) are gathered into and measured by the din of waters (*doupon eklue*) that the shepherd hears, far away from the floods as he is (*tēlose en ouresi*). The shepherd and the din that he hears become the center around which an otherwise unintelligible chaos crystallizes, becomes organized. This is not the place—nor is there any need—to elaborate upon the elegance with which this much power and fury are compressed into a mere seven verses or to commend the extraordinary emphasis and precision that this economy effects. We are interested only in the fact that the simile, which exists only to define the quality and the quantity of the warriors' fury, fulfills its function so successfully and with such inimitable economy because Homer's shepherd, by experiencing these floods at this distance, convinces us of the intensity of this fury.

Vergil's simile is as different from Homer's in its tone and texture as it is in its aims. We find once again an extraordinary compression, but in Vergil's passage the compression neither works to achieve unity of feeling nor does it gather the diversities of which it is made into a complicated but controlled picture. The echo of *Iliad* 4.446 ff., combined as it is with echoes of *Iliad* 2.455 ff. and 5.87 ff. (fire and the beautiful labors of the young men, respectively), creates a richly textured and disquieting complexity that exactly expresses the anxiety and foreboding of Aeneas as he wakes from his troubled sleep. Vergil's simile, unlike Homer's, does not define action, sharpen the appetite for seeing and knowing, and suggest an unseen and stable immensity behind what is seen and heard; rather, in blurring its image, in stressing the shepherd's ignorance of what, precisely, is happening, it renders a confused and indistinct emotion. Where Homer offers lucid configurations that nearly satisfy the mind and eyes and thus persuade us of the plausibility of his scene, that intensify its chaos and terror in proportion as they order them, Vergil's simile mirrors the movements of a consciousness that gradually wakens to stimuli it dreads and cannot comprehend. *Stupet inscius pastor accipiens sonitum* transforms the clear immediacy of *poimēn eklue doupon* into a vague, shapeless anxiety. Forest fire or flood? *De alto saxo* emphasizes the reason for the shepherd's uncertainty and his incipient dread (there may be danger to his charges), where *tēlose* emphasizes rather the magnitude of the noise the shepherd hears. Vergil's shepherd, isolated on his high mountain crag, hears a noise whose cause he cannot identify; he can only sense a danger that is the more menacing because he does not understand what it is that is threatening him and his flock. Aeneas is neatly compared to a shepherd as he hears the noise of a forest fire or a flood; this precision of analogy, this neatness, is not present in Homer's simile and is not needed there.[66] Yet it is the very elegance of Vergil's simile, the involvement of Aeneas in the simile, that curiously diminishes its dramatic vigor and clarity of outline. The action and therefore the image of the action have been internalized in such a way that this simile, unlike Homer's, is not used to intensify the pleasure, strength, and mystery of perception, but rather to emphasize what cannot be seen and to intensify the uncertainty and the apprehension that can occur when something that needs to be seen cannot be seen. What we apprehend is the indistinct, wavering, unordered emotions that an unintelligible disorder have called into existence. In deliberately and emphatically transforming Homer's dynamic clarity, his bright representation of action, into blurred and wavering uncertainties, Vergil underscores at this crucial point in Book 2 both Aeneas' immediate situation and the permanent dilemma of his ignorance and the strange, un-Homeric world in which he moves. Here and frequently elsewhere in the poem (and not merely in the first six books) it is precisely drama and action that are excluded from our view in favor of soliloquy and vacillation. In Book 2, after this moment, and elsewhere in the poem, Aeneas will try to act but will be stopped from acting effectively[67] by circumstances that he cannot possibly comprehend. And here, as elsewhere in the poem at crucial moments in the action, pathos predominates over action; and shadows and half-lights over form.

2. εὗρον ἔπειτ' Ὀδυσῆα διίφιλον· ἀμφὶ δ' ἄρ' αὐτὸν
   Τρῶες ἕπον ὡς εἴ τε δαφοινοὶ θῶες ὄρεσφιν
   ἀμφ' ἔλαφον κεραὸν βεβλημένον, ὅν τ' ἔβαλ' ἀνὴρ
   ἰῷ ἀπὸ νευρῆς· τὸν μέν τ' ἤλυξε πόδεσσι
   φεύγων, ὄφρ' αἷμα λιαρὸν καὶ γούνατ' ὀρώρῃ·
   αὐτὰρ ἐπεὶ δὴ τόν γε δαμάσσεται ὠκὺς ὀϊστός,
   ὠμοφάγοι μιν θῶες ἐν οὔρεσι δαρδάπτουσιν
   ἐν νέμεϊ σκιερῷ· ἐπί τε λῖν ἤγαγε δαίμων
   σίντην· θῶες μέν τε διέτρεσαν, αὐτὰρ ὁ δάπτει·
                                    (*Iliad* 11.473–481)

Then they found Odysseus, dear to Zeus, hemmed in by Trojans, as red jackals ring an antlered stag that a man has wounded with an arrow. The man it escapes, flees onward while its blood beats warm and the strength of its legs endures; but when the quick arrow has mastered it at last, then ravenous jackals fall to devouring it in a shadowed copse in the mountains. But a lion some power guides against them, a voracious beast and angry, and the jackals scatter terrified, and the lion feasts. . . .

> uritur infelix Dido totaque vagatur
> urbe furens, qualis coniecta cerva sagitta,
> quam procul incautam nemora inter Cresia fixit
> pastor agens telis liquitque volatile ferrum
> nescius; illa fuga silvas saltusque peragrat
> Dictaeos, haeret lateri letalis harundo.
> $\qquad$ (*Aeneid* 4.68–73)

> Unhappy Dido burns. Across the city
> she wanders in her frenzy—even as
> a heedless hind hit by an arrow when
> a shepherd drives for game with darts among
> the Cretan woods and, unawares, from far
> leaves winging steel inside her flesh; she roams
> the forest and the wooded slopes of Dicte,
> the shaft of death still clinging to her side.

In Homer's simile there are four elements: the stag, the hunter (*anēr*), the jackals, and the lion. The sequence of events that they enact and the causes and the effects of these events show a graceful economy in their design and articulation. One might object that the final event, the lion's feasting on the abandoned stag (*autar ho daptei*), has no clear correspondence with the action in the poem that it exists to illumine, but this objection would tend to ignore the central focus of the simile—the danger that Odysseus is in and the flight of the Trojans as Ajax and Menelaus come to his aid. With this focus clearly in mind, we see that the lion's triumph over the jackals illumines the courage both of Odysseus as he defends himself and of Ajax as he comes to rescue his fellow soldier. And it is this sense of triumph that the simile radiates. From a series of what at first seem random happenings—the wounding of the stag, its discovery by the jackals, the marvelous appearance of the lion (*lin ēgage daimōn*)—there emerges a sudden splendor, the defeat of the craven, the salvation of Zeus' chosen (*Odysēa diiphilon* [473]). The simile is from first to last dramatic, and it dramatizes the plight of Odysseus, his courage and his change of fortune, from hazard to safety, with dynamic clarity.[68]

It would be imprudent to say that Vergil, in borrowing from

this simile, was consciously ironic in selecting from it precisely those features that are undramatic: the deer and the archer. Yet one need not ignore the perhaps unintended yet not unwelcome irony that a reader may feel in comparing the two similes. Homer's stag, though wounded, is not without its own force and stamina; it escapes the hunter and runs valiantly till it drops. Then, when it falls, its suffering is tactfully ignored. The archer, identified merely as a man, wounds his intended prey, which then escapes him. But these figures exist only to make plausible the encounter between the jackals and the lion; their actions set in motion the central action of the simile, but whatever feelings they may have about what they do and suffer are excluded from the mimesis— they do not matter. But in Vergil's simile the qualities of these figures (*cerva-incauta; pastor-nescius*) and the pathos of their situation (it is *not* an encounter, much less a conflict) are all that do matter. Evocative mood replaces drama as pathos replaces action. This is, of course, not a criticism of Vergil; for he, like Homer, is obeying the decorum that his materials and his imagination have shaped. There is no action for a simile to mirror in this material. But there is a disordered, all but unintelligible feeling to suggest. Dido is, of course, in motion, but that motion (*vagatur*) is not directed to a goal; her aimless physical motion is expressive of disordered movement in a soul deprived of volition and action. This kind of failure of reason and freedom cannot be plausibly represented by clear pictures, so, for all its economy and power, Vergil's simile excludes clarity and concentrates on appealing to the *alogos aesthēsis*, that aspect of the reader's mind and heart that can perceive—though it cannot comprehend—this kind of experience when it is adequately suggested in all of its imprecision and disorder.[69]

If one asks why the hind is *incauta* and why the pastor is *nescius*, one asks questions that are irrelevant to the simile, though they are not irrelevant to the narrative. Dido is *incauta*, and Aeneas is *nescius* (as is frequently the case with Aeneas). They are involved in an inexorable, destructive process that neither they nor we will ever quite understand. At the moment that Vergil presents us with this simile, we experience this process as Dido herself experiences it, in all its horror and incomprehensibility. The process and the simile that help us imagine that process are horrible in exact proportion as they are, however vivid, incomprehensible. A random meaningless accident (*procul incautam fixit pastor nescius*). The pastor had a purpose in what he was doing (*nemora in Cresia agens telis*), but he is somehow (and the vagueness is important) *nescius* in performing his action. This ignorance intensifies the pathos of the situation that the hind's failure of caution has made possible. But even when we have understood this much, our minds are still worried with the question, But why did it happen? Vergil has a special fondness for this kind of question (even as Homer, who is not primitive either, ruthlessly avoids such questions). Vergil also has a fondness for toying, ironically, with inadequate answers to his questions. The hind was *incauta*, the shepherd was—what? Stupid? Careless? Juno is angry? Jupiter is angry? Or wise? That's fate? [70] The pieces of the puzzle are fingered anxiously, distractedly, then finally laid aside—the pieces do not fit. Why should a hind who has no notion that there is a distant shepherd who is careless with weapons take the trouble to be cautious or be somehow criticized for being incautious? Why does a shepherd shoot at random? Why is a shepherd shooting? Either of set purpose or at random? Do poetic shepherds shoot? This shepherd, of course, outside the simile, is shepherd of his nation, but that does not explain his being *nescius* inside the simile any more than the imprudence of Dido outside the simile explains the imprudence of the hind inside the narrative (and we are bound to ask, Was Dido truly imprudent, is that the right word for it, outside the simile, in the poem that the simile comments on?).[71] If the *harundo* is *letalis*, does the *cerva*, in fact, die? Homer would probably have shown us the dying and dead hind. Why, except for the *harundo*, is the scene laid in Crete? Is it geography of liars as well as the geography of dreadful arrows that is in question?

I am aware that these questions may sound at once petulant and overscrupulous, but what I want to suggest in framing them in this way is that it is by virtue of the vagueness, the near incoherence of its images, that the simile achieves the power and the resonance that it undoubtedly possesses and that it was undoubtedly designed to possess. *Incauta* and *nescius* take on a suitably eerie and inarticulate force in the twilight landscape of this stylized and shadowy Crete that a clearer place and a clearer picture could not bestow on them. And the force of this simile resonates far beyond its brief compass; its pathos, like the pathos of Dido and of Aeneas himself, can be deeply felt not only throughout Book 4 but also at various moments throughout the poem, wherever there is unintelligible suffering and inexplicable ignorance—can be felt, here and elsewhere, but cannot be understood. Where Homer permits us to participate in his contemplation of things as they are, Vergil persuades us to brood on images and on

the intimations and uncertainties that these images suggest. Homer
tends to imagine actions and to let us decide what they may mean;
Vergil tends to imagine moods and to let us ponder their discrepancies and their insubstantialities.

3.　αἱ δ' ἄλλαι ψυχαὶ νεκύων κατατεθνηώτων
ἕστασαν ἀχνύμεναι, εἴροντο δὲ κήδε' ἑκάστη.
οἴη δ' Αἴαντος ψυχὴ Τελαμωνιάδαο
νόσφιν ἀφεστήκει κεχολωμένη εἵνεκα νίκης,
τήν μιν ἐγὼ νίκησα δικαζόμενος παρὰ νηυσὶ
τεύχεσιν ἀμφ' Ἀχιλῆος· ἔθηκε δὲ πότνια μήτηρ,
παῖδες δὲ Τρώων δίκασαν καὶ Παλλὰς Ἀθήνη. . . .

ὣς ἐφάμην· ὁ δέ μ' οὐδὲν ἀμείβετο, βῆ δὲ μετ' ἄλλας
ψυχὰς εἰς Ἔρεβος νεκύων κατατεθνηώτων.
ἔνθα χ' ὅμως προσέφη κεχολωμένος, ἤ κεν ἐγὼ τόν·
ἀλλά μοι ἤθελε θυμὸς ἐνὶ στήθεσσι φίλοισι
τῶν ἄλλων ψυχὰς ϝιδέειν κατατεθνηώτων.
　　　　　　(*Odyssey* 11.541–547, 563–567)

There hung about me others of the departed, each sadly asking
news of his loved ones. Only the spirit of Aias the son of Telamon
kept aloof, he being yet vexed with me for that I had been pre-
ferred before him when by the ships we disputed the harness of
Achilles, the arms which his Goddess-mother had set as prize, and
which the sons of the Trojans and Pallas Athene adjudged. . . . So
I appealed, but he answered not a word: only went away towards
Erebus with other spirits of the departed dead. Yet likely he
would have spoken despite his wrath—or I to him again—only
my heart was wishful to see other souls of the many dead.

> inter quas Phoenissa recens a volnere Dido
> errabat silva in magna. quam Troius heros
> ut primum iuxta stetit agnovitque per umbras
> obscuram, qualem primo qui surgere mense
> aut videt aut vidisse putat per nubila lunam,
> demisit lacrimas dulcique adfatus amorest. . . .
> tandem corripuit sese atque inimica refugit
> in nemus umbriferum, coniunx ubi pristinus illi
> respondet curis aequatque Sychaeus amorem.
> nec minus Aeneas casu concussus iniquo
> prosequitur lacrimis longe et miseratur euntem.
> 　　　　　　(*Aeneid* 6.450–455, 472–476)

Among them, wandering in that great forest,
and with her wound still fresh: Phoenician Dido.

And when the Trojan hero recognized her
dim shape among the shadows (just as one
who either sees or thinks he sees among
the cloud banks, when the month is young, the moon
rising), he wept and said with tender love. . . .
At last she tore herself away; she fled—
and still his enemy—into the forest
of shadows where Sychaeus, once her husband,
answers her sorrows, gives her love for love.
Nevertheless, Aeneas, stunned by her
unkindly fate, still follows at a distance
with tears and pity for her as she goes.

Vergil's grand invention in this simile and for this scene, *aut videt aut vidisse putat lunam*, defines his mastery of this kind of controlled imprecision as perhaps no other image in the poem can define it. Instead of the adjective *nescius*, which we have found enforming the two previous passages, we here find a clause that suggests Aeneas' confusion, surprise, and guilt without specifying any of these feelings or emphasizing any of them. The facts of ignorance and uncertainty are now compounded with their consequences: here, Dido's death and the hopeless, endless grief of her punishment (*errabat silva in magna*, where the tense of the verb, or rather, its aspect, suggests perfectly the slow-motion, uncompletable aimlessness of her movement); Aeneas, in a way that he cannot now and never will understand, has been partially instrumental in bringing this punishment upon her, and *aut videt aut vidisse putat* reflects the obscure complex of emotions that suddenly besets him on realizing that indeed this is she, Dido. He is shocked to see her, he hopes that it is she whom he sees; he fears seeing her; he wants to see her; he feels guilt in seeing her, for, among other things, such is the diminishment of her beauty, such is her ruin, that he would be appalled by her state even if he were not involved in its accomplishment, as he is, despite his unconvincing, almost pathetic denial of guilt: *nec credere quivi / hunc tantum tibi me discessu ferre dolorem* (463–464)—

> And I could not
> believe that with my going I should bring
> so great a grief as this.

He feared it was true, and now he knows it is true. This complexity of his feelings about himself (and her) is heightened by the fact that Dido is, in a sense, unreal; this ambivalence of existence not only increases his guilt; it also increases the desperation of this moment: two modes of being, of his being and her unbeing, are juxtaposed in a way that creates an uneasy, undefinable dread—a dread that the uncertainty of the simile, with the obscure brightness wavering into and out of vision, underscores.[72]

The quality of this dread may be defined by comparing this scene with its model in the *Odyssey*, in which Odysseus sees Ajax. The feelings of Odysseus on meeting with Ajax are naturally far less mixed than those of Aeneas on meeting Dido. Odysseus feels guilt, and he clearly feels some pity for the doomed warrior whom he had bested in the contest for Achilles' arms. Yet his embarrassment in seeing Ajax evokes in him not only guilt and pity; it also evokes qualities that are characteristic of Homeric poetry: the suavity and very real courtesy of his speech to his rival. This courtesy, like the close of the scene in which common sense bids Odysseus to put a good face on the encounter, lessens the unreality of the moment as well as its uneasiness. There are moments of horror in this Homeric hell, but nowhere does it show a moment like the one in Vergil's hell, when Aeneas and the reader are suddenly struck with an intimation both of the fact of Dido's terrible insubstantiality and of the reasons for it. (The reader's sense differs from Aeneas' in that he knows more about her death than Aeneas could possibly know, and this irony increases the horror of Aeneas' situation.) Pure clarities could reveal neither the indeterminate state of being that Dido suffers nor the mixed and ineffable emotions that assail Aeneas (and us) as he encounters Dido in her new modes of being and unbeing. But the pathos, the grief, the horror, and the incomprehensibility of the entire scene are precisely mirrored in the blurred clarities of this incomparable simile, where light, half-light, darkness, knowledge, ignorance, guilt, love, despair, realities, and unrealities circle one another in a shifting, uncertain, yet dazzling configuration of the known and the unknown, the seen and the unseeable.[73]

4. ἀλλὰ μάλ' οὐ Μήδειαν ἐπὶ γλυκερὸς λάβεν ὕπνος.
πολλὰ γὰρ Αἰσονίδαο πόθῳ μελεδήματ' ἔγειρεν
δειδυῖαν ταύρων κρατερὸν μένος, οἷσιν ἔμελλεν
φθῖσθαι ἀεικελίῃ μοίρῃ κατὰ νειὸν Ἄρηος.
πυκνὰ δέ οἱ κραδίη στηθέων ἔντοσθεν ἔθυιεν,
ἠελίου ὥς τίς τε δόμοις ἐνιπάλλεται αἴγλη
ὕδατος ἐξανιοῦσα, τὸ δὴ νέον ἠὲ λέβητι
ἠέ που ἐν γαυλῷ κέχυται· ἡ δ' ἔνθα καὶ ἔνθα
ὠκείῃ στροφάλιγγι τινάσσεται ἀίσσουσα·
ὣς δὲ καὶ ἐν στήθεσσι κέαρ ἐλελίζετο κούρης.
                              (*Argonautica* 3.751–760)

84

But Medea no delightful sleep surprised. No, rather fear that was engendered by desire for Jason fed unending wakefulness. She pictured how the stark strength of the bulls must crush her lover there on Ares' field, trampled by outrageous destiny. And as this doom she figured, thick and fierce her heartbeat quickened. As when a shaft of sun flickers upon the walls, reflected from water just poured into kettle or pail, now here, now there, it flutters in rippling pattern, so within her breast the wild heart swayed and shivered.

> talia per Latium. quae Laomedontius heros
> cuncta videns magno curarum fluctuat aestu
> atque animum nunc huc celerem, nunc dividit illuc
> in partesque rapit varias perque omnia versat:
> sicut aquae tremulum labris ubi lumen aenis
> sole repercussum aut radiantis imagine lunae
> omnia pervolitat late loca iamque sub auras
> erigitur summique ferit laquearia tecti.
>
> (*Aeneid* 8.18–25)

And so it went through all of Latium;
and when the Trojan hero has seen this,
he wavers on a giant tide of troubles;
his racing mind is split; it shifts here, there,
and rushes on to many different plans,
turning to everything: even as when
the quivering light of water in bronze basins
reflected from the sun or from the moon's
glittering image glides across all things
and now darts skyward, strikes the roof's high ceiling.

There is doubtless a fine irony in Vergil's borrowing and expanding the simile that Apollonius had used to illumine the fear and the love of the young Medea for Jason in order to represent the far different emotions of his middle-aged and eminently responsible warrior; but we need not, and indeed we should not, press this irony very far.[74] In shaping this witty indecorum between the Alexandrian lady and the Roman founding father, Vergil may be doing nothing more than emphasizing his own awareness of the delicate and difficult tension that exists between much of his form (Alexandrian *maniera*) and much of his content (Roman *gravitas*). It is amusing that the maiden's torments have been juxtaposed momentarily with the epic hero's torments, but the amusement disappears as quickly as it came into a quite serious use of Apollonius' simile. What matters to us here is the ways in which Vergil has altered his Alexandrian model, his shifting its contours in accordance with his own habits of perceptions in order to create an image that is at once far more complex and far more obscure than the fresh and charming picture that Apollonius had invented.

In Apollonius' image the trembling light defines a single emotion, the fear that Medea feels for Jason's safety. It is true that this fear is caused by her love for him (*polla gar Aisonidao pothōi meledēmat' egeiren* [752]) and is intensified by the guilt she feels in contemplating the necessity of betraying her father and her country for Jason's sake (*deilē egō, nun entha kakōn ē entha genōmai?* [771]) but, subtly as these other emotions are elsewhere developed in this section of the poem, this simile illumines not the divisions of her soul but the intensity, the unity of her dread for her beloved's life (*deiduian taurōn krateron menos* [753]). The divisions of the spirit, the conflicting drives that torment her will be immediately presented in the narrator's own comments (760–769) and in the brilliantly modulated soliloquy (771–801) in which she ponders her feelings and their probable consequences. But the simile itself exists to define only the totality of the anxiety she feels for the safety of the man with whom she has fallen in love. And because its aim is clear-cut, its form is clear-cut. The purity and the essential simplicity of the girl's nature, suddenly shaken by an unaccustomed violence, are compared to the quick-darting, violent reflections of sunlight on water that has been poured into a receptacle and has not had time to settle and so permit a stable reflection. It is the violence and the speed of his images that interest Apollonius; the objects that these qualities exist in—the sunlight, the basin, the milk pail, the house —are sketched with utter simplicity—they are merely instruments to reveal the wildness of her dread, which is brilliantly compressed in the speed and force of the final sentence of the simile: *hē d'entha kai entha / ōkeiēi strophalingi tinassetai aissousa*).

Vergil introduces his simile with the divisions of Aeneas' spirit: *atque animum nunc huc celerem, nunc dividit illuc / in partes rapit varias perque omnia versat* (20–21). The simile continues to examine the immensity and the uncertainties of those divisions. The single reference to swiftness in the simile proper (*pervolitat*) is gathered into, and finally lost in, a pattern which emphasizes the delicate wavering, the subtle agitation of the reflection as it shifts over the walls and ceilings of a vast hall. In Vergil we see sunlight or moonlight trembling in a brazen bowl, light that darts about the high, wide walls and strikes the ornate ceiling; in Apollonius we see mere sunlight in a pail that flickers wildly on the walls of a room. The calculated imprecision and vague grandeur of Vergil's simile—when compared with the precision, the simplicity, and the clear focus of Apollonius' simile—reveal the kind of anxiety that Vergil has imagined for this section of his poem. The intensity of Medea's fear persuades us both of the depth of her love for Jason and the depth of her guilt in respect of the treason she intends. The simile that represents her fear, then, is dramatic not only in its form but also in its function, for in offering a plausible and forceful description of her state of mind at this moment in the poem, the simile helps to explain her dilemma, the choice she makes, and the action she performs as a result of that choice. But Vergil's simile, though it is not merely an example of his *Stimmungskunst*, does not, and does not pretend to, illumine a specific conflict or advance or clarify the poem's action. Aeneas is indeed worried about his immediate dilemma, but that dilemma is compounded with great confusion and uncertainty. For Aeneas is, as usual, worried not only about the immediate obstacles and dangers that confront him and his people but also about the morality of the difficulties that he finds himself entangled in: *tristi turbatus pectora bello* (29).[75] We need not make merry over the post-Socratic philosopher who has suddenly been shoved onto a Homeric battlefield. We might rather remember that even after his ascent from Hell, Aeneas remains, and will remain till the end of the poem and beyond it, a heroic figure *because* he broods on and is profoundly troubled by the human condition in general and the brutality of power and glory in particular. At this crucial moment in the poem—when war is now certain, the causes for that war beyond comprehension, the outcome of the war doubtful but tragic whoever triumphs—this haunting simile and the sleeplessness of Aeneas that it defines reminds us of Aeneas' special, perhaps unique, humanity and magnanimity. The vastness and the darkness of the world he moves in and his doubts about what he must do are exactly rendered in this most beautiful and original of Vergil's similes. *Radiantis imagine lunae*: a trembling, fitful splendor, moving at random, overwhelmed by a space whose magnitude it can suggest but cannot illumine.

B. PLACES AND THINGS

5. di, quibus imperium est animarum, umbraeque silentes
   et Chaos et Phlegethon, loca nocte tacentia late,
   sit mihi fas audita loqui, sit numine vestro
   pandere res alta terra et caligine mersas.
   ibant obscuri sola sub nocte per umbram
   perque domos Ditis vacuas et inania regna:
   quale per incertam lunam sub luce maligna
   est iter in silvis, ubi caelum condidit umbra
   Iuppiter et rebus nox abstulit atra colorem.

                                        (*Aeneid* 6.264–272)

You gods who hold dominion over spirits;
you voiceless Shades; you, Phlegethon and Chaos,
immense and soundless regions of the night:
allow me to retell what I was told;
allow me by your power to disclose
things buried in the dark and deep of earth!
They moved along in darkness, through the shadows,
beneath the lonely night, and through the hollow
dwelling place of Dis, his phantom kingdom:
even as those who journey in a forest
beneath the scanty light of a changing moon,
when Jupiter has wrapped the sky in shadows
and black night steals the color from all things.

Homer offers us no parallel for this passage, and it is possible that
there is nothing to compare it with or to in all ancient literature
unless we should go for our analogy to some choruses of Greek
tragedy. For this simile, which appeals to the eye only by method-
ically depriving it of the images that it presents and which en-
hances this deliberate failure of vision with an extraordinary
musicality, is Vergil's most elaborate and most rigorous exercise
in the negative image.[76] And if Vergil did not invent this poetic
device, he nevertheless brought it to such perfection that one is
tempted to regard it not only as his hallmark but also as his
special preserve.

   As is often the case with Vergil's similes, this simile functions
as a transition both in respect of mood and of narrative structure.
Following on the great invocation, a prayer for help in describing Hell, these lines at once set Aeneas and the Sibyl on their
downward journey and define the difficulties that both Vergil and
his readers are about to experience as they attempt to imagine

the "unknown modes of being" that Vergil, in trying to write his poem, has learned are part of its materials. For Vergil's Hell, unlike Homer's, is not only a place but also a state of mind and of feeling; not only the location of an event or series of events that are experienced in time but also a mode of existing which cannot be described or even perceived in terms of the ordinary categories that belong to the realities of time and space. This is not to say that Homer's hell is not awesome and terrifying or that Homer has failed to imagine a special mode of being that contrasts with the realities that his living Odysseus experiences, but his hell does not, like Vergil's, awaken considerations that exist outside his narrative in such a way as to achieve a life of their own: it remains, and this is another of Homer's extraordinary achievements, a natural place that exists for the sake of containing the natural actions that comprise Odysseus' visit to the underworld. Because action is constantly central to Homeric poetry, the normal operations of light and motion and perception, though they can be temporarily suspended in order for Homer to depict supernatural intrusions into the human order, cannot be essentially altered or for long ignored. But Vergil's hell exists both for the sake of the narrative it frames and for the sake of other kinds of realities, and indeed it exists not so much to help in imitating a specific action as to examine (though not to explain) the circumstances that surround that action and its significance. In an extraordinary way, one that is seldom found in literature, the story of what Achilles and Hector do is almost precisely what their story is about: in the *Iliad* the *muthos* almost is the *praxis*.[77] However much we may ponder the ramifications of what they do and suffer, we are gathered back into that fierce, transparent, incomparable moment in which who they are and what they choose is all that matters; from all the violence and the passion of the poem a still center forms, a moment of unpersuadable justice, a single clear picture in which, for a moment, human life itself becomes clear. Homer's reality is, in other words, immanent.

But neither the journeys of Aeneas—whether to hell or elsewhere—nor his conflicts with Dido or Turnus are quite what the *Aeneid* is about. Nor does the poem, like a simple allegory, point beyond itself to something for which it may be said to stand. Instead it points beyond itself, with a kind of crystalline structure, to things for which it cannot stand; or, to put it another way, Vergil despairs of immanence, recognizes the need for transcendence, yet knows that he and his world are incapable of transcendence.[78] This does not make his poem pessimistic or cynical or despairing, for his poem is heroic in the face of this desolation,[79] but his heroes and the world they move in are, in a sense, unknowing and unknowable. On one of its levels, then, the *Aeneid* is about a world that lacks transcendence and about the kind of courage (and other virtues) that are necessary in such a world.

The varying degrees of the failure of light or motion or knowledge that are combined in the simile before us are expressive of a distrust of immanence and of the classical mimesis that is dependent upon a belief in immanence. I give a rough paraphrase of the purely narrative content of the simile: they began their journey; they found their going slow and hard; because they moved in a deceptive near-darkness, worse than pitch dark, toward something that they feared and did not understand at all. Vergil could have used the tools of his diction and verse to raise something like that from versified prose to good poetry or even great poetry. But he was interested in imagining more than a stage in his characters' journey, this *part* of the action; he was interested in trying to imagine, *and to show the difficulty of imagining*, the incomprehensibility not only of the underworld but also of Hell. Thus, though the sentence begins with a verb of motion and though this verb is clarified by *quale iter est per lunam*, there is no real sense of motion.[80] The figures drift on an illimitable and static[81] *via negativa* where light is being constantly promised and constantly denied. Then, suddenly, light is annihilated by the darkness that surrounds it: *et rebus nox abstulit atra colorem*. Into this darkness the figures disappear, and we watch instead the ominous and clouded creatures of hell who are fixed in the landscape of hell until, again suddenly, Aeneas returns to view in order to make a characteristically courageous and futile gesture:

> corripit hic subita trepidus formidine ferrum
> Aeneas strictamque aciem venientibus offert
> et ni docta comes tenuis sine corpore vitas
> admoneat volitare cava sub imagine formae,
> inruat et frustra ferro diverberet umbras.
>
> (*Aeneid* 6.290–294)

> And here Aeneas, shaken suddenly
> by terror, grips his sword; he offers naked
> steel and opposes those who come. Had not
> his wise companion warned him they were only
> thin lives that glide without a body in
> the hollow semblance of a form, he would
> in vain have torn the shadows with his blade.

What Vergil has succeeded in imagining here is "darkness visible" and "vast profundities obscure." He had undertaken this problem because as he worked at his poem he learned that, whatever the Homeric underworld was, his own vision of it must emphasize the fact that human beings cannot comprehend it. He also realized that he could not present this incomprehensibility by using the traditional means of plausible representation that had enabled the Homeric poet to present the kind of underworld that he chose to imagine. The poet of the *Odyssey* knew that hell is not accessible to human reason or even to the ordinary categories of human perception. With his usual tact (not simplicity or sentimentality or mindless optimism), he chose not to obscure the action of his poem by presenting his readers with a confusing hell that would distract them from the matter at hand or would raise issues that he could not answer and that would inevitably confuse the focus of his entire *muthos* and *praxis*.

But Vergil had set himself another problem. If human perception and human action are uncertain, problematical, it then becomes useless to expend one's energy in shaping images of human action. Thus Vergil's poem becomes (at least in part) a meditation on the human condition and on the ways in which rational liberty is jeopardized by the obscurity of our beginnings and our ends, by the frailty of our freedom and our reason, and, above all, by the powers of darkness. If some such view of the human condition was not unknown to the authors of the *Iliad* and the *Odyssey*, for reasons we may never understand sufficiently they chose to emphasize aspects of man's condition that Vergil chose not to emphasize because his sense of the *praxis* he was meditating led him into other worlds. The Homeric poets had begun to glimpse in their different ways an idea of rational liberty that Aeschylus, Sophocles, Plato, and Aristotle were, in their different ways, to bring to its fruition. In the *Aeneid*, because of the act of writing the *Aeneid*, Vergil regretfully—indeed despairingly—moves away from this idea of rational liberty towards a new emphasis for the problem of reason and freedom, and this new emphasis will find its own fruition centuries later in the high moments of Western Christendom. But long before that flowering, Aeneas and the Sibyl, moving yet not really moving in the static false light and false darkness of their descent into hell, represent all the figures of this poem and all that they suffer and do: quests that are not quite achieved, affirmations that promise more than can be performed, torches that sputter out, light that flickers and fades, and—in the teeth of this hazard—sufficient courage to confront the unreasoning night, though not sufficient strength to master it, to survive it, or to be transformed by it.

6. exoritur trepidos inter discordia cives:
   urbem alii reserare iubent et pandere portas
   Dardanidis ipsumque trahunt in moenia regem,
   arma ferunt alii et pergunt defendere muros:
   inclusas ut cum latebroso in pumice pastor
   vestigavit apes fumoque implevit amaro;
   illae intus trepidae rerum per cerea castra
   discurrunt magnisque acuunt stridoribus iras;
   volvitur ater odor tectis, tum murmure caeco
   intus saxa sonant, vacuas it fumus ad auras.
                              (*Aeneid* 12.583–592)

Dissension takes the panicked citizens:
some say the city is to be unlocked,
the gates thrown open to the Dardans; they
would drag the king himself up to the ramparts;
while others carry arms, rush to defend:
as when some shepherd tracks a swarm of bees
that shelter in a porous cliff, and fills
their hive with bitter smoke; they rush about
their waxen camp in panic; buzzing loud,
they whet their wrath; across their cells the black
stench rolls; rocks echo with the stifled murmurs;
smoke trickles up into the empty air.

ὡς δὲ μελισσάων σμῆνος μέγα μηλοβοτῆρες
ἠὲ μελισσοκόμοι πέτρῃ ἔνι καπνιόωσιν,
αἱ δ' ἤτοι τείως μὲν ἀολλέες ᾧ ἐνὶ σίμβλῳ
βομβηδὸν κλονέονται, ἐπιπρὸ δὲ λιγνυόεντι
καπνῷ τυφόμεναι πέτρης ἑκὰς ἀίσσουσιν·
ὣς οἵγ' οὐκέτι δὴν μένον ἔμπεδον, ἀλλ' ἐκέδασθεν
εἴσω Βεβρυκίης, Ἀμύκου μόρον ἀγγελέοντες·
                              (*Argonautica* 2.130–136)

When shepherds or bee-keepers come to smoke a beeswarm from its home in hollow rocks, for a time the bees abide, crammed thick together, grumbling with ferocious drone, but then, crazed by lurid flames, from their hive they sputter; so the Bebrycians, failing to hold their ground, dispersed in flight and roamed through the countryside, spreading the word of how Amycus died.

The simile of Apollonius describes the Bebryces in the moment before their flight from the Argonauts and the disorder and panic of their flight. Compared with Vergil's simile, that of Apollonius shows, once again, a fine simplicity in its style and structure and a kind of homely naturalism that is delicately and charmingly at odds with the epic surface of the scene that it defines. Vergil's alterations of his model are few in number, but the change they effect is massive and powerful. The image of the furious bees reflects not only the despair and violence of a city divided against itself but also the ultimate doom of that city; placed just before the suicide of Amata, the darkness, stench, and noise, drifting up into the sky, shape a nameless ugly foreboding. Vergil's bees, unlike those of Apollonius, do not flee from their hive; they remain trapped within their ruined home, once comrades, now each other's victims and prisoners, and their loud futile buzzing steadily exacerbates their anger with each other with the precision of a hellish machine. Then, suddenly, the fear and the rage, the acrid smell, the shouting, and the blinded smarting eyes[82] vanish into smoke and thin air. The thriving industrious *civitas* becomes a nightmare of civil war, then dissolves into nothingness. And the bees, ideal symbols of the ideal citizens, have become, by virtue of their unreason, instruments of the destruction of all they have built and of themselves. The image is shocking because it deliberately perverts this special Vergilian symbol of the *civitas* at the climax of the poem, and in this way it denies a fundamental concept of the poem, that of the idea of the City, the necessity and the sanctity of *communitas*.

> This is, and is not, Cressid!
> Within my soul there doth conduce a fight
> Of this strange nature, that a thing inseparate
> Divides more wider than the sky and earth. . . .

Vergil here shreds the fabric of his own best dream, the unity of the City (*fervet opus redolentque thymo fragrantia mella. / O fortunati, quorum iam moenia surgunt!* [1.436–437]),

> the work is fervent, and the fragrant honey
> is sweet with thyme. "How fortunate are those
> whose walls already rise!"

and bitterly proffers the recurrent nightmare vision of the City of Rome ruining itself. It is true that from this destruction new unions will come and that this concern with and belief in rebirth from destruction is also at the heart of the poem. But in the harmonics of

Book 12, it is the failure of hope that is increasingly emphasized, and here it is the brightness of the hope that defines the peculiar horror of this image, which the violent catachreses, *ater odor* and *murmure caeco*, magnify so fearfully. This darkness not only engulfs the image and dissolves it into nothingness but also organizes an elaborate perversion of the senses and their perceptions—black smell and blind growling. The corruption of the body politic is mirrored in the corruption of the human faculties and the blind, maddened anger of corrupted bees—darkness and bestial, annihilating rage accompany the destruction of the City. Chaos is come again.

7. ὣς ἔφατ', οὐδ' ἀπίθησε ποδήνεμος ὠκέϊ' Ἶρις,
βῆ δὲ κατ' Ἰδαίων ὀρέων ἐς Ϝίλιον ἰρήν.
ὡς δ' ὅτ' ἂν ἐκ νεφέων πτῆται νιφὰς ἠὲ χάλαζα
ψυχρὴ ὑπὸ ῥιπῆς αἰθρηγενέος Βορέαο,
ὣς κραιπνῶς μεμαυῖα διέπτατο ὠκέϊ' Ἶρις.

(*Iliad* 15.168–172)

Thus he spoke, and swift Iris, her feet like the wind, did not disobey, and she went down from Ida's hill to holy Ilium, and as when from clouds snow speeds or cold hail, driven by the blast of Boreas, who is born of the bright air, so, quickly, eagerly, flew on swift Iris.

harum unam celerem demisit ab aethere summo
Iuppiter inque omen Iuturnae occurrere iussit.
illa volat celerique ad terram turbine fertur.
non secus ac nervo per nubem impulsa sagitta,
armatam saevi Parthus quam felle veneni,
Parthus sive Cydon, telum immedicabile, torsit,
stridens et celeres incognita transilit umbras:
talis se sata Nocte tulit terrasque petivit.

(*Aeneid* 12.853–860)

And quickly Jupiter sends one of these
from heaven's height, commanding her to meet
Juturna as an evil emissary.
She flies off; cloaked in whirlwinds, she is carried
to earth. Just as an arrow that is driven
from bowstring through a cloud, an arrow tipped
in gall and venom, an incurable shaft,
shot by some Parthian—a Parthian
or a Cydonian; as it hurtles, hissing,
it passes through swift shadows, seen by no one:
so did the child of Night rush on; she sought
the earth.

The easy clarity of Homer's simile is emphasized by the speed and zest of its closing verse—*so rapidly in her eagerness winged-Iris, the swift one. From clouds, flies, snow or chill air, under the blast of bright sky-born Boreas. So, swiftly, being eager, flew quick Iris.* The images gather their brightness, speed, and force into a simple configuration that emphasizes swiftness. But Homer was writing about an Olympian descending as we might expect an Olympian to descend. The stylistic norms and narrative conventions that are involved here (whatever they may have been) did not, of course, make Homer's problem easier than Vergil's. This combination of compression, vigor, and freshness is not easy to come by, particularly if we suppose that the original audiences for this poem were used to—not only expected but also demanded—warmed-over leftovers tossed in the *pot au feu*. The difficult thing for Homer was to transform banalities into something fresh and pure, to compress the brightness and the momentum into two verses of image and one verse of analogy.[83] He brought it off.

But Vergil's problem was no less difficult in its own way; for he is trying once again to imagine an aspect of hell—this time, the Dira in action. The problem of imagining the creatures of hell in flight is difficult enough in itself; for, though they have the requisite supernatural power for such flight and though the conventions of mythology allow for their flight, in what one is tempted to call rational (that is to say, Homeric) epic, flight is reserved for the Olympians. For the creatures of hell it is an unnatural activity because the conventions of hell and the habits of perception that are based on those conventions are set against it: hell and its creatures are fixed in hell; escape, not to mention flight, is denied them (as Milton knew very well). The poet who undertakes to imagine such an activity is seeking not so much to break with convention as to expand it. Vergil's problem with the Homeric iconography of divine flying messengers is that, as we have seen, for Homer speed is of the essence. But speed is not of the essence for the Dira or for what she has been sent to accomplish; nor has brightness or force much to do with what she is and what she is about. The Homeric brightness has been totally excluded from the Vergilian simile, and the force and the speed, though they have not been totally excluded, have suffered a strange and ugly mutation in being combined with the qualities that are of the essence for Vergil's image: darkness, deception, poison, unseen death.

The syntax of the simile is remarkable for its deliberate failure of smoothness, a smoothness that the norm for this scene might be thought to require in some degree. To begin with, the simile is, quite properly, introduced with the negative *non secus ac*. The subject of the sentence and of the simile, *sagitta*, appears at the end of the first line, combined with a participial phrase, *nervo per nubem impulsa*. It is then qualified with another participial phrase, this time in the accusative, *quam armatam Parthus sive Cydon torsit*. And it is finally qualified by two participial adjectives, *stridens* and *incognita*, in the final verse of the image, just before the conclusion of the analogue. The basic sentence of the simile then, *sagitta transilit celeres umbras*, is comparable to the Homeric simile in its emphasis on speed, but the entire sentence is leaden and motionless.[84] Furthermore, brief as it is, it is not comparable to the Homeric simile in brightness, which it carefully excludes. The verse that offers the analogy, *talis se sata Nocte tulit terrasque petivit*, is comparable in force to the model, but as the core's brightness is weakened by *umbras*, so the force of the final verse is weakened by the ironic denial of *aithrēgeneos* (bright-sky-born) in *sata Nocte*. The Homeric core is longer than the Vergilian core, but, with the possible exception of *chalaza psychrē* and *aithrēgeneos*, it contains no qualifications, for the core is the sentence: it has reduced all of its qualifications to its elements. In Vergil's simile, the essential elements are scattered through its qualifications: *per nubem* = darkness, which reinforces the darkness that is found both in the core and in the analogy; *Parthus sive Cydon* = deception; *armatam felle veneni* and *telum immedicabile* = poison and unseen death, which is the simile's real center. When we add to the jagged and cumbersome syntax the remarkable spondaic movement of the first two verses (856, spondees in second, third, and fourth feet; 857, spondees in first four feet), we have a simile that is distinctly opposed to the Homeric model in every possible way. In so opposing and transforming his model, Vergil succeeds in imagining through his simile the monstrous inversions that this scene requires. Good mannerism is, whatever its enemies may believe, intensely concerned with decorum. In this simile, the clarity and power of the model would be useless in themselves, but our memory of them heightens the terror of this hellish parody of Homeric health. That is decorum too.

8. ὡς δ' ἐν ὀνείρῳ οὐ δύναται φεύγοντα διώκειν·
   οὔτ' ἄρ' ὁ τὸν δύναται ὑποφευγέμεν οὔθ' ὁ διώκειν·
   ὡς ὁ τὸν οὐ δύνατο μάρψαι ποσὶν οὐδ' ὃς ἀλύξαι.
                                        (*Iliad* 22.199–201)

And as in a dream a man cannot chase after someone who flees
from him, and he who flees cannot shake off his pursuer, and he
who pursues cannot pursue: so Achilles could not overtake Hector,
nor could Hector escape.

> ac velut in somnis, oculos ubi languida pressit
> nocte quies, nequiquam avidos extendere cursus
> velle videmur et in mediis conatibus aegri
> succidimus (non lingua valet, non corpore notae
> sufficiunt vires nec vox aut verba sequuntur):
> sic Turno, quacumque viam virtute petivit,
> successum dea dira negat. tum pectore sensus
> vertuntur varii: Rutulos aspectat et urbem
> cunctaturque metu telumque instare tremescit;
> nec quo se eripiat, nec qua vi tendat in hostem,
> nec currus usquam videt aurigamque sororem.
>
> (*Aeneid* 12.908–918)

> Just as in dreams of night, when languid rest
> has closed our eyes, we seem in vain to wish
> to press on down a path, but as we strain,
> we falter, weak; our tongues can say nothing,
> the body loses its familiar force,
> no voice, no word, can follow: so whatever
> courage he calls upon to find a way,
> the cursed goddess keeps success from Turnus.
> Then shifting feelings overtake his heart;
> he looks in longing at the Latin ranks
> and at the city, and he hesitates,
> afraid; he trembles at the coming spear.
> He does not know how he can save himself,
> what power he has to charge his enemy;
> he cannot see his chariot anywhere;
> he cannot see the charioteer, his sister.

For this last long simile in his poem Vergil once again invents
a radical transformation of his model. Homer is interested, in the
simile, in emphasizing the all but equal strength and valor of his
two opposing figures, and if there is a slight imbalance in this
near equilibrium, it is to be discovered in the frustrations of the
pursuer who dreams, not with the pursued.[85] I say "dreams" because the equilibrium that obtains between the pursuer and the
pursued, while it may be frustrating and unpleasant for the pursuer, does not become horrible. Homer's dream is not a night-

mare, as it might be if it were the pursued who was dreaming. In Vergil's simile, of course, it is the pursued who dreams, and his dream is one of the great nightmares of poetry; this nightmare is a suitable recapitulation of what has immediately preceded it, and is a transition to, and adumbration of, the closing moments of the poem, for both the nightmare and the closing action of the poem are presented from the viewpoint of Turnus. So it is fitting that his growing terror, his despair, and his sudden and final inability to act should be crystallized in this simile.

Vergil has expanded one verse of image in Homer's simile to five verses, and, where Homer had excluded Apollo from the single analogical verse, Vergil has emphatically included the Dira within his analogy: *successum dira dea negat*.[86] In short, Homer's simile, which consists of only two verses, has been expanded by Vergil to six and a half verses. But significant as the quantitative change may be in showing the degree to which the model engaged Vergil's imagination, it is the qualitative change that matters. From the grave and gentle irony of *oculos ubi languida pressit / nocte quies* to the final image of terrifying helplessness, *nec vox nec verba sequuntur* (one cannot even cry for help), Vergil shapes a carefully modulated picture of the process of becoming nothing. The simile, then, is not so much concerned with helping us to visualize the drama of the chase (only *nequiquam avidos extendere cursus* recalls the essence of Homer's simile: *ou dunatai pheugonta diōkein*[87]) as it is with imagining the nameless and invisible sense of what it is like to be overtaken by one's doom. In the midst of the hopeless, violent struggle the strength drains away and speech itself, and with it reason and perception, fails. The inhuman, unintelligible darkness comes. It is not so much the despair of Turnus that is being imagined here as the indefinable, larger despair that haunts the entire poem and threatens to overwhelm it. The metaphysical center of the simile has been brilliantly located and defined by H. R. Steiner: "Die Gesetze von Raum und Zeit nicht mehr gelten scheinen . . . es gibt uns zu verstehen, wie einer, der in groessten Lebensbedrohung steht, sein Dasein als unwirklich, wie einen Traum erlebt: Wirklichkeit wird fuer ihn zum Traum, Traum aber zu grausam-unerbittlicher Wirklichkeit."[88] The insubstantiality that has been warded off throughout the poem, though it seemed to be about to vanish for good, now returns in full force. Reality dwindles to dream, and the nightmare from which we have been fighting free throughout the poem (*velle videmur*—for at this moment Vergil includes his readers in his poem) has become the reality. No Homeric lucidities or articulations here, for the laws of time and space—like the human capacities for motion, action, and speech—themselves have become void. Action, truth, and their images drain away to nothingness. It is the perfect flowering of the Vergilian imagination, this perfect representation of the monstrous and unreasoning night. The *via negativa* is now, against all likelihood, as reliable and as expressive a mode of mimesis as the *via positiva* that Homer's art had brought, in Western poetry, to its first great perfection. This formulation and perfection of the negative image go beyond inwardness or subjectivity or elaborations of the potentialities of poetic mood and poetic music; they rather involve an exploration of the relentless, impenetrable darknesses inside us *and* outside us. The lyricism is sometimes tender and fragile, but it is also sometimes ferocious and unyielding in its search for our real weaknesses and real enemies as well as for the lies and myths we tell ourselves about them. After Vergil, not only the grand desolations of Dante and Milton but also the smaller desolations of Tennyson will be possible:

> But, ever after, the small violence done
> Rankled in him and ruffled all his heart,
> As the sharp wind that ruffles all day long
> A little bitter pool about a stone
> On the bare coast.

The darkness without and within, the big darkness and the small —Vergil has found ways of imagining them; darkness, all kinds of darkness, is finally made visible. And the boundaries of poetry are extended immeasurably.

4. AENEAS AND THE MONUMENTS

It has long been an unspoken article of faith in modern aesthetics (by modern in this context I mean, roughly, after the first generation of English Romantics) that art is a kind of salvation; that a Wallace Stevens or a Proust saves himself from modern damnation (boredom) at the very least and maybe all of us along with him. Adam Parry, sensing perhaps that Vergil has some affinities with the great symbolists, attributes this heresy to Vergil by attributing it to Aeneas. Parry sees that politics do not save Aeneas and, basing his argument on the scene in which Aeneas surveys the representations of the Trojan War that he chances upon in the temple Dido has built for Juno, suggests that Aeneas finds not only comfort but also redemption in beholding the evils and sufferings of his ruined city magnified and distilled to intelligibility by the discipline of art.[89] The truth of the matter is that Vergil's judgment on the nature and function of art is not unlike his judgment on the nature and function of politics and history: it comforts, yes, in a sense; but it also deludes and betrays. In this final section on language and imagery of the *Aeneid* we shall look at the three scenes in which Aeneas is portrayed as viewing artistic representations of history (I include, for reasons I shall defend, the pageant of great Romans in Book 6), and we shall be paying particular attention both to the beauty of these representations and to the intellectual and spiritual significance that they contain.

a)   constitit, et lacrimans "quis iam locus," inquit, "Achate,
quae regio in terris nostri non plena laboris?
en Priamus! sunt hic etiam sua praemia laudi;
sunt lacrimae rerum, et mentem mortalia tangunt.
solve metus, feret haec aliquam tibi fama salutem."
sic ait, atque animum pictura pascit inani
multa gemens, largoque umectat flumine vultum.

                          (*Aeneid* 1.459–465)

He halted. As he wept, he cried: "Achates,
where on this earth is there a land, a place
that does not know our sorrows? Look! There is Priam!
Here, too, the honorable finds its due
and there are tears for passing things; here, too,
things mortal touch the mind. Forget your fears;
this fame will bring you some deliverance."
He speaks. With many tears and sighs he feeds
his soul on what is nothing but a picture.

Some readers have snickered at Aeneas' tears, but, aside from the very small hyperbole of *largo flumine*, there is nothing particularly remarkable about Aeneas' display of emotion, and he does not really outdo Odysseus in the copiousness of his tears:[90]

    ταῦτ᾽ ἄρ᾽ ἀοιδὸς ἄειδε περικλυτός· αὐτὰρ Ὀδυσσεὺς
    πορφύρεον μέγα φᾶρος ἑλὼν χερσὶ στιβαρῇσι
    κὰκ κεφαλῆς ἐέρυσσε, κάλυψε δὲ καλὰ πρόσωπα·
    αἴδετο γὰρ Φαίηκας ὑπ᾽ ὀφρύσι δάκρυα λείβων.
    ἦ τοι ὅτε λήξειεν ἀείδων θεῖος ἀοιδός,
    δάκρυ᾽ ὀμορξάμενος κεφαλῆς ἄπο φᾶρος ἕλεσκε
    καὶ δέπας ἀμφικύπελλον ἑλὼν σπείσασκε θεοῖσιν·
    αὐτὰρ ὅτ᾽ ἂψ ἄρχοιτο καὶ ὀτρύνειαν ἀείδειν

Φαιήκων οἱ ἄριστοι, ἐπεὶ τέρποντο ϝέπεσσιν,
ἂψ Ὀδυσεὺς κατὰ κρᾶτα καλυψάμενος γοάεσκεν.
ἔνθ' ἄλλους μὲν πάντας ἐλάνθανε δάκρυα λείβων·
Ἀλκίνοος δέ μιν οἶος ἐπεφράσατ' ἠδὲ νόησεν
ἥμενος ἄγχ' αὐτοῦ, βαρὺ δὲ στενάχοντος ἄκουσεν.
αἶψα δὲ Φαιήκεσσι φιληρέτμοισι μετηύδα·

(*Odyssey* 8.83–96)

Of this was sung the song of the very famous minstrel: but Odysseus with two strong hands drew the broad purple cloak over his head to hide his goodly face. He was ashamed to let the tears well from his deep-set eyes publickly before the Phaeacians. Each time the divine singer broke off his song Odysseus dashed away the tears, freed his head from the cloak, and poured from his loving cup a libation to the God. But as soon as the song began again, at the bidding of the Phaeacian chiefs to whom the verses were unalloyed delight, then would Odysseus again hide his head and stifle his sobs. The other company failed to see how his tears ran down: only Alcinous remarked it, for he sat next him, and could not but notice and overhear his deep-drawn agony. Wherefore at an early chance he broke in upon the oar-loving Phaeacians. . . .

If there is a problem with the Vergilian passage, and I believe there is, it is not one of excessive emotionality on Aeneas' part; it is rather a question of how we are made to view that emotion. In the scene in the *Odyssey* the hero's tears are a means to an end: not only does Odysseus' attempt to hide his tears say something about him as a human being, it also says something about him to Alcinous. In short, we share with Alcinous the sight of Odysseus weeping, so that his tears become a part of the narrative structure. In Vergil's scene, on the other hand, the particular tears of Aeneas serve to emphasize what is in fact the artistic content of this scene, namely, *lacrimae rerum*. Here, as often, the emotions of the characters are not ways of revealing the characters, who, in turn, reveal the *muthos* in their words and actions; here both characters and *muthos* exist to reveal emotion and meditations on emotion. The ubiquitous and insubstantial Achates presumably witnesses these tears; indeed, perhaps he adds some tears of his own. We don't know. He exists in this scene only by virtue of a vocative, for we have not caught a glimpse of him since the *corripuēre* and the *ascendebant* of verses 418 and 419; in this scene, as in others, he is a heavily stylized, almost ironic epical ornament. In a sense, then, Aeneas, *saeptus nebula*, is alone as he gazes on the images of the desolation of his native city. Visually, the scene is rather complex.

We see a man obscured by a divine mist looking at pictures that blur his eyes with tears: the frame and the focus are, especially if we compare them with the Homeric "model," uncertain. Yet this blurred focus, this strange opacity, is not undeliberate, for it exactly suits the complexity and the obscurity of the emotions that Vergil wants to evoke.

I have suggested that sorrow is the content of the scene, the particular sorrow of this man's loss as he contemplates a graphic record of his loss, but it is also a general sorrow, everybody's loss, as Aeneas himself insists by his somber abstractions, *rerum* and *mortalia*. But this sorrow, whether particular or general, is not unequivocal. Against sorrow, Vergil and Aeneas set elusive intuitions of renewal. Aeneas comes to the very spot where Dido had first learned to hope again:

> hoc primum in luco nova res oblata timorem
> leniit; hic primum Aeneas sperare salutem
> ausus et adflictis melius confidere rebus.
>
> (450–452)

> Within this grove, the sights—so strange to him—
> have, for the first time, stilled Aeneas' fear;
> here he first dared to hope he had found shelter,
> to trust more surely in his shattered fortunes.

The source of Dido's intuitions of salvation are unclear; presumably they were in some way granted her through the grace of Juno to whom she dedicates the temple which stands in the grove.[91] The source of Aeneas' renewal of hope is the depiction of the Trojan War; he marvels at its skillful artistry and he sees

> Iliacas ex ordine pugnas
> bellaque iam fama totum vulgata per orbem,
> Atridas Priamumque et saevum ambobus Achillem.
>
> (456–458)

> the wars of Troy set out in order:
> the battles famous now through all the world,
> the sons of Atreus and of Priam, and
> Achilles, savage enemy to both.

That Aeneas should find frescoes whose content is the Trojan War and whose manner suggests an Augustan wall painting[92] is at once a puzzling impossibility and an anachronism that need not disturb us; it is no wittier than Demodocus' mastery of the Trojan epic cycle in *Odyssey* 8. But a comparison with the scene from the Odysseus poet is nevertheless useful here. Odysseus is grieved by being made to recall what he has lost and suffered, for these things are a constant grief to him and the poetic mimesis of the causes of his grief further heightens the misery of his present situation. In short, Odysseus feels nothing but grief, and that is as easily comprehensible as it is deeply felt by him and by us. Aeneas, however, feels both grief and a kind of strange inarticulate joy simultaneously, and he (and we with him) is gathered up into a dialectical movement of sorrow and relief. I am not saying that this scene is good merely because it is complicated, ambiguous, or equivocal (there are bad complexities as well as good complexities), nor am I saying that the Odyssean scene is bad or simple-minded because it is simple (there are good simplicities as well as bad ones): rather, I am trying to drive home the absolute difference in tone and purpose between these two scenes.

What, precisely, is Aeneas so happy about? Presumably the glory of what was done and suffered in the last days of Troy boosts his spirits in the somewhat conventional antique way: he thinks of the immortality conferred by art. But even this positive view of his situation and state of mind is subject to certain reservations. First, he is standing by the temple of his archenemy, and the meaning of this enmity eludes him here as it constantly eludes him elsewhere in the poem. In a way that also eludes him (and some readers), the frescoes that amaze and hearten him are a kind of victory monument to Juno: they depict crucial, pathetic moments in the ruin of Troy, a ruin in which Juno, of course, takes a savage, ineffable delight. After the initial victory of Hector (*namque videbat, uti bellantes Pergama circum / hac fugerent Grai, premeret Troiana iuventus* [466–467]), the paintings show only the defeats and humiliations of the Trojans; the death of Rhesus; the death of Troilus, with *infelix*, a kind of leitmotif for dissolving pathos, introducing the brilliant pathos of *lora tenens tamen; huic cervixque comaeque trahuntur / per terram, et versa pulvis inscribitur hasta* (477–478), where evanescence and fatal beauty are, as often, blurred together; the futile supplications of the Trojan women before Athena; the mangling of Hector,

> tum vero ingentem gemitum dat pectore ab imo
> ut spolia, ut currus, utque ipsum corpus amici
> tendentemque manus Priamum conspexit inermes;
>
> (485–487)

> And then, indeed, Aeneas groans
> within the great pit of his chest, deeply;

for he can see the spoils, the chariot,
the very body of his friend, and Priam
pleading for Hector with defenseless hands;

his own valiant but fruitless battles with the Greeks (*se quoque principibus permixtum agnovit Achives* [488]), which are unobtrusively blended into the gouache of events; the courage and ineffectuality of Memnon; and, finally, in a superb adumbration of Camilla's *aristeia* and death, the shimmering picture of Penthesilea in all her glory and, notwithstanding her force and courage, her delicate vulnerability:

> ducit Amazonidum lunatis agmina peltis
> Penthesilea furens, mediisque in milibus ardet,
> aurea subnectens exsertae cingula mammae,
> bellatrix, audetque viris concurrere virgo.
>
> (490–493)

> Penthesilea in her fury leads
> the ranks of crescent-shielded Amazons.
> She flashes through her thousands; underneath
> her naked breast, a golden girdle; soldier-
> virgin and queen, daring to war with men.

Her glory and her valor are beautifully defined, but the strength of the woman is subtly offset by the near-oxymoron, *bellatrix-virgo*; she is the equal of the male warriors in some ways (*mediis in milibus ardet*), and she is undeniably courageous (*audetque viris concurrere*), but for all that, she is a girl fighting men, and there is something sad (and patronizing) about the emphasis of the detail, her fitting the armor on the vulnerable breasts. With this image the frescoes come to an end. It is a beautiful picture, and in its compression and its delicate modulations it is one of the greatest passages in Vergil; but I maintain that it is possessed of a devastating melancholy. So, we are still left pondering the question, What in the world does Aeneas see here that cheers him up?

For the present, my answer to the question raised by this paradoxical scene is suitably paradoxical. There is nothing in the pictures to cheer Aeneas, and in fact he is not cheered. He deludes himself into feeling heartened because the realities he confronts are, literally, intolerable. *En Priamus! sunt hic etiam sua praemia laudi.* The verse may be read—indeed must be read—in two ways: (1) an affirmative way, in which the sufferings of Priam have won the immortality and clarity of art and are therefore in some sense justified, in some sense redeemed (*feret haec aliquam fama salutem*); (2) a rather bitter negative way, "So this is the reward of integrity and courage; we have shored up some kind of solace and redemption [note *aliquam*] against our ruin." The bitterness is no doubt largely unconscious, for he is trying to put a good face on the situation, this miserable sudden reminder of his despair. *Solve metus.* Yes, because *metus* is what he feels in addition to sorrow and despair. To fear, sorrow, and despair is now added hope, but it is, as the pictures themselves show, an utterly deceitful hope. The beauty of the imagery, its clarity and unity, may bestow solace on Aeneas (and on us), but it is a temporary and finally deceptive solace: *Animum pictura pascit inani. Animum pascit* is a gentle catachresis, yet it is sufficient to convey much of the complexity and the confusion of Aeneas' emotional state; joined as it is with the more violent oxymoron, *pascit pictura inani*, it reveals not only the confusions of Aeneas but also the confusions and, indeed, the essential fraudulence of art and of the realities that art mirrors. *Inani* means, of course, "having no life," but it also means "deceptive, illusory, empty, meaningless." In part Vergil reminds us that art is illusion, that his poem is illusion, but, since this scene—like the scenes we are about to examine—is concerned with art that imitates history, we are also being reminded that history, the thing imitated, is as illusory as the art that imitates it: image of an image. That the Trojans have won immortality in the frescoes of Juno is cold comfort, for their function there is to enhance the victory of Juno over the Trojans. In a moment, it is true, with the appearance of Dido, there will be a promise of *salus*, but that promise will at last be found to be false. Here there is an adumbration of the final and equivocal defeat and triumph of Juno at the end of the poem. The kind of *salus* that Aeneas desires and thinks he is being granted is not to be found here or anywhere in the poem, not even at its close. This does not mean that Aeneas is a fool; it means that the old epic and tragic cosmos—though still visible through the shimmering, ironic opacities of Vergilian pathos—endures in this scene and in this poem the onslaught of the *Weltwende* that finds its clearest definition in the names of Christ and Caesar.

b)   egregium forma iuvenem et fulgentibus armis,
             sed frons laeta parum, et deiecto lumina vultu. . . .

                              (6.861–862)

sed nox atra caput tristi circumvolat umbra.

(866)

heu pietas, heu prisca fides, invictaque bello
dextera! non illi se quisquam inpune tulisset
obvius armato, seu cum pedes iret in hostem
seu spumantis equi foderet calcaribus armos.
heu, miserande puer, si qua fata aspera rumpas!
tu Marcellus eris, manibus date lilia plenis;
purpureos spargam flores, animamque nepotis
his saltem accumulem donis, et fungar inani
munere.

(878–886)

　　　　　　　　　　　one still young,
of handsome form and gleaming arms, and yet
his face had no gladness, his eyes looked down:

　　　　　　　　And yet, around his head
black night is hovering with its sad shade!

I weep for righteousness, for ancient trust,
for his unconquerable hand: no one
could hope to war with him and go untouched,
whether he faced the enemy on foot
or dug his foaming horse's flank with spurs.
O boy whom we lament, if only you
could break the bonds of fate and be Marcellus.
With full hands, give me lilies; let me scatter
these purple flowers, with these gifts, at least,
be generous to my descendant's spirit,
complete this service, although it be useless.

We have seen, in the previous passage, how the *salus* that
Aeneas ardently desires is at once founded on and nullified by
picturae inanes. Those who would speak of the increasing self-
confidence of Aeneas, of the growth of his firmness of purpose
as his situation itself grows more clear, need, I think, to reexamine
the verses quoted above more carefully. We are once again presented with dissolving pathos (*manibus date lilia plenis / purpureos spargam flores, miserande puer*), with the distinctively
Vergilian play with dark and light (*fulgentibus, laeta* negative,
lumina / nox, atra, tristi umbra), and finally, with *inani munere*.
The contrafactual verbs (*tulisset* and *iret*) and the potential-
future-more-vivid (*rumpas*) not only define the pathos of Mar-

cellus' death; they also suggest a tragedy, indeed a bitterness, that threatens to overwhelm the magnificence of Roman achievement.[93] It is not merely that the death of Marcellus deprives Rome of one of her (potentially) greatest leaders at a time when such leadership is a cause for profound concern; it is more nearly a question of blighted hope, a perfection that was promised but never performed, which necessarily, at one level, entails the ruin of *pietas* and *fides*. In this sense, Anchises' grief and the brilliant imagery that reveals the melancholy and futility of his ritual mourning at the side of the corpse of Marcellus dissolve the procession of famous Romans and the triumphal moods that this procession creates: *munere inani.* Something was destined to be, must have been, was about to be, but finally was not. It is a curious thing that Aeneas turns away from this vision of the vanishing Marcellus and his father's grief with no word and no gesture: *sic tota passim regione vagantur / aeris in campis latis, atque omnia lustrant* (886–887). It is true, of course, that the pathos could not have been heightened by a response from Aeneas, that, indeed, any further elaboration upon it must necessarily qualify or mitigate it. The lesson of Homeric art is, precisely, that a suffering that is acknowledged and shared, though it may remain unintelligible, becomes nearly tolerable. In this regard, it is perhaps not too much to say that the whole quality of the *Iliad* would be utterly changed (probably for the worse) if it did not conclude with the superb triple threnody. This incapacity for shared suffering and the comparative rarity of dialogue in the *Aeneid*, the inclination to internalize sorrow rather than to communicate it and so release it, underscore here the essential solitude of Aeneas and the concomitant futility and despair of his perceptions and understanding. This does not mean that Aeneas is a fool. Rather it means that images do not truly communicate the meaning that we expect them to communicate. Our feeling, as Aeneas turns away casually to view the other marvels of the underworld, is that both history and art have failed to explain what happens and does not happen in history.

It may be objected that the vision that Anchises proffers to Aeneas is strictly a political meditation and has no place in a discussion of Aeneas' response to artistic representations and Vergil's own attitude towards the nature and power of art. I would counter this objection in two ways. First, Aeneas is in this scene—much as he is in Book 1 and Book 2—a beholder of a sequence of images, a continuum of historical points which is organized by artistic (as well as historical) principles. Second, in addition to being once again a visitor in a museum without walls, Aeneas is specifically told by Anchises, in some of the most famous verses of the poem, that the figures he is now viewing represent specifically Roman arts of law and order as against Greekling tomfoolery: *hae tibi erunt artes—pacisque imponere morem / parcere subiectis et debellare superbos* (852–853). Vergil does not (perhaps unfortunately) allow himself many moments of levity in his epic, but in these lines he indulges himself and us in a witty and understated *recusatio* not unlike that which we find at the end of Horace's *Odes* 2.1. In that poem Horace wittily regrets his being unable to do what he has in fact just done, namely, write a superb tragic lyric on the subject of war. Here, a Roman epic poet disclaims the possibility of vying with the Greeks, an activity which, of course, has been an obsession throughout his career as a poet. But the *recusatio*, of course, is not merely witty. The *recusatio* not only emphasizes the fact that Vergil has vied with (and perhaps rivalled and overcome) the Greeks[94] (... *spirantia mollius aera ... vivos ducent de marmore vultus* [847–848]) in his presentation of the great Romans; by throwing doubt on the value and validity of the artistic process, it also prepares the way for the dissolving pathos that we encounter in the Marcellus passage. It is no secret that Vergil's splendid triumphal frieze of the heroic Romans—not despite, but in large measure by virtue of, the fascinating convolutions of its sequence of design—is so shaped as to frame Augustus precisely in its center (Augustus [791–807] is placed between 756–790 [= 34 lines] and 808–846 [= 38 lines]). For all its ornament, then—and that ornament, after all, was what many Romans seem to have liked—the architectonics of the frieze are as clearly shaped as their patriotism is vigorous and sincere. Yet this wavering clarity, which from the swirl and glitter of its dynamic achieves a splendid unity, melts into forgetfulness as soon as the transitional *recusatio* has disavowed its form and ruthlessly vindicated its content. Finally, with the pathetic vanishing of Marcellus and what he signifies, even the content of the vision will disappear. The luminosity of art is fraudulent, the meaning of history is fraudulent. What then is real? The content and the form of historical art are both gathered into the oblivion that reigns under the sign of ivory.

What then is real? The answer to this question, in so far as *docta insapientia* can provide any answer, has been adumbrated in the prelude to the triumphal frieze (724–751) where Anchises gives Aeneas an explanation of the origins and the eschatology of the world in general and man in particular. The explanation eludes precise philosophical categories not because Vergil was ignorant of such categories (he could have given us pure Platonism or pure Stoicism or a judicious mixture of them had he been of a mind to do so), but rather because these systems would be utterly inappropriate to the kind of world he is trying to imagine. The imagery of Platonic transfiguration and of Stoic celestial apotheosis may provide an ironic frisson or two, but the heart of this vision—however optimistic its ultimate significance—is at odds with the historical celebrations that it introduces, for it calls into question the value and meaning of existence and action in this world.

> igneus est ollis vigor et caelestis origo
> seminibus, quantum non noxia corpora tardant
> terrenique hebetant artus moribundaque membra.
> hinc metuunt cupiuntque, dolent gaudentque, neque auras
> dispiciunt clausae tenebris et carcere caeco.
> quin et supremo cum lumine vita reliquit,
> non tamen omne malum miseris nec funditus omnes
> corporeae excedunt pestes, penitusque necesse est
> multa diu concreta modis inolescere miris.
>
> (730–738)

> Fiery energy
> is in these seeds, their source is heavenly;
> but they are dulled by harmful bodies, blunted
> by their own earthly limbs, their mortal members.
> Because of these, they fear and long, and sorrow
> and joy, they do not see the light of heaven;
> they are dungeoned in their darkness and blind prison.
> And when the final day of life deserts them,
> then, even then, not every ill, not all
> the plagues of body quit them utterly;
> and this must be, for taints so long congealed
> cling fast and deep in extraordinary ways.

And so on, through a description of the varieties of purgatory and purification, until the dross of earth is utterly refined away, the purity of fire restored, and the cycle is ready to begin again. I think it would be quite incorrect to suppose that Vergil himself is committed to this unpersuasive dilution of Plato blended with Zeno, but I think it would be foolish to suppose that the statement is merely the work of a philosophical dilettante who wishes to provide some tone and filigree for his epic at an opportune moment. What had been ingenious and artistic metaphors in the meditations of Plato have decayed into half-baked articles of superstition in Vergil's time. This does not mean that Vergil himself assented to them, but it does mean that he was to some degree aware that some of his readers were increasingly beginning to assent to them. Part of the task that Vergil magnificently set himself was to write an epic poem for people who were beginning to inhabit a world that Dodds has described so well for us (see n. 12 and n. 126).

> The adoration of the visible cosmos, and the sense of unity with it which had found expression in early Stoicism, began to be replaced in many minds by a feeling that the physical world—at any rate the part of it below the moon—is under the sway of evil powers, and that what the soul needs is not unity with it but escape from it.

I shall save speculation as to the degree to which Vergil sympathized with the views described by Dodds until my closing chapter. For the moment, it is sufficient to say that the strange Neopythagoreanism or Proto-Gnosticism or whatever that had begun to haunt the Graeco-Roman world by the time Vergil was born shows certain affinities with the place described in Anchises' speech, for in it, too, the world is seen as "a place of darkness and penance" where catharsis is of the essence. The counterpoint of "Stoicizing monism" and "Platonizing dualism" that we find in this speech and the blending (or, rather, tense juxtaposition) of "cosmic optimism" and "cosmic pessimism" may illumine the unequivocal affirmation of the Augustan frieze that follows them, but they may also suffuse the triumphal frieze with an ineradicably somber hue that threatens to darken the sense of triumph. Certainly the rejection of the physical world that is sketched in these verses finds certain near echoes in the closing panel of the frieze, where the glory of Marcellus slowly alters into what amounts to a picture of his nonbeing. The optimism and pessimism do not fuse in a satisfactory way in the prelude to the frieze, and this anguished failure of reconciliation dominates its finale. There the quality and the intensity of the pathos that dissolves the image of Marcellus—combined as they are with the sumptuous glorification of Rome and Augustus—offer an excellent angle of vision for the surface and the *praxis* of the poem as a whole. The pathos does not nullify the grandeur, but the grandeur does not redeem the pathos.[95] Nor does the counterpoint between the pathos and the grandeur function in such a way as to win through to an equilibrium that would permit us to say either, Yes, now we

understand the glory of Rome because we understand the terrible
price that has been paid, by guilty and innocent alike, for that
glory; or, Yes, now we understand the anxiety and nightmarish
vision of this poem because we see that the glory, however real
at one level, is fraudulent at its core. The poem refuses us (one
ought not to say, cheats us of) the power of either unequivocal
affirmation or unequivocal denial or even of the harmonies of
discordia concors that we get from a Homer or a Shakespeare.
There are two visions here, but in the popular phrase, there is no
double vision. We are not suddenly brought up sharp—saddened,
solaced, and enlightened. The two images refuse to merge into a
steady whole that will permit us to understand the grounds of
their opposition and, by this understanding, to view them separate
but unified, each a necessary eternal part of the process. Rather,
the arcs that should complete the circle, in precise proportion as
they seem to near one another, keep swerving off in opposite
tangents. Vergil thus creates by art and political meditation a pattern that—alternately affirming and denying the healing powers
of poetry and of history—underscores the dialectical process of
both imagery (art) and of human behavior in time (history).
This stern dialectic issues in no synthesis, which is at once a reason
for bafflement and for the renewal of belief, for a kind of negative
affirmation that is eminently suited to, say, the Christian temper.

c)   ὣς ἄρα φωνήσασα θεὰ κατὰ τεύχε' ἔθηκε
προσθεν 'Αχιλλῆος· τὰ δ' ἀνέβραχε δαίδαλα πάντα.
Μυρμιδόνας δ' ἄρα πάντας ἕλε τρόμος, οὐδέ τις ἔτλη
ἄντην ἐϲιδέειν, ἀλλ' ἔτρεσαν. αὐτὰρ 'Αχιλλεὺς
ὡς ἔϝιδ', ὥς μιν μᾶλλον ἔδυ χόλος, ἐν δέ ϝοι ὄσσε
δϝεινὸν ὑπὸ βλεφάρων ὡς εἰ σέλας ἐξεφάανθεν·
τέρπετο δ' ἐν χείρεσσιν ἔχων θεοῦ ἀγλαὰ δῶρα.
αὐτὰρ ἐπεὶ φρεσὶ ϝῆσι τετάρπετο δαίδαλα λεύσσων,
αὐτίκα μητέρα ϝὴν ϝέπεα πτερόεντα προσηύδα·
                 (*Iliad* 19.12–20)

Thus the goddess spoke, and she placed the armor in front of
Achilles, and the splendid panoply clattered as it touched the
ground. Then trembling clutched the Myrmidons nor dared any of
them glimpse the armor, and they were terrified. But Achilles,
when he saw the armor, a fiercer rage endured, and his eyes shone
forth from his lids with dreadful radiance, like a firestorm, and he
rejoiced as he took in his hands the bright gifts of the god. But
when he had sated his pleasure in gazing on the splendid armor,
straightway his mother he addressed with winged words.

ille deae donis et tanto laetus honore
expleri nequit atque oculos per singula volvit,
miraturque interque manus et bracchia versat
terribilem cristis galeam flammasque vomentem ....
illic res Italas Romanorumque triumphos,
haud vatum ignarus venturique inscius aevi,
fecerat Ignipotens; illic genus omne futurae
stirpis ab Ascanio pugnataque in ordine bella.

                              (8.617–620, 626–629)

talia per clipeum Vulcani, dona parentis,
miratur; rerumque ignarus imagine gaudet,
attollens umero famamque et fata nepotum.

                                       (8.729–731)

Aeneas cannot have enough; delighted
with these gifts of the goddess, this high honor,
his eyes rush on to everything, admiring;
with arm and hand he turns the helmet over,
tremendous with its crests and flood of flames ....
For there the Lord of Fire had wrought the story
of Italy, the Romans' victories,
since he was not unskilled in prophecy
or one who cannot tell the times to come.
There he had set the generations of
Ascanius, and all their wars, in order.

Aeneas marvels at his mother's gift,
the scenes on Vulcan's shield; and he is glad
for all these images, though he does not
know what they mean. Upon his shoulder he
lifts up the fame and fate of his sons' sons.

Justly famous as Lessing's comparison of the shield of Aeneas
and the shield of Achilles must be, mainly by virtue of its fine
perception of an essential aspect of Homeric narrative technique,
the comparison nevertheless ignores the fact that Vergil's shield
is possessed of a marvelous, unique sound and fury and that in its
balance and compression it is one of the finest things in Vergil's
poem. Lessing's judgment is essentially correct: compared with
the Homeric passage, the Vergilian passage shows, for all its richness of detail and brilliant, exciting momentum, a curiously static
quality. But, though this final effect of frozen grandeur may have
much to do with the fact that we see it as a finished product rather
than as a shield in the process of being made, it also has to do

with the fact that the responses of the shield's recipients differ so markedly from one another. We behold the excitement of Aeneas before we see the shield for ourselves; that is, his response to the beauty of the shield functions as a preparation for its grandeur. We experience the response of Achilles after we have experienced the shield for ourselves, and this order of presentation is, in a sense, more natural, since it aids us in understanding the response of Achilles; indeed, we experience with him the intensity of his pleasure in the weapons. The response of Aeneas, as it is initially pictured, is not tepid by any means, but it lacks the fine ferocity that Homer gives us (*hōs min mallon edu cholos, en de woi osse / dweinon hypo blepharōn hōs ei selas exephaanthen*).[96] The crucial point in this comparison, then, is the activity of Achilles against the essential passivity of Aeneas's response. *Miratur* is used both at 619 and at 730 to define the quality of that response, and the word has figured prominently in the two other passages that we have examined in this section, where Aeneas's wonder at the beauty he beholds defines his innocence and his ignorance when in the presence of realities that overshadow him (1.456, *miratur; haec dum Dardanio Aeneae miranda videntur* [1.494]; 6.854, *sic pater Anchises, atque haec mirantibus addit*). Achilles feels, then, a mixture of sensual delight and vengeful anger in the presence of his new weapons; Aeneas feels only awe for the shield, which represents the great celebration of Augustus to which the whole movement of the passage splendidly builds (8.714 ff.). And while the excitement that Achilles feels when he examines his new weapons causes him to burst into a speech in which he announces his determination to begin avenging Patroclus immediately, Aeneas—in his wonder and self-effacing joy—remains typically silent. We have seen this innocence and this ignorance of his situation before; here these qualities are more than usually moving, for the humility of his gesture contains in it the entirety of the Roman feeling for past and future, for responsibility.[97]

Yet for all the marvelous fusion of magnanimity and humility, there is something strangely disturbing about the wonder, the ignorance, and the joy: *miratur rerumque ignarus imagine gaudet.* For one thing, the superb harmonies of the shield in its celebration of Rome and Augustus are abruptly ended in the simplicities of the spare coda. This surprising shift in mood and cadence is heightened by an antithesis that is specially suitable to Aeneas' condition in this scene and throughout the poem: *rerum / imagine* —realities and images. Vulcan, the maker of the shield, is *haud vatum ignarus venturique inscius aevi*; but the person for whom

the shield is made and who will use it in fulfilling his destiny and
fostering the destiny of his countrymen does not really know
what his shield signifies; his awe here, like his awe in the underworld, is a function not only of the grandeur of what he sees but
also of his necessary inability to comprehend the significance of
what he sees. In a crucial sense, then, the beauty of the shield
(and the beauty of the poetry) is equivocal, fails finally to en-
lighten or to redeem Aeneas (or us), however much it may awe
him (and charm us). *Respicit ignarus rerum ingratusque salutis*
(10.666); *Obstipuit varia confusus imagine rerum* (12.665):
the condition of Turnus and his ignorance of his surroundings
and of the meaning of his fate may be more extreme than the
ignorance of Aeneas, but essentially both men move in a world
where appearances are not only deceptive but also potentially
fatal and where—for them and for the reader too—the flux of
perceptions, however beautiful they may sometimes be, is never
finally caught up into a pattern that is at once intelligible and
trustworthy. Aeneas and Turnus, like the other characters in the
poem, inhabit a world where the brighter the shining of glory or
prophecy, the surer and the more terrible the darkness will be.
Near the core of Vergil's imagination is a fascination for the pro-
cesses of "disastrous twilight," the sudden flaring of a glory that
exists to reveal the darkness that encloses the sublunar world.

5. THE END OF BOOK 12

τὸν δὲ καταθνῄσκων προσέφη κορυθαίολος Ἕκτωρ·
"ἦ σ' εὖ γιγνώσκων προτιόσσομαι, οὐδ' ἄρ' ἔμελλον
πείσειν· ἦ γὰρ σοί γε σιδήρεος ἐν φρεσὶ θυμός.
φράζεο νῦν μή τοί τι θεῶν μήνιμα γένωμαι
ἤματι τῷ, ὅτε κέν σε Πάρις καὶ Φοῖβος Ἀπόλλων
ἐσθλὸν ἐόντ' ὀλέσωσιν ἐνὶ Σκαιῇσι πύλῃσιν."

ὣς ἄρα μιν ϝειπόντα τέλος θανάτοιο κάλυψε·
ψυχὴ δ' ἐκ ῥεθέων πταμένη Ἀϊδόσδε βεβήκει,
ϝὸν πότμον γοάουσα, λιποῦσ' ἀνδροτῆτα καὶ ἥβην.
τὸν καὶ τεθνηῶτα προσηύδαε δῖος Ἀχιλλεύς·

"τέθναθι· κῆρα δ' ἐγὼ τότε δέξομαι, ὁππότε κεν δὴ
Ζεὺς ἐθέλῃ τελέσαι ἠδ' ἀθάνατοι θεοὶ ἄλλοι."

(*Iliad* 22.355–366)

Then, as he lay dying, Hector of the flashing helmet addressed
Achilles: "Yes, I see you very well, as you are, and this is as I
sensed it must be, nor was it possible that I could persuade you,
for in your breast the heart is iron. But think carefully now of

what you are doing, or I may be made the occasion of the gods' anger on you when Paris and Phoebus Apollo shall destroy you, stalwart though you are, at the Scaean gate." As he was speaking, his death's limit engulfed him, and his soul, speeding from his limbs, went down to Hades, grieving for its destiny, relinquishing the manhood and the youth. But dead though he was, him Achilles addressed: "Die and lie dead. My own deathdoom I shall embrace whenever Zeus and the other immortals see fit to achieve it."

This speech is not imitated in *Aeneid* 12, and the absence of this speech from the *Aeneid*'s close is significant both for the kind of emphasis and the modulations that Vergil wants for his scene and for the harmonics of Book 12 as a whole. Hector attempts to supplicate Achilles only after he has been mortally wounded; it is not, then, life that he asks for but only a decent burial. In this second speech, after his entreaty has been rejected, he shows at once a courage that is specifically his own and a ferocity that matches Achilles'. In short, Hector goes down swinging; there is not the vaguest hint that he is merely the victim of a force, whether human or divine, that has bereft him of his nobility and humanity, qualities which are tragically emphasized in the closing words of the formula that pictures his death (*lipous' androtēta kai hēbēn* [relinquishing manhood and youth]). Because of Vergil's compression and alteration of his model, this heroic emphasis disappears and is replaced with an ugly, unheroic pathos: *ille humilis supplex oculos dextramque precantem / protendens 'equidem merui nec deprecor' inquit* (930–931);[98] *ast illi solvuntur frigore membra / vitaque cum gemitu fugit indignata sub umbras* (951–952).

> Then humble, suppliant, he lifts his eyes
> and, stretching out his hand, entreating, cries:
> "I have indeed deserved this; I do not
> appeal against it;"
>
> . . . .
>
> His limbs fell slack with chill; and with a moan
> his life, resentful, fled to Shades below.

It is no secret that there is a general dissatisfaction or uneasiness with this famous closure. One may try to rationalize the dissatisfaction by proving the villainy of Turnus or by showing that the death of Turnus, the manner of his death, symbolizes the defeat of Juno; for those who are content to read the poem as an ethical melodrama, such solutions are apparently adequate—once we have separated the good guys from the bad guys and the bad guys get what is coming to them, the beauty of the poem is found to be intact. Thus, a solution we would find banal in any ephemeral movie of our choice is found to be adequate in the hands of an acknowledged master of Western epic. By the same token, it does no good to make Aeneas a monster, for that is to do little more than play the same game in a slightly more fashionable way: find the villain but call him anti-hero. But in writing his poem, Vergil sought to imagine a world—or, rather, a complexity of worlds —that one or another kind of villain could not account for. So, relegating villains to the pleasant melodramas that are their proper sphere, we can undertake to ask in what the beauty of Vergil's closure consists and what that particular beauty signifies. Here as elsewhere in this study we begin asking our questions by focusing on Vergil's transformation of his Homeric models. Our essential questions, then, will be these: Why does Vergil imagine his Turnus as a victim? Why does the victimization of Turnus become the central issue of the poem's climax? Why is imagination of a pathetic Turnus beautiful—if it is—not despite, but because of, the uneasiness and the dissatisfaction that it effects in us?

The fact that Turnus is a victim has been foreshadowed since his first appearance in Book 7 when Allecto infects him with madness after having infected Amata with a similar madness. But the full reality and full significance of this madness become wholly apparent only at 12.614 ff. when we see the onset of that failure of nerve that will let the madness have its way unimpeded by any rational or courageous gesture. It is well to remember here that the madness and victimization of Dido show a similar pattern of adumbrations, retardations, and slow growth from their onset to their climax. So, after the representation of Turnus' failure of nerve, Turnus' victimization is obliquely yet carefully connected with the retarding minor themes of the maddened ruined *civitas* and with the madness and death of Amata:

> "ei mihi! quid tanto turbantur moenia luctu?
> quisve ruit tantus diversa clamor ab urbe?"
>
> (12.620–621)

> "What sorrow so disturbs our walls, what is
> this roar that races from the distant city?"

At this point Juturna, disguised as the charioteer, Metiscus, attempts to reassure her brother and to encourage him against Aeneas. But her speech neither cheers him nor incites him:

> O soror, et dudum agnovi, cum prima per artem
> foedera turbasti teque haec in bella dedisti,
> et nunc nequiquam fallis dea. sed quis Olympo
> demissam tantos voluit te ferre labores?
> an fratris miseri letum ut crudele videres?
>
> (632–636)

> O sister, I knew you long since, both when
> you first disturbed our pact by craftiness
> and plunged into these wars; and when you tried—
> in vain—to trick me, hiding your godhead.
> But who has willed that you be sent from high
> Olympus to endure such trials? Was it
> to see your luckless brother's brutal death?

In this speech, two things are emphasized: (1) Turnus' recognition that, despite divine help, his position is hopeless; (2) his understanding that, in ways he cannot understand, the action that was intended to help him is now helping to destroy him. He has, that is to say, not only recognized Juturna in her disguise, but he has also recognized that some power higher than Juturna's has effected the ruin of the truce and has shaped a situation that is dangerous and humiliating to his country and fatal to him. His recognition of his sister and what she is doing accompanies, in a properly tragic way, a decisive change in Turnus' fortunes, for it is his knowledge—that is to say, his sudden realization that he does not, cannot, comprehend what is happening—that saps his will. From this point on (until the final moments of the poem) Turnus continues his struggle valiantly, but he fights now with the valor of a deeply confused and clearly doomed man from whose lips the final speech of Hector would be an impossibility.

In permitting Turnus to recognize Juturna and in permitting him to recognize the presence of Juno behind her (though he does not know that the presence is Juno's), Vergil is able to emphasize one of the central patterns that he is shaping for the closure: fulfillment of *devotio* of Turnus and the ironic *evocatio* of Juno. For it is around these two familar historical and religious concepts that Vergil designs the end of his epic, and it is the interplay of these two concepts that gives the closing of the *Aeneid* both its unique momentum and its unique and chilling resolution.

It is at the end of his superb rejoinder to the speech of Drances that Turnus consciously devotes himself in single combat for the triumph of his country and the salvation of his countrymen,

"vobis animam hanc soceroque Latino
Turnus ego, haut ulli veterum virtute secundus,
devovi. solum Aeneas vocat; et vocet oro,
nec Drances potius, sive est haec ira deorum,
morte luat, sive est virtus et gloria, tollat."

(11.440–444)

"To you, the Latin elders and Latinus,
the father of my bride, I, Turnus, second
to no one of our ancestors in courage,
have dedicated this my life. They say
Aeneas calls on me alone; I pray
that he may call. Do not let Drances fight
instead of me, if either heaven's wrath
is turned against us and demands a death
or there is glory to be gained by courage."

and this *devotio* is emphatically reaffirmed at the opening of
Book 12:

"aut hac Dardanium dextra sub Tartara mittam,
desertorem Asiae (sedeant spectentque Latini),
et solus ferro crimen commune refellam,
aut habeat victos, cedat Lavinia coniunx."

(12.14–17)

"either I
send down this Dardan, Asia's renegade,
to hell with my right hand—while Latins sit
and watch—and by my single sword blot out
the slur that stains us all; or we are beaten
and held by him, he takes Lavinia."

I do not envy the reader who believes that this *devotio* is the proof
of Turnus' arrogance or stupidity or, on a less personal level, that
it is merely the product of the madness and chaos that Juno has
effected for Turnus and for the Latins.[99] Turnus is doing all that
is humanly possible and wagering all that is humanly possible for
purposes that transcend his personal desires and ambitions: he is,
if any hero is, heroic. But he has not reckoned with Juno, and the
bitter truth of his poem is that no one—not Dido, not Aeneas,
perhaps not even Jupiter—has reckoned with her or can reckon
with her. There is a fine irony in Turnus' *devotio* because, when
he utters it, he still hopes, unconsciously and irrationally, for personal triumph and salvation over and above the national triumph
and salvation for which he offers himself as sacrifice. At the time

of this *devotio* he cannot, of course, know that the Latin people will indeed triumph by their union with the Trojans, the union that his sacrifice will make possible; nor can he know how dreadful that sacrifice will be—dreadful in exact proportion as he is the unwitting and unwilling pawn of Juno in her struggle against the destiny of Aeneas and the Trojans. By the time he guesses some of the horror, it is, of course, too late, but he goes forward to his own doom and to his nation's salvation as steadfastly as the gathering terrors of the closure will allow. The fact that Turnus is ignorant of what Juno is doing with him and to him does not fully relieve him of the burden of his merely personal mistakes any more than the fact that Aeneas is ignorant of what Juno is doing relieves him of responsibility for his mistakes of omission and commision. That Turnus' mistakes are more numerous and more grave than those of Aeneas does not prove that he is a bad man; it proves only that he is more radically deceived by Juno, more abused by her, than even Aeneas is. Finally, though he may not seem very likable to many readers (some readers do not like Achilles very much), he is not therefore wicked, and his courage and his plight are not to be listed among Vergil's ambivalences and obscurities. In any case, if anything can mollify Turnus' detractors, his final unselfishness, his gallantry, and his fear as he prepares to perform the *devotio* should succeed in mollifying them. For what he has guessed by the time that we view him in the scene in question is a dreadful thing: he comes to realize—and we watch and participate in his realization—that he and his country are caught in the toils of the powers of darkness. That Juno is, depending on at what level one reads the poem, either an instrument of those powers or symbolic of those powers or controls or is herself those powers—this dominance of Juno Turnus does not know, nor does Aeneas. But we know it, and our knowing what they do not know as we watch them move towards their separate tragedies intensifies the power and terror of the poem.

It is the way that Vergil gathers the powers of darkness in upon Turnus that gives to Book 12 its incomparable and sinister momentum and its brilliant imagination of catastrophe. Here again a comparison with Homer is in order. Whatever one takes as the central pattern of the *Iliad*, there can be little doubt that the duel between Achilles and Hector, together with the actions that lead up to it and the action and emotions that reverberate from it to the last line of the poem, is an essential aspect of that centrality. Crucial here are not only the perfection and the steady ease of the logical and emotive preparations for the duel and the clarity and the controlled and delicate realism with which the duel itself is imagined; crucial also is the grace of the modulations from the terror and the inexorable truth of the duel into the understanding and illuminations of which its aftermath is composed. In this aftermath the essential beauties both of Hector and of Achilles are steadily and thoroughly affirmed and defined. Neither man is praised at the expense of the other, and, irreconcilable as the virtues they represent may be while they both live, inevitable as the collision of these virtues may be, it is the duel of Achilles and Hector—its causes, its effects, and its meaning—that crystallizes the *praxis* of the poem. The virtues of both men survive the catastrophe of their collision and, enduring a ruthless transcendence, achieve a still coinherence which remains, priceless and unattainable, the norm for tragic poetry in the West.[100]

Various good readers of the poem (for my present purposes, I am thinking of Weil and Bespaloff, among the most recent) have succeeded in penetrating some of the mysteries of the *Iliad*. But how the poet of the *Iliad* learned to imagine this much calm born from this much violence and hatred remains, and probably will remain, one of the great mysteries of literature. This mystery is not our concern here. But this calm, issued as it is from such rage and destruction, must be our concern, for it is precisely this calm that will enable us to gauge the degree to which calm of any kind has been consciously excluded from the *Aeneid*.

Immediately after Achilles, in his speech to the corpse of Hector, has answered Hector's final challenge (355–366) and has addressed the Achaeans who have come to gaze with wonder at the greatness of Hector even in death (367–374), we watch Achilles accomplish his mutilation of Hector's corpse, and we watch Hecuba as she sees what Achilles has done (395–407). Now begins the series of laments that move us away from the unintelligible immediacy of Hector's death and Achilles' savagery. In a pattern that partly mirrors the action just before the beginning of the duel, first comes Priam's lament for his son, then follows the lament of Hecuba, then, breaking the reflection with a delicate slowness, comes Andromache; her thoughts on embroidery and hot baths, she guesses from the growing noise the bad truth, goes to the wall, sees the terror everyone else has seen, and, in one of the great moments of poetry, moans a paradigm of isolation and despair, a formless frenzy that is heightened by her desperate attempts at reasoning. This is not, of course, the moment of calm, but it completes the adumbrations of calm. After the deep rage that gropes for words and tries to fasten, hopelessly, on any reality that can make sense of what this death is and means, after the supreme precision of Andromache's speech, come the casual radiance of the funeral games for Patroclus, the tough, uncertain, desperate confrontation of the father and his son's murderer, and then, again, a triple threnody that mirrors the threnodies of Book 22, and, stretching beyond the anguish, transcends despair to achieve, at last, the calm.

The central grief has been purged with grief. Against all hope or possibility, the threnodies render the grief bearable. We see, or rather we sense, that the life of Hector has been perfected in his death, his goodness and his authenticity verified by the sorrow that their absence causes. What is evil or stupid about the sorrow has been purged away; what is good about the sorrow—and we sense that there is something good about this sorrow, something that has no name and that we sometimes experience vicariously and dimly in tragic poetry—what is good about the sorrow remains. How "the resentment that rots of the soul" leaves Achilles or Hector or Andromache is something that is susceptible neither to rational analysis nor to poetic mimesis. That it has been transcended, transfigured to a nameless faith or praise, is beyond question, because this is what the poem clearly shows. After all this rage and madness, human reality is somehow intact, has somehow escaped the near corruption of its integrity, is, against all hope, somehow sane and free; for evil and the mutability of fortune are understood, in a way neither reason nor poetry can explain, as somehow unreal. How this happens remains a mystery because not even the purity and power of Homer's language can imitate that action. But one can suggest that, without the leisure and the economy of Homer's modulations, we could not be persuaded that these desolations have been survived and these integrities have been rediscovered and renewed. It is because of Homer's mastery of long and slow diminuendo, his firm yet gentle modulations, that we can believe and accept the subdued and somber good news he offers in the trio of threnodies where the anguish heals and restores. It is the mastery that Milton possessed when he turned from Vergil to Sophocles:

> Nothing is here for tears, nothing to wail
> Or knock the breast, no weakness, no contempt,
> Dispraise, or blame, nothing but well and fair,
> And what may quiet us in a death so noble.
> (*Samson Agonistes* 1721–1724)

Even the most casual reader of the *Georgics* would be unlikely to deny that Vergil understood such modulations and such diminuendoes, for in that poem he uses the poetic solutions that these devices proffer frequently and with assured ease; and in much of the *Aeneid* these same devices are clearly operative. But from the closure of this poem, precisely where we might have expected to find them, they have been utterly excluded. And this absence of diminuendo and healing threnody, of lamentation that does not so much purge grief as clarify it, is heightened by the steady divine interventions that dwarf human actions in Book 12 and end by darkening them. In Homer's handling of the duel between Achilles and Hector, the interventions of Apollo and Athena, like the interventions of other deities in the poem, illumine the human actions by reminding us of the deathless perfection against which the heroic figures enact their beautiful and awesome, yet imperfect and wholly mortal, drama. And the interventions of Apollo and Athena are not so obtrusive as to negate the courage or the moral autonomy of either Achilles or Hector. After Apollo has been forced to abandon Hector because of the judgment of Zeus' scales (209 ff.), and after Athena, disguised as Deiphobus, has lured him to the place of his death, Hector, on realizing what has happened to him, so far from quailing, breaks into an angry denunciation and reaffirms his determination to fight to the death, whatever the odds against him may be (297–305). In other words, though he feels cornered, he does not, strange to say, feel trapped. His death is, as he sees it, probably inevitable, but he has come to that death not so much because Athena has lured him to it as because he himself, in his courage and in his sense of responsibility, has chosen to come to it. For in the world of the *Iliad*, the deceptions of the gods, like Fate itself, are part of the natural order that includes within it men's freedom and their reason. But the interventions of Juno in Book 12, like her earlier appearances in the poem, constitute a violent and malevolent disruption of the natural order, and the effect of this disruption is to ensnare Turnus, strip him of the glory that his *devotio* might have brought him had the truce not been ruined, gradually sap him of his will and his reason, and at last, almost as by whim, secure his annihilation. In Book 12 neither Juno nor Juturna nor Jupiter with his scales nor, certainly, the Dira lights up the actions of Aeneas and Turnus, by reminding us, in the midst of their violence and unreason, of an order of reality whose truth and eternity are the measure of what human beings do with themselves and their lives. Rather Juno and her instruments and Jupiter himself stifle the reality of the human action and deprive it of whatever dignity and significance it might otherwise have. In Book 12 the divine is not, as it is in *Iliad* 22, a frame which magnifies the greatness as well as the terror of the action that it encloses; it is rather itself a part of that action, and so great a part of it that the action is finally engulfed by and dissolved into it.

Vergil creates this pattern of darkness by bringing his Homeric models into new configurations, by conflating them, by compressing them, and so transforming them. Specifically, Vergil unites the wounding of Menelaus and the breaking of the truce in *Iliad* 4 with the deception of Zeus and his reconcilation with Hera in Books 14 and 15, and he underscores this audacious conflation of the Homeric models with an original and terrifying invention— the Fury, the Dira, who becomes the instrument of Jupiter's strange and macabre justice. The peculiar horror of this configuration of Homeric models arises, in large measure, from the essential innocence of the models themselves. The opening of *Iliad* 4 is possessed of that fine comic lustre that Homer created for his deities to play in: the breaking of the truce and the wounding of Menelaus are part of a grim joke that Zeus is playing on Hera,[101] and, though the events have, as usual, an essential function in the articulation of the poem's story, they function no less as a means of relaxation and entertainment. But in Vergil's poem the truce and the wounding are not merely articulations of the *muthos*; they are the beginning of its climax, and, given the total seriousness of that climax, divine intervention at this point in the poem is crucial to the poem's essential meaning. What Zeus does in *Iliad* 4 alters the course of events in a minor way; what Juno does in *Aeneid* 12 shapes what finally happens to Turnus and what finally happens to Aeneas himself. And what finally happens to both of them, though it does not alter perhaps the design of fate or the course of history, is an essential part of what the *Aeneid* is about—two kinds of heroism that fail of their proper fruitions, which is a reversal, though not a criticism, of what the *Iliad* is about.

In Vergil Jupiter is not (or at least seems not to be) deceived by Juno, but he is reconciled to Juno (or she to him) as Zeus in *Iliad* 15 is reconciled to Hera. In effect, the meeting between Juno and Jupiter in Book 12 is shaped as an *evocatio*.[102] Jupiter is persuading Juno (it is not, of course, a supplication) to abandon the doomed city and to take up residence in the future city whose existence she has, throughout the poem, done everything she could think of to obviate. Her last stratagem, the ruin of the truce, has in fact not yet quite failed, so far as we can see, but Jupiter persuades her to desist from her efforts not so much by proving to her that she has no hope of winning but rather, in the usual way for *evocatio,* by warning her that her cause is lost and by enhancing his warning with a handsome bribe.[103]

It is important to emphasize how abrupt this encounter between the two deities is, how lacking in preparation, and how easy is the resolution it effects. Juno has apparently made up her mind to abandon Juturna and Turnus and to abate her wrath against Aeneas and the Trojans (or ignore it) before Jupiter seeks her out (wherever he was during the earlier action of Book 12,[104] wherever she has been since we saw her last, at 134–160, when she sent Juturna to see that the truce was ruined and to help her brother). Furthermore, combined with the abruptness of this encounter and the obscurity of the reasons for Juno's change of mind and heart, the tone of this scene has a peculiarly random and bittersweet calm that seems (but finally is not) ill-suited to the violence and the austerity of the mood, theme, and action that surround it. At the opening of Book 15 Zeus is, not surprisingly, very angry at having been hoodwinked by Hera, and she, after listening meekly to the fury of his specific plans for her punishment, is naturally very frightened. Her response, of course, flatters his masculine pride (though this was not Hera's intention), and he smiles that incomparably, deliciously mindless smile of his (47 ff.), and tacitly forgives her by sending her to tidy up the mess she has made. And so they are reconciled and, more important for our purposes, we see the effects of that reconciliation in her actions, for, sulky in defeat, still alarmed, petulant, spoiled, and irresistible as ever, she unwillingly sees to it that what she has done begins to be undone (78–80, and, in particular, 100–102).

When Jupiter encounters Juno (791–792) he is not angry; he is perhaps somewhat exasperated, but his voice is the voice of firm reason:

> "ventum ad supremum est; terris agitare vel undis
> Troianos potuisti, infandum accendere bellum,
> deformare domum et luctu miscere hymenaeos:
> ulterius temptare veto."
>
> (803–806)

> "This is the end.
> You have harassed the Trojans over land
> and wave, have kindled brutal war, outraged

124

Latinus' home, and mingled grief and marriage:
you cannot pass beyond this point."

That is, considering all the things that Juno has in fact done or tried to do in this poem, putting it rather mildly. No threats, no recriminations; rather, a simple, rational statement of the facts: what she has done and what she may do no more. And, against all that we might expect from her on the basis of her previous behavior, she yields instantly to reason and to fact:

> sic dea submisso contra Saturnia voltu:
> "ista quidem quia nota mihi tua, magne, voluntas,
> Iuppiter, et Turnum et terras invita reliqui. . . ."
>
> (807–809)

> the goddess, Saturn's daughter, yielding, answered:
> "Great Jupiter, it was indeed for this—
> my knowing what you wish—that I have left
> both Turnus and the earth, unwillingly. . . ."

We shall return to the significance of *submisso voltu* in a moment. What concerns us now, because it must somehow puzzle us, is Juno's apparently new respect for Jupiter's will and what has occasioned that respect *even before he addressed her*. For her utter composure suggests that in this instance at least she is telling something like the truth: she had at some point, for reasons that remain mysterious to us, decided to desist from her efforts at annihilating the Trojans before Jupiter presented her with his reasonable and composed ultimatum. We may wonder, too, when it was that she began to hate war (*et nunc cedo equidem pugnasque exosa relinquo* [818]) and how she can possibly be so pleased with the terms of the *evocatio* (834–840). She has made a mistake, has indeed made several mistakes; now she sees that what she wanted was wrong and that the course of action that she had pursued in attempting to possess what she wanted was futile. She changes her mind, has changed her mind; Jupiter is pleased because it has been so easy, because she has, despite his experience with her, quickly yielded to sweet reason. He is pleased that he has, at long last, his way. He smiles at her,

> olli subridens hominum rerumque repertor:
> "es germana Iovis Saturnique altera proles:
> irarum tantos volvis sub pectore fluctus."
>
> (829–831)

> And Jupiter smiled at her then; the maker
> of men and things said: "Surely you are sister
> to Jove, a second child of Saturn, for
> deep in your breast there surge such tides of anger."

and this is one of the most sinister moments in this increasingly sinister poem.[105]

He smiles because she has shown, not by her capitulation (whose insincerity he probably guesses) but by the constancy and intensity of her anger, that she is, like him, a true Olympian.[106] He smiles because, like the Zeus of *Iliad* 15, he has caught his wife in an amusing lie and can therefore toy as he pleases with her partial admission and her ridiculous pretense at submission (Hera, of course, is not pretending). But unlike the smile of Zeus, the smile of Jupiter is touched with a nameless evil, for the deception of Hera was little more than an escapade, but the deception of Juno was a last-ditch attempt to destroy peace and harmony for the Trojans and Latins alike, and to secure, by whatever means, at whatever cost, her desperate and ugly revenge. In smiling at Juno and her lie and her hypocrisy, Jupiter in effect sanctions what she is doing and what she is. Finally, the deception practiced by Hera was not essential to the central action of the *Iliad*. But Juno's action alters the central action of the *Aeneid* and shapes its final catastrophe, which is defined by the particular ugliness of Turnus' despair and of Aeneas' anger.[107] The suffering and violence that Juno's final intervention creates differ from the previous suffering and violence that she has caused because they lead into the final catastrophe. Jupiter knows that Juno is responsible for the breaking of the truce (and with it, the possibility of a somewhat rational and essentially nonviolent solution to the dilemma) and for the wounding of Aeneas,[108] but, somehow, he does not care about this last and greatest piece of daimonism. He pretends to be satisfied with her explanations and with her announcement that her plans have changed; he effects, or seems to effect, the *evocatio* that he desires, and Juno herself is gladdened (*laetata*) by this turn of events.

Is she gladdened, like the Eumenides, because she is to get a new cult statue? Or, having risked so much, is she pleased at having got off so lightly and at knowing that she has accomplished much of her purpose? With the truce broken and *ira* still raging, the triumph of Aeneas will inevitably be marred. Or is she glad because she knows that, since Dido's curse is still operative, the suffering of the Trojans cannot be revoked by her temporary acquiescence to Jupiter's command, that there will be other times and other places for her to attempt what she wants to accomplish? The expression on her face as she answers Jupiter's first speech suggests submission, and in a speech that centers on a lie hidden in a half-truth she promises submission even before she has heard the grand wages that sin has earned her. When she hears that she has not only escaped all punishment for her crimes but is also to be rewarded for not persisting in them, she assents to Jupiter's offer with delight: *adnuit his Iuno et mentem laetata retorsit.* The mild catachresis, *mentem retorsit*, is naturally taken as Lewis and Short take it, "she changed her mind." But suppose it means also, *his mentem retorsit*? That is, she openly assents to what Jupiter says, but, in her mind, she turns away from his words, rejects them? [109] Twists her mind back from them would be a neat—and normal—antithetical balancing of *adnuit his*, and the mental action would negate the outward sign that she makes. I do not say that this is clearly the meaning of the Latin, though I doubt that the Lewis and Short reading is clear either; I only suggest that the ambiguity is possible, and, in view of Juno's characteristic duplicity, is suitable as a conclusion to this scene. The fact that Juno did not, so far as Roman sentiment was concerned, became reconciled to Rome at this time, and possibly never became fully reconciled to Rome at any time, is clear from Servius' difficulties in interpreting *mentem retorsit*.[110] Juno is happy, perhaps, but Juno happy is not much less frightening than Juno unhappy. Neither Servius nor Horace is quite at ease with her happiness, and perhaps we should not be quite at ease, either. For though Juno now disappears from the poem, the poem began with her and in effect it ends with her. The climax of the poem starts gathering its momentum the moment she departs, and that climax involves the destruction of Turnus, her unwilling victim and unknowing pawn; he is destroyed by the Dira, who is, in the hellish imagery that expresses her, a figure that is parallel to Allecto and that therefore represents not so much the will of Jupiter as the will of Juno.[111]

Jupiter sends the Dira to preside over Turnus' death and so to accomplish, at long last, the triumph of Aeneas and the Trojan settlement in Italy. But it looks as though Turnus is the object of Jupiter's wrath, that he is somehow being punished for every crime that has been committed since Aeneas and the Trojans landed in Italy. There is no question that Turnus is guilty of several acts of arrogance, and there is no question that he has totally misunderstood what is fated to happen, namely, that Aeneas, who is not an interloper but the instrument of Fate, is destined to settle in Italy. But Turnus, if he lacks Aeneas' knowledge of true destiny, shares with Aeneas his ignorance of what Juno and Allecto have been trying to do. In this sense, the ugliness of his death and the behavior of the Dira (and of Jupiter in sending her) seem, to put it as mildly as possible, excessive.[112] Servius' note on the Dira suggests that at least some ancient readers of the poem were hard pressed to explain what Vergil's Fury was and what she signified. How, in fact, can there be an Olympian Fury? Was not manifest Unreason banished from heaven long since?[113] Vergil's Dira—whom he boldly, even recklessly locates at the foot of Jupiter's throne—is a figure out of a chorus in Greek tragedy or an Etruscan painting,[114] but in Vergil's poem the Dira is not merely an image or a group of images; she takes on a vast and profound life, plunges into the action of the poem, and presides over its dreadful climax. It is this sudden, chilling embodiment of the powers of darkness and the forces of unreason that makes the final intervention of the divine in the *Aeneid* as sinister as it is original.

The anger of Jupiter (though it is not emphasized as anger, which is disturbing) and the possible justice of this anger have parallels in Homer, and once again Vergil's originality and, more important, his power in this passage arise from the masterly conflations and compressions of the Homeric models.

ὡς δ' ὑπὸ λαίλαπι πᾶσα κελαινὴ βέβριθε χθὼν
ἤματ' ὀπωρινῷ, ὅτε λαβρότατον χέει ὕδωρ
Ζεύς, ὅτε δὴ ἄνδρεσσι κοτεσσάμενος χαλεπήνῃ,
οἳ βίῃ εἰν ἀγορῇ σκολιὰς κρίνωσι θέμιστας,
ἐκ δὲ δίκην ἐλάσωσι, θεῶν ὄπιν οὐκ ἀλέγοντες·

(*Iliad* 16.384–388)

As all the black earth is overwhelmed by a whirlwind on a harvest day and Zeus sends forth his most brutal rains if mortal men have goaded him to fury, twisting judgments in their turbulent convocations, banishing justice, indifferent to the chastening gods. . . .

When Zeus from the heavens unrolls the rainbow that glints darkling to be a signal of war or of uncomfortable winter, he forces mortal men to cease from their labors on the earth, and he troubles their flocks. . . .

(*Iliad* 17.547–550)

his actis aliud genitor secum ipse volutat
Iuturnamque parat fratris dimittere ab armis.

dicuntur geminae pestes cognomine Dirae,
quas et Tartaream Nox intempesta Megaeram
uno eodemque tulit partu paribusque revinxit
serpentum spiris ventosasque addidit alas.
hae Iovis ad solium saevique in limine regis
apparent accuuntque metum mortalibus aegris,
si quando letum horrificum morbosque deum rex
molitur, meritas aut bello territat urbes;
harum unam celerem demisit ab aethere summo
Iuppiter inque omen Iuturnae occurrere iussit.
illa volat celerique ad terram turbine fertur.

(Aeneid 12.843–855)

This done, the Father, left alone, ponders
another plan: to have Juturna driven
far from her brother. It is said there are
two fiends who bear the name of Furies; they
were born in one same birth with hell's Megaera
out of untimely Night, who wrapped all three
in equal serpents' folds and added wings
that take the wind. These wait before the throne
of Jove, the threshold of the cruel king,
and spur the fears of feeble mortals when
it happens that the king of gods flings down
dread sorrow and diseases or when he
sends war to terrify unrighteous cities.
And quickly Jupiter sends one of these
from heaven's height, commanding her to meet
Juturna as an evil emissary.
She flies off; cloaked in whirlwinds, she is carried
to earth.

In the first Homeric passage the justice and power of Zeus' anger
are emphasized; in the second, the justice of his anger is ignored
in favor of a macabre vision of natural beauty and subtly destructive menace. In Vergil's imitation, the violence and the macabre
are accented, and the justice disappears, leaving only a trace behind it. In her ferocity and her bestial vindictiveness, the Dira
whom we see at work in 861 ff. and 875 ff. surpasses the Homeric
models, for Vergil has gathered them into a single impression and
uses that impression to underscore a crucial dramatic action—
Juturna's agonized abandonment of her brother.

In the Homeric correspondence Apollo abandons Hector immediately after the scales of Zeus have determined that the time

for Hector's defeat and death has come (22.209–215), whereupon Athena comes to Achilles and tells him how she will lure Hector to fight with him. The scales of Zeus represent characteristically Homeric impartiality and inevitability, and they illumine Hector's doom, focus on it, announce it. But Vergil uses the scales not to heighten the climax of the struggle between the two heroes or to fix its decisive moment; rather he employs it, almost ironically, to ornament the beginning of the duel, and he therefore phrases the picture of the scales ambiguously:

> Iuppiter ipse duas aequato examine lances
> sustinet et fata imponit diversa duorum,
> quem damnet labor et quo vergat pondere letum.
>
> (12.725–727)

> There Jupiter himself
> holds up two scales in equal balance, then
> he adds two different fates, one on each hand:
> whom this trial dooms, what weight sinks down to death.

He thus deprives it of the immediacy and inevitability that enform the Homeric model. In a similarly bold and ironic reformation of his model, Vergil separates the withdrawal of Turnus' divine champion Juturna from the impartial decision of the scales and juxtaposes it with Juturna's terrified recognition of the Dira. Thus, though the Dira may be connected with Jupiter, and though she may—without Aeneas' knowledge—become his ally (for she is now paralleled with Athena in the Homeric model), she cannot be associated with the imagery of justice and pure fate. She represents and brings with her into the poem and its closure the full fruition of the evil, incomprehensible darkness that has drifted through the poem but has never, until now, overwhelmed it. What the Dira effects in the closure is a strange configuration of confusion, impotence, and terror. Turnus is not a fool or a coward, nor does Aeneas turn into a savage fiend, though in our last view of him, he, the enemy of unreasoning passion and senseless violence, is *furiis accensus et ira / terribilis*.[115] Rather, when the Dira appears in the poem, both heroes must come to the heart of the poem, to an unknown, terrifying desolation in which their particular virtues are less than useless and all goodness and all truth are broken and lost. The poem ends, on one level at least, with the triumph of Juno. Small wonder that she can depart from Jupiter with joy.[116]

This is not the place to try to discover what the *Iliad* is or is not about, to try to gather its polycenters into its core, for we are concerned here only with closure. In terms of its closure we can say that at least one of the things that the *Iliad* is about is the testing and the affirmation of two radically different concepts of heroic behavior as these are represented by the figures of Achilles and Hector, respectively, and we can say that these concepts are tested, both of them, by a ruthless imagination of the human condition and are affirmed by an equally pitiless imagination of what is true and what is just. But if this dialectical scrutiny brings us to contemplate two opposed, yet equally valid concepts of heroism, and if the collision of these concepts is a crucial aspect of the *praxis* that the *muthos* of Achilles and Hector imitates, then the closure of the *Iliad* will reflect the idea that both modes of heroism are equally noble and equally valuable; that they offer, in different ways, paradigms of the self-respect that human beings must aim for if their lives are to be worth living: Achilles in his intractable (or nearly intractable) individualism that verges towards, but does not finally fall into, a magnificent yet ruinous selfishness; Hector in his indomitable (or nearly indomitable) sense of responsibility that verges towards, but does not finally fall into, a magnificent but ruinous self-sacrifice. Thus, through the process of a dramatic dialectic, the norms and the spectrum of heroism are illumined *sub specie aeternitatis*. That is at least one of the things that the *Iliad* is about and something that its closure makes visible.[117]

But this dialectical contemplation of man's bondage and his dignity (with a slight emphasis on his dignity—and it is a superb slightness) is not one of the things that the *Aeneid* is about, and the poem's closure shows that it is not. In presenting the closing action of the poem almost entirely from the point of view of the hero who becomes more and more a victim as he nears his death, by intensifying this pattern with a steady and careful imagination of what the Dira is and what she does, Vergil contemplates and forces us to contemplate not so much man's dignity and courage as his vulnerability and, most especially, the mysterious forces that cause him to jeopardize his dignity and waste his courage:

> cunctanti telum Aeneas fatale coruscat
> sortitus fortunam oculis et corpore toto
> eminus intorquet.

> (919–921)

> In Turnus' wavering Aeneas sees
> his fortune; he holds high the fatal shaft;
> he hurls it far with all his body's force.

Aeneas volvens oculos dextramque repressit;
et iam iamque magis cunctantem flectere sermo
coeperat. . . .

(938–941)

Aeneas stood, ferocious in his armor;
his eyes were restless and he stayed his hand;
and as he hesitated, Turnus' words
began to move him more and more. . . .

These are two very different kinds of hesitation, but both moments of hesitation are expressive of a deep and total failure of will, of a confusion—indeed of a despair—that the world of Juno, Allecto, and the Dira make all too comprehensible to us:

murali concita numquam
tormento sic saxa fremunt nec fulmine tanti
dissultant crepitus. volat atri turbinis instar
exitium dirum hasta ferens orasque recludit
loricae et clipei extremos septemplicis orbes.

(921–925)

No boulder ever catapulted from
siege engine sounded so, no thunderbolt
had ever burst with such a roar. The spear
flies on like a black whirlwind, carrying
its dread destruction, ripping through the border
of Turnus' corselet and the outer rim
of Turnus' seven-plated shield.

Both the hyperbole that is used to describe the wounding and the terror of the imagery (*atri turbinis instar, exitium dirum*) figure forth a world where healing threnody for, and final affirmation of, Turnus would be pointless, a world from which threnody and affirmation are rigorously and decorously excluded. And in the absence of lamentation for and celebration of Turnus and what he stands for, our sense of Aeneas and what he stands for becomes inevitably weakened and confused. I do not mean that Aeneas fails at the end of the poem, does something utterly incomprehensible or utterly wicked, becomes a bad man, undoes all the good that he has done throughout the poem, or that we cannot imagine him going on, after the poem, to continue to do good things and to perfect his unique greatness, that extraordinary combination of courage, compassion, and patience which is one of

Vergil's most lasting, difficult, and brilliant inventions. I mean, rather, that what Vergil chooses to emphasize at the close of his poem is a moment when Aeneas gives way to an anger which, however perfectly justified, is directed against a man who is no longer, in any way, a match for him, and who is, though Aeneas cannot know this, a victim of a mindless, evil design. And when that anger has been unleashed, both men become victims of a kind of mechanical malevolence that negates the dignity and the courage of both of them.

Sub specie aeternitatis the poet of the *Iliad* has subjected the rival concepts of heroism to dialectical scrutiny in order to vindicate both concepts and to offer both as paradigms of human goodness in a world that is harsh and dangerous but that is, at the same time, not hostile to man's effort and integrity. But in choosing to view the actions of his figures *sub specie historiae* Vergil found himself more and more constrained to imagine a world in which the prevalence of anger and unreason and sheer ignorance is so great that the human spirit is seen to be awesomely vulnerable and human effort is seen to be matched against dark forces that are as insuperable as they are mysterious. In such a world as this it is not impossible to talk of man's greatness of spirit, but it is more to the point to suggest that merely to be decent or adequate in such a world is hard enough—*gloria, laus,* and *fama* are for other times and other places. In a way that Aristotle might have approved of, Homer's subject was in large part how men may behave under certain circumstances; what their capacities for good and evil—but, finally, especially for good—may be. It is idle to guess what Aristotle might have thought of the *Aeneid*, but it is perhaps worth suggesting, in summarizing this description of the poem's closure, that Vergil's subject is, in large measure, how men and nations have behaved in the past, how they tend now to behave, and why.[118] Vergil's main subject may originally have been the actions of Aeneas and the virtues that Aeneas demonstrates in his actions; but the longer Vergil pondered his contents and design, the more his poem came to be about the nature of history.[119]

It is for this reason that Juno comes to stand more and more at the center of his design, that the Dira orchestrates his poem's closure, that *devotio* and *evocatio* are the warp and woof of Book 12, and that neither the solace of threnody nor the celebration of valor and integrity can release Turnus or Aeneas from the darkness that fastens upon them and holds them as the poem closes. Vergil's poem is about human beings at their most desperate and most vulnerable. Their weakness and their despair will finally be the measure of their gallantry; in this sense, the *Aeneid* is not pessimistic at all. But since the poem is not so much about human beings as they *may* be as it is about human beings as they are in their efforts to live together, in groups and in nations; since the poem is about what happens in history, Juno is not a bad choice for the axial figure of its pattern, and the Dira is not a bad choice for the figure that conducts the poem to its catastrophic ending. This patterning allows us to see human courage as it is measured by human vulnerability, and this image, in turn, allows us to contemplate the record of man as a political animal with a fairly steady focus, neither fearing too much nor hoping for too much. Strangely enough, in using the figure of Juno at the center of his design for history, Vergil is able to secure balance, perspective, equilibrium. Lacking this emphasis on demonic violence, we could not see so well the need for calm. That is what the *via negativa* points to: *l'absence de Dieu.*

IV

THE WORLDS VERGIL LIVED IN

He err'd not, for by this the heavnly Bands
Down from a Skie of Jasper lighted now
In Paradise, and on a Hill made halt,
A Glorious Apparition, had not doubt
And carnal fear that day dimm'd Adams eye.

MILTON

Great writers are never the products of the times they live in, though they often seem so because they reflect—indirectly but brilliantly—the events, the common attitudes, hopes, and fears of their contemporaries. But they do not merely react to events or passions or "doctrines of the times" as purely popular writers do; they also react against events and contemporary attitudes and use these critical reactions to shape something permanent and true out of the ephemeral. All these true truisms mean here is that the term "the Augustan Age" identifies a propaganda device that was very successful and is now a handy but somewhat deceptive category for people who are engaged in writing or lecturing about the poetry or the art or the political events or social patterns that existed within a certain span of time. The only world that Vergil lived in was the poetic one he created out of the various dying and evolving worlds that he inhabited with his contemporaries. In this chapter I shall examine some of the raw materials that these partial worlds offered Vergil when he began to fashion, and as he kept fashioning, his epic; in looking at these raw materials I have two aims.

First, I think it is important to qualify the idea that Vergil is an Augustan poet. Whatever its connections with the Ara Pacis, which it partly inspired, it would be more nearly correct to say that the *Aeneid* created the Augustan Age than to say that the Augustan Age produced, in any way, the *Aeneid*. It was the passionate concern and the imagination of Vergil that supplied an intellectual coherence to a period of time that would otherwise have lacked it, and of the few contemporaries of Vergil who cared about that coherence, Augustus took from it only what interested him. It was the mind and heart of Vergil that brought intellectual and aesthetic order to the confused and anxious times in which he lived.

Second, since in many of the configurations it presents, Vergil's epic is about degenerations and renewals; since in at least one of its aspects it ponders the tragic failure of classical humanism to confront its own weaknesses and the new dangers that threaten it from without, it seems useful for a reading of the poem to emphasize that Vergil lived in an age when the shared metaphors that any society requires in order to exist were disintegrating and when, therefore, Vergil and his contemporaries were beginning to inhabit separate and divided worlds. This problem did not worry Lucretius, who had no use for this kind of metaphor or for the kind of society that required metaphors for its existence. But the tough independence of Lucretius, rare in any age, was clearly very rare in the late republic and early empire, and Vergil was worried about the disintegration of the shared metaphors and their community. The *Aeneid* records, among other things, Vergil's effort to close with and to master this worry over the divisions of a unity he believed in. And the dying and divided worlds that Vergil lived in were only renewed and unified by Vergil's hard-won ability to admit the fact of their death and division. When we talk of the Augustan Age, whether we know it or not, it is often this single act of self-discipline and courage that we have in mind.

I. *QUOD CREDAS*: THE SOCIAL ORDER

Vergil was roughly fifteen years old when Catullus and Lucretius were engaged in creating their different poetic emigrations from the ruining city: the one turning, with something like the cultivated despair of a modern symbolist, towards an elaborate and beautiful nihilism; the other hammering out a music and a vision that could contain and express his austere loneliness and his inner freedom from fear and from society.[120] Since it is well known that the Romans thought that society was reality, it will be seen that both of these poets, each in his own way, had invented a desperate remedy. When Vergil was just over twenty years old, the war between Caesar's men and Pompey's men began. He was twenty-six when Caesar was murdered and Cicero, in a final burst of idealism and practicality, attempted to sum up in *De Officiis* what the republic had tried to be and what it could have been and should have been. At twenty-eight he began his pastoral experiments, and he continued to work at them during a period when, it seemed, there was some hope for Rome after all. These he completed when he was thirty-three, and—when hope had begun to waver and fade again—he began what was to be his technical masterpiece, the *Georgics*, which was completed when he turned forty-one, and hope had returned again. What all this means, even perhaps for those who despise biographical criticism, is that Vergil grew to his young manhood and began and continued his poethood under the constant reality, or the constant threat, of civil war.

This brief sketch of the political situations in which Vergil disciplined his gifts and perfected his powers gives little warrant to the notion that during the twenties "the Augustan settlement was hailed with almost universal enthusiasm" or that Roman "defeatism and despair were succeeded by unbounded confidence and hope."[121] It is true that the *Aeneid* frequently shows marks of enthusiasm and a good deal of hope and that nowhere in the poem do we confront anything that smacks of the anonymous wit's grand muttering: "omnia mutasti Saturnia saecula, Caesar, / incolumi nam te ferrea semper erunt."[122] This ironic view of the permanence of the Augustan settlement could not be precisely formulated until long after Vergil was dead, until Ovid imagined it thoroughly because he had had the unfortunate advantage of living under the completed settlement and had begun to guess what price had been paid for it and would continue to be paid. Writing in the twenties, Vergil may well have felt varying degrees of confidence in Augustus, but even Vergil, a tragic lyricist with little satiric impulse, watched the first decade of the principate with the anxiety and foreboding that constantly enform his epic.[123] Nor is the reason far to seek. Marvelous as Augustus clearly was, capable and even fair-minded as he often seemed (and very frequently was), not even this miracle could obliterate the century of terror. Suppose Augustus should die before the miracle was consummated? Suppose, in a way more dreadful still, he should alter his purposes? It is the clear terrible truth of civil war and the fact of uncertainty about anything in human affairs that shape this poem and stick in the mind when we put the poem aside. (But the myth demands certainty.)

The war that fills the last half of the *Aeneid* is, unequivocally, a civil war. When Allecto has completed her dirty work and is, much against her will, about to be sent back where she belongs (*invisum numen, terras caelumque levabat*), she announces her grand success in this fashion: *en perfecta tibi bello discordia tristi: / dic in amicitiam coeant et foedera iungant* (7.545–546). She refers to the fact that the Trojans and the Latins, who were fated to become one people in a great *civitas*, have had their union tainted from the outset by Juno's interference:

> verum ubi nulla datur caecum exsuperare potestas
> consilium, et saevae nutu Iunonis eunt res,
> multa deos aurasque pater testatus inanis
> "frangimur heu fatis" inquit "ferimurque procella!
> ipsi has sacrilego pendetis sanguine poenas,
> o miseri. te, Turne, nefas, te triste manebit
> supplicium votisque deos venerabere seris;
> nam mihi parta quies omnisque in limine portus
> funere felici spolior."
>
> (7.591–599)

> But when no power is granted him to check
> their blind resolve, when all moves at the will
> of savage Juno, then—again, again—
> father Latinus calls upon the gods
> and on the empty air; he cries: "The fates
> have crushed us, we are carried by the storm.
> Unhappy men! The penalty for this
> will yet be paid with your profaning blood.
> O Turnus, vengeance, bitter punishment
> for this unholy act will wait for you;
> too late your prayers will venerate the gods.
> My rest is near, my harbor is in view;
> a happy burial is all I lose."

Thus Latinus, ignorant of Allecto and Juno and crying out to the *empty* air, singles out Turnus for chief blame. Aeneas—ignorant of Allecto, Juturna, and Juno—will, in his desperation, blame Latinus:

> ipse inter primos dextram sub moenia tendit
> Aeneas, magnaque incusat voce Latinum,

testaturque deos iterum se ad proelia cogi,
bis iam Italos hostes, haec iam altera foedera rumpi.

(12.579–582)

Aeneas

himself is in the vanguard, stretching out
his hand beneath the ramparts; and he shouts
his accusations at Latinus, calls
the gods to witness that he had been forced
to battle; twice the Latins have become
his enemies; twice they have broken treaties.

Turnus will blame Juturna, out of real desperation, for he has
guessed the truth:

"o soror, et dudum agnovi, cum prima per artem
foedera turbasti teque haec in bella dedisti,
et nunc nequiquam fallis dea. sed quis Olympo
demissam tantos voluit te ferre labores?"

(12.632–635)

"O sister, I knew you long since, both when
you first disturbed our pact by craftiness
and plunged into these wars; and when you tried—
in vain—to trick me, hiding your godhead.
But who has willed that you be sent from high
Olympus to endure such trials?"

Yes, Turnus, Latinus, and Juturna are all, in a sense, to blame for
the breaking of the *foedera*[124] and for the appearance of *discordia*,
but behind the violence, confusions, and misunderstandings that
open the second part of the poem with Book 7 and close it with
Book 12, *saevae nutu Iunonis eunt res*, even though as Juno
herself admits with splendid, chilling accuracy as she dismisses
Allecto:

"te super aetherias errare licentius auras
haut pater ille velit, summi regnator Olympi;
cede locis; ego, si qua super fortuna laborum est,
ipsa regam."

(7.557–560)

"The lord of high
Olympus will not let you wander free
about the upper air. Be gone from here.
I can attend to all that now remains."

But if Jupiter objects to Allecto as *agent provocateur*, what does he think of what his wife is about to do?

> nec minus interea extremam Saturnia bello
> imponit regina manum.
>
> ilicet infandum cuncti contra omina bellum,
> contra fata deum, perverso numine poscunt.
>
> tum regina deum caelo delapsa morantis
> inpulit ipsa manu portas et cardine verso
> belli ferratos rumpit Saturnia postes.
>
> (7.572–573, 583–584, 620–622)

> Meanwhile the royal daughter of Saturn gives
> a final touch to war.
>
> At once, despite the signs and oracles
> of gods, through some perverted power all
> ask for unholy war.
>
>   Then the queen of gods,
> when she had glided from the heavens, forced
> the slow gates; on their turning hinges Saturn's
> daughter burst the iron doors of war.

Vergil's brilliant reshaping of Ennius' verse (Saturnia replaces Discordia) and the theologically perverse, almost Gnostic oxymoron (*contra fata deum perverso numine*) strongly emphasize that what is happening in Book 7 and what will soon happen in Book 12 means, inevitably, the corruption of the city. For Juno to become Discordia, for her *numen* to become *perversum*, this represents a condition in the life of the city and a tendency in human affairs that finds no solution whatever in the poem. The poem may indeed point beyond itself to solutions (clearly it points to the need for solutions), and, to the extent that it does, it may be said to show some degree of hope or even of confidence. But if Juno does not win in this poem (and it is not clear that she does not), she does not lose either. And if she does not lose, the dark forces of social corruption have not been dissipated and the realities of human savagery and selfishness remain.

Yet out of a century of civil war, of social corruption, savagery, and selfishness, come these bare, clumsy truths: *disce, puer, virtutem ex me verumque laborem, / fortunam ex aliis* (12.435–436); *quaecumque est fortuna, mea est: me verius unum / pro vobis foedus luere et decernere ferro* (12.694–695). In this view, *virtus, labor verus*, and this attitude to *fortuna* are seen as adequate instruments of political integrity because they must be. Given the times Vergil lived in and his other materials, this is sublime. Many readers of the *Aeneid* who talk of its greatness may think they have in mind the triumphal marches of Books 6 and 8 (a few, of course, really know what they like and deserve what they get), but what in fact has stayed with them is the stubborn, humble wisdom of *disce, puer* and *quaecumque est fortuna*, which is magnificent and sublime because it can chasten our common and erroneous notions of what magnificence and sublimity are. In its social allegories the *Aeneid* makes clear that the greatness of a *civitas* has nothing to do with glory and grandeur and has everything to do with taking responsibility. Very few poets have dared to imagine the evils of a *civitas* that will not accept responsibility, and no poet has imagined them more closely or more successfully than has Vergil. To sentimentalize and trivialize his achievement by appeals to the Augustan settlement or to Christianity and classical culture is to defame his artistry. Augustus or no, the social world Vergil lived in was tragically divided between the corrupt and ruined freedom of its past and the corrupt security of its new, unfamiliar Hellenistic future. It is the nature, causes, and consequences of this kind of division that Vergil's social *praxis* bids us ponder.

2. *QUO TENDAS*: THE METAPHYSICAL ORDER

Even had the Augustan settlement been as clear to its creator and to its poet as it has seemed in other times, the world view or world views of Vergil and his original readers would obviate the kind and the degree of stability and clarity that many readers have read into Vergil's intentions and into his final design. Behind this reading of the poem, both from the angle of its politics and from the angle of its "philosophy," there lies the belief that Vergil's Rome, like Cicero's, is grounded in and nourished by Platonic and Stoic intimations of order.[125] Yet if, as I suggest, the genuine intellectual and rational strength of this period in Rome is to be found in Lucretius, and if the failure and debility of the Platonism and the Stoicism of late republican Rome are to be found in Cicero's courageous, but on the whole unsuccessful, attempts to rationalize the vanishing political order by appeals to the failing philosophical systems of the past, then it may be no disservice to Vergil and no misreading of his poem to suggest that one of Vergil's problems in writing his epic was that the philosophical, ethical, and religious unities that had survived even into the recent past were precisely what he did not have to build on.[126] Vestiges of the old unities remain, it is true, and Cicero uses them as best he can in constructing his own magnificent and desperate synthesis, even as Augustus uses both Cicero and some of the forms and contents of the vanishing and the vanished republic to construct his new political unity. But the work of Cicero is the summing up of a world that has almost disappeared at the time of its writing, and the work of Augustus is the planning and the seeding of a world that will not come to its great flowering, as Gibbon rightly insists, until almost a century after Augustus' death. In terms of his spiritual and philosophical materials, then, as in terms of his political materials, Vergil is dealing wth fragments of the past and dreams of things to come. Many poets—maybe most good poets—have the same problem or a similar problem, but most poets who attempt a foundation epic or who write poems in which they seek to justify their culture or to gather to unity the components of their culture have something more nearly like a fixed tradition to work with than Vergil had. And particularly if we suppose that Vergil's chief aim was to justify Rome's manifest destiny, we might expect that he would need the foundation of a sound theodicy. As we have seen in our examination of Jupiter's last appearance in the poem, Vergil seems to go out of his way to demonstrate the perils and confusion of the religious traditions from which such a theodicy might be fashioned.

One measure of the perils and confusion of that tradition is to be found in the failure of Augustus to complete the religious and moral reforms that he deemed necessary for the success of his entire *renovatio*. And in this regard it is worth emphasizing the connections that obtain between Augustus' political goals and methods on the one hand and the waning of Graeco-Roman rationalism and the rise of superstition and the mystery religions on the other.[127] Though Augustus himself wanted no part of the mystery religions and though he fought the growth of superstition, thinking of himself (correctly enough) as a conservative Roman gentleman, the world that he and Vergil lived in and the political artifact that he was busy shaping had in fact lost all but the final letter of rational Graeco-Roman religion. This ruin of traditional religion Vergil uses with fine effect in designing his story of cosmic unreason and of human efforts to combat that unreason. It would be foolish to suggest that there are not sometimes unironic echoes of the old Olympian rationalism joined with authentic echoes of Plato, Zeno, and indigenous Roman spirituality, but these memories of old spiritual wisdoms jostle with, and are often overwhelmed by, the recurrence of the new antirationalism as well as by the genuine mystical yearnings that arose in Rome and throughout the empire at the time when Augustus was at work on his settlement and Vergil was at work on his poem.[128]

Paradoxically enough, Cybele appears as an Olympianized deity in the *Aeneid*, and there may be some degree of irony—whether intentional or not we need not try to decide here—in Vergil's ascribing to the Asiatic goddess a benevolence and a providence that would normally belong to the Olympians.[129] That the goddess from Aeneas' homeland should be, with his mother, his protectress is natural enough, but the comparative impotence and remoteness of the Olympians in this poem (Juno is the great exception) contrast strikingly with Cybele's compassion and power. Yet it is not in Cybele that we see adumbrations of the new religious sensibility and proofs of the disintegration of the old sensibility. It is rather in two quite different modes of apprehending the divine, both of which contrast sharply with the tradition that Augustus was determined to restore. The first mode we find in the Neopythagorean moods (it is too much to call them doctrines or beliefs) that we find in Book 6 and that have been Platonized and Stoicized by Vergil's critics with little success. The second mode consists of the chthonian and daemonic elements that appear both in Book 6 and (frequently) throughout the last six books of the poem.[130] To this second mode Vergil often adds an Etruscan coloring, for with the revival "of interest in astrology and the Eastern cults, men turned also to the lore of Etruria; the more so since this might be considered more respectable: anomalously, Etruscan customs now appear to have been regarded as romanized and part of Italic tradition, in contrast to the wilder beliefs that were reaching Rome from the East."[131]

The heyday of Orientalism is a long way off when Vergil is writing the *Aeneid*, but what Auerbach calls "the darkening of the atmosphere of life"[132] has already begun in Vergil's lifetime, and his poem reflects these beginnings and uses them. I am not suggesting that Vergil himself was swept away by this riptide of the Zeitgeist, and I am not trying to play *post hoc propter hoc*. Rather, I am emphasizing, because it seems not to have been sufficiently emphasized in this regard, that much of what Vergil has to work with in the way of "doctrines of the times" involves dark emotionalism or water-color mysticism, both of which are hostile to Lucretian affirmation of man's liberty and of the intelligibility of the world he lives in; to Cicero's (and Augustus') affirmation of the *res publica*; to Plato's or to Zeno's ways of saying, "And all shall be well and all shall be well and all manner of thing shall be well"; in short, to every shade and variety of classical rationalism and classical humanism. This is the new world where figures as different as Isis, Cybele, Nigidius Figulus, and Posidonius may feel at home.[133] It is with these figures that the future lies, and at least some of the things they stand for (both good and bad) are present in the *Aeneid*, however inchoately, for the first time in a major ancient mimesis. The *Aeneid* is not an irrational or an antirational work, but it combats irrationality in ways that are new in antiquity because by Vergil's time unreason has assumed new faces and new strength while reason has lost much of its real strength.

We have examined some of these losses, particularly as they appear in Book 12, in the previous chapter. We now turn to the description of Allecto in Book 7. Juno hails her at 331 in this fashion: *hunc mihi da proprium, virgo sata Nocte, laborem.* One cannot always tell what the writer of literary epic intends with his formulas, but it seems not unreasonable to suppose that *sata Nocte* was intended to resonate to the verse in Book 12 (860) which describes the flight of the Dira: *talis se sata Nocte tulit terrasque petivit.*[134] These figures, Allecto and the Dira, frame the action of the second half of the *Aeneid*; both are creatures of darkness that are connected with irrational and utterly incomprehensible works of destruction, and both are, whatever their specific models might be, Vergil's reimaginations of nightmarish beings that Greek rationalism had utterly excluded from its normal modes of conceiving the human world. Both are Furies, but in their behavior they show not only the dark violence of hellish powers but also the gratuitous sadism that marks a special kind of hell. Evil for them is good; they look not to a deliberate and voluntary rejection of good for a sanction for their acts, since an almost mechanical perversion of good is its own sanction. In short, for Allecto and the Dira (though not, of course, for Jupiter and not quite for Juno) evil is not a means to an end, it is an end in itself; it is therefore, by definition, unintelligible. But this unintelligibility is not horriyfing as Allecto and the Dira see it (or, in the case of the Dira, as we are made to see it, for we see her with the corrupt objectivity with which she sees herself): for them it is a delight and a glory. In other words, we are passing from the world of Graeco-Roman rationalism into the worlds of Seneca's tragedies, of Lucan, of Apuleius, and of barbaric Christianity.

exim Gorgoneis Allecto infecta venenis
principio Latium et Laurentis tecta tyranni
celsa petit tacitumque obsedit limen Amatae,
quam super adventu Teucrum Turnique hymenaeis
femineae ardentem curaeque iraeque coquebant.
huic dea caeruleis unum de crinibus anguem
conicit inque sinum praecordia ad intima subdit,
quo furibunda domum monstro permisceat omnem.
ille inter vestes et levia corpora lapsus
volvitur attactu nullo fallitque furentem,
viperam spirans animam; fit tortile collo
aurum ingens coluber, fit longae taenia vittae
innectitque comas et membris lubricus errat.
ac dum prima lues udo sublapsa veneno
pertemptat sensus atque ossibus implicat ignem
necdum animus toto percepit pectore flammam,
mollius et solito matrum de more locuta,
multa super nata lacrimans Phrygiisque hymenaeis. . . .

$$(7.341-358)$$

At once Allecto, steeped in Gorgon poison,
makes first for Latium and the high palace
of the Laurentian chieftain. There she sits
before the silent threshold of the queen,
Amata, who is kindled by a woman's
anxieties and anger, seething over
the Trojans' coming, Turnus' thwarted wedding.
Then from her blue-gray hair the goddess cast
a snake deep in Amata's secret breast,
that, maddened by the monster, she might set
at odds all of her household. And the serpent
glides on, between the queen's smooth breasts and dress,
and winds its way unnoticed; by deceit
it breathes its viper breath into her frenzy.
The giant snake becomes a twisted necklace
of gold, a long headband to bind her hair,
and slithers down her limbs. And while its first
infection, penetrating with damp poison,
has gripped her senses and entwined her bones
in fire, before her soul has felt the force
of flame throughout her breast, Amata speaks
softly, as is the way of mothers, weeping
over her daughter and the Phrygian wedding.

The passage is extraordinary for its macabre beauty and for the description of how a human soul is sapped of its reason and robbed of its power of choice that glimmers under that beauty. There is no objection to someone's supposing that this is a picture of Amata's psyche before she does what she does and says what she says (that is clearly the sense of *quam super adventu . . . coquebant*), but I point out that this is not the sort of thing that goes on in *Iliad* 1 when Athena stops Achilles from killing Agamemnon; it is more like the sort of thing that goes on when Cupid poisons Dido's mind and heart in *Aeneid* 1: the effect is wholly psychological but the cause is supernatural, evil, and invisible (*attactu nullo*).[135] These deliberate confusions of supernatural cause presented as physical cause that issues in psychological turmoil and impairment of volition are elaborated in Allecto's attack on Turnus, for she appears to him in a dream; in his dream he ridicules her and she hurls a torch into his body:

> sic effata facem iuveni coniecit et atro
> lumine fumantes fixit sub pectore taedas.
> olli somnum ingens rumpit pavor, ossaque et artus
> perfundit toto proruptus corpore sudor.
> arma amens fremit, arma toro tectisque requirit;
> saevit amor ferri et scelerata insania belli,
> ira super . . . .
>
> (7.456–462)

> And saying this, she cast a torch at Turnus,
> fixing the firebrand within his breast,
> and there it smoked with murky light. Great fear
> shatters his sleep, sweat bursts from all his body
> and bathes his bones and limbs. Insane, he raves
> for arms, he searches bed and halls for weapons.
> Lust for the sword and war's damnable madness
> are raging in him and—above all—anger . . . .

Is the torch less real than the snake because Turnus dreams and Amata wakes? Are the torch and the snake less real than the poison of Cupid? No, Cupid and Allecto are no more states of mind or symbols of states of mind than the Dira of Book 12 is a state of mind. All of these agents of evil become states of mind for those whose minds and volitions they have perverted; but they nevertheless remain realities that exist in the space and the time of the poem which they inhabit together with the human figures.

postquam acies videt Iliacas atque agmina Turni,
alitis in parvae subitam collecta figuram,
quae quondam in bustis aut culminibus desertis
nocte sedens serum canit importuna per umbras,
hanc versa in faciem Turni se pestis ob ora
fertque refertque sonans clipeumque everberat alis.
illi membra novus solvit formidine torpor
arrectaeque horrore comae et vox faucibus haesit.

(12.861–868)

As soon as she can see the Trojan
ranks and the troops of Turnus, suddenly
she shrinks into the shape of that small bird
which sometimes sits by night on tombs and lonely
rooftops, where it chants late, among the shadows,
its song of evil omen; so transformed,
the foul one howls before the face of Turnus,
flies back and forth; her wings beat at his shield.
Strange stiffness, terror, took the limbs of Turnus;
his hair stood up; his jaws held fast his voice.

As the dreadful thing beats at the face of Turnus, his terror gathers into itself all the terrors that have preceded it: the unseen horror is at last physically present, and the daughter of darkness has become visible. This sickening apotheosis of hell gains some of its subtle horror from the surrealistic catachresis, *subitam figuram* (note also the fine oxymoron, *atro lumine*, in the previous passage), but its special success derives from the emphasis on a peculiarly sinister quality that all the ministers of evil in the poem share and that surpasses even the brilliant imaginations of evil and madness that we find in Greek tragic choruses. What Turnus meets face to face, what evokes in him nightmarish impotence and despair, is not a traditional bogey cleverly magnified; it is rather a wild, vindictive negation of goodness, an active, gloating privation of goodness and being.

If I suggest that much of this strange, new vision of evil came from Etruria, I am not suggesting that the Iris of Book 4 exists because Vergil saw Vanth in the François tomb or that the snakes and torches of Allecto were inspired by the death demons we know from Etruscan tombs.[136] Nor did Vergil need to see the Orcus tomb to imagine Allecto or the Dira. I am not even suggesting that this Etruscan coloring in the *Aeneid* is present there because Vergil grew up in Mantua, though I do not think it is a waste of time to speculate on this possibility.[137] The Etruscan revival, combined with the growth of the mystery religions and the rise of Neopythagoreanism, was useful to Vergil because it provided him with poetic materials for his imagination of a darkening world. The ministers of darkness (Iris in Book 4 and Cupid in Book 1, as well as Allecto, the Dira, and Juno herself) are not new creations in the sense that they have no models in Greek mimesis, but they are new in their reveling in evil, their pleasure in the mindless destruction (which is what I am calling their Etruscan coloring), and, more important, they are new in their ability to dominate the *muthos* of a poem and to threaten to dominate the *praxis* of a poem. The primacy and triumph of evil are intolerable thoughts in the classical moments of Graeco-Roman culture, so intolerable that the least hint of mere dualism is combated ferociously. In Vergil's poem, for the first time, the possibility that hell can triumph is found to be worth pondering.[138] As political integrities are seen in this poem not as actualities but as potentialities to be realized only with desperate effort against terrible odds, so the primacy of goodness and truth is seen as vulnerable to dreadful and incomprehensible hazards. I do not say that this is what Vergil and his audience believed or felt most of the time; I only suggest that this intimation of the possible failure of rational order and rational freedom in the universe, in human history, and in individual existence is clearly part of the materials of Vergil's poem, and, in my reading of the poem, this intimation of the danger to rational order in the universe and rational freedom in human lives comes near to being the central *praxis* of his poem.[139]

In shaping this material, in closing with evil as it presents itself in human history and in the lives of men, Vergil no more affirms the triumph of unreason and *ira* in the universe and in history than he affirms their defeat. It is from its capacity for approaching metaphysical and political despair without quite despairing that the *Aeneid* wins through to its extraordinary courage and power; it is because the poem knows how "to grieve and not to grieve" that it leaves us disturbed and unsolaced without leaving us frozen in wan hope. Vergil proffers us a desperate, patient strength we can believe in because he gives us no calm and not much hope:

> obstipuit varia confusus imagine rerum
> Turnus et obtutu tacito stetit; aestuat ingens
> uno in corde pudor mixtoque insania luctu

et furiis agitatus amor et conscia virtus.
ut primum discussae umbrae et lux reddita menti. . . .

(12.665–669)

Confused by all these shifting images
of ruin, Turnus stood astounded, staring
and silent. In his deepest heart there surge
tremendous shame and madness mixed with sorrow
and love whipped on by frenzy and a courage
aware of its own worth. As soon as shadows
were scattered and his mind saw light again. . . .

These seem to me among the most precise, the most compassionate, and the most tragic verses in the entire poem. They sum up
what Vergil knows best about us and what he is best able to imagine about what he knows. I doubt that any other poet could
have combined these elements—our real weakness and our real
strength—with such sympathy, such dispassion, and such power.
At this moment, on the edge of defeat and despair, an affirmation
of coherence and *virtus* is possible because Vergil has completed
his imagination of what we have to fear and what we have to fight
against that fear with. The *Aeneid*, I have tried to suggest, is
polycentric, and every reader will find the center that suits him or
her. For what it is worth, this is mine.

3. *QUOD AGAS*: THE MORAL ORDER

*. . . intellegit ibi vitium vas efficere ipsum
omniaque illius vitio corrumpier intus
quae collata foris et commoda cumque venirent;
partim quod fluxum pertusumque esse videbat,
ut nulla posset ratione explerier umquam;
partim quod taetro quasi conspurcare sapore
omnia cernebat, quaecumque receperat, intus.*
Lucretius 6.17–23

. . . then he realized that it was the pot itself that caused
the evil, and he realized too that anything that entered
into the pot, however wholesome it might be, must be
destroyed when it was poured in because of this innate
evil. He saw that this was so partly because the pot
was chipped and leaked, so that it could never, by any
stratagem, be filled, and he saw that it was partly so
because it tainted everything that was poured into it,
caused everything it contained to acquire a foul taste.

Flawed in his own nature, flawed no less in the works of his mind, heart, and hands—that is man as seen by Epicurus if he remains unpurged by strictly rational truths. Though not unparalleled in Graeco-Roman thought, this denial that human beings can will or reason their way to happiness and justice in society by using natural gifts that have been disciplined by tradition shows a radical departure from the norms of classical humanism in its rejection not only of the ideal of responsible and purposeful action in society but also of the concept of an eternal, rational order that defines and guides human action in its beginnings and its ends. If there is indeed a problem with Vergil's poem, it is only the problem that he received as his donnée and struggled with, heroically, for a decade: the conflict between the Epicurean analysis of the problems of evil (an analysis which Vergil seems, for the most part, to have accepted) and his ambivalent faith in the idea of salvation in and through history.[140] Had Vergil been less convinced by the Epicurean diagnosis of human suffering, and had he been more vividly impressed by the possibilities of the rebirth and renewal of societies and by the meaning of history, perhaps he might have been able to reconcile the Epicurean *summum bonum* with the more conventional, classical *summa bona*. But Vergil, to his honor, but not to his peace of mind, could not reconcile these opposing sanctuaries, and he remained, to the end of his poethood, a haunted wanderer.

For the Epicurean temperament, the social order, which is a kind of perversion of friendship, can do little good but can do and invite endless harm. Since the Epicurean ideal is freedom from ignorance for the individual, the body politic only serves to nourish what it feeds upon—fear of catastrophe, dependence upon changing circumstance—in short, painful, destructive illusions about things as they are and men's proper good. An Epicurean can manage, without deluding himself, to find and safeguard the garden that is his because, very strictly speaking, it does not matter in what city his garden may be; he is, by definition, a fierce and proud internal émigré. And in planting and tending his garden, he relegates the city to what he regards as its proper and actual place—outside, on the margins of reality, among the other necessary and unnecessary illusions. In the garden the problems of evil can be handled because the *vitia* are seen as at once natural and within us, that is to say, they are capable of remedy. They do not have a life of their own, they are not mysterious dangers lurking outside the walls of the garden, waiting, hoping to destroy. Lucretius had written a great poem, in a sense an epic poem, about the fight of the human spirit to liberate itself from the illusion that illusions are real; Vergil's reading of that poem was probably the most important thing in his life as a poet (to call that reading an event would be misleading since it is clear that the reading was habitual and unending). Our problem, then, was Vergil's. Why should a man who read *De rerum natura* so passionately and who absorbed it so thoroughly undertake to write a poem that is not merely about what happens in history but is also about the vindication of the meaning of history in general and the meaning of the City in particular (in Epicurean terms, about how illusion is vindicated by illusion)? Why should an Epicurean attempt to write not merely a foundation epic but *the* Foundation Epic (imagine, if you will, a Shaker who "believed in the green light" at work on the Great American Novel)?

These questions admit of no exact answer, but they invite speculation. Suppose Vergil's heart was divided. Suppose he read and reread his Lucretius as a religious atheist might peruse his Saint Paul—desperate, faithful in his disbelief, hoping, at some moment, for the illumination, because the fears that were being so uncannily catalogued were, precisely, his own fears, and almost believing that he might discover the fears were, as the writer kept insisting, groundless? But suppose that, unpersuaded that the objects of his dread were unreal, he kept turning toward a belief in a divinely rational design wherein the small evils, though real, were part of a pattern, were christened by truth and justice, were gathered into the large goodness, invisible yet ineffably secure. If the stern freedoms of Epicurus could not save, then perhaps the rational cosmos and the renewed city, their microcosm, might win what a single human being had not strength to win—freedom from evil and fear, freedom for goodness and joy.

Basing my arguments on these speculations, I would suggest (it is no more than suggestion, for I do not pretend to be dealing with facts) that the disintegrations of the world he lived in, which were not really balanced by the uncertain political restorations of that world, caused Vergil to despair of the good myths of order and reason and to seek both comfort and strength in the disciplines of Epicurus. But, for whatever reasons, the wisdom of Epicurus could not solace the intensity of Vergil's dread, and he returned to the good myths (and the bad myths) of the Cosmos and the City.[141] And continuing in this vacillation and indecision, he wrote a great epic which succeeds partly because its author has the honesty to admit not only the intensity and durability of his fears but also the depths of his weakness and indecision. It is, I submit, the nakedness, the purity of his initial pity for himself that persuades us to believe in its transformation into compassion for us.[142]

Having accepted his donnée—the pull toward embracing Epicurean freedom and the counterpull toward justifying the rational cosmos and its *civitas*—Vergil discovered in shaping his poem the tragic paradoxes that give the *Aeneid* its particular texture, resonance, and range. The evils that Lucretius focuses on in the passage quoted above: the negative evil, which is a privation or absence of good; and the positive evil, which is flawed action proceeding from mistaken perceptions and judgments, must, in an epic poem, be hypostatized into actions performed by characters. First as symbols in a fiction, then, disastrously, as false entities in a myth, the darkness within becomes the darkness without. When objectified in this way, the natural weaknesses and natural ignorance of Aeneas, Dido, and Turnus become Juno and her ministers: on the social level, *discordia*; on the moral level, *violentia* and *ira*; on the metaphysical level, a blind momentum towards destruction and nothingness, evil for the sake of evil. All of this is unacceptable in an Epicurean poem because what was, before the mythologizing, merely a tendency and a possibility has become a fact, has become almost an unalterable law of denatured nature. Illusions, evil illusions, the privation of and the desire for the annihilation of being have become first realities, then reality itself. And in a Stoic or Platonic or Aristotelian poem, any of which might be, in varying degrees, tolerant of such allegory at the outset, this hypostatization of evil would be no more acceptable than it is in the Epicurean epic: the metaphors must remain convenient metaphors. But for Vergil they do not and cannot. Since he is prevented by his grasp of Epicurus and by the tragic history of his country from giving full allegiance to the concept of the rational cosmos, reified evil refuses to be subordinated to the grand and rational design, insists on its own way, rushes off into the deeper darkness, bearing with it the meaning of history and the dream of rational freedom. Thus in the *Aeneid* there grows a constant impulse toward awful dualism that mocks the splendid unities of classical humanism, with its belief in an intelligible universe and in purposeful human activity inside that universe. The metaphors for evil have become, here below, the truths.[143]

In his fear, in his vast Epicurean sensitivity to pain and suffering, Vergil nevertheless turned from the calm, austere garden back to the world where unreasoning power is a reality that must somehow be persuaded or suffered and where pain must be inflicted or endured. The garden was impossible because he could not teach himself not to hear the screams and riot outside. Yet when he ventured out to help, he found that he had neither the toughness nor the stamina to withstand the onslaughts of reality even for himself, much less to hearten his fellow sufferers or to restrain the monsters or tame them. It is this extraordinary sensitivity to pain that will not permit him to ignore suffering and that will not permit him to condone it by explaining it away. So the darkness that he had sought to evade first in the garden and then in the city moved against him. Terrified though he was, he stood firm to report what he saw, and, as the poem bears witness, the depth of his terror is the index to the greatness of his courage.

An Epicurean hero, excruciatingly responsive to pain, moves through a world where *hou an kratēi archein* (Thucydides 5. 105.2) is law, where sick fantasies seem on the verge of becoming essential realities, and where men's natural limitations become so magnified that their virtues seem in danger of being transformed into the opposing vices. The same Epicurean hero, his freedom and reason perfected in Stoic obedience to the commands of good patriotism and holy destiny, moves in a world where freedom and reason lose their significance as justice and truth, which are their proper agents, glimmer fainter and dissolve in vengeance and deception. Aeneas is an extraordinarily good man, but in the world where he is fated to suffer and to act, goodness is (or is perhaps) not enough, nor is reason, nor is freedom. Courage, in a sense, is almost enough, and Vergil's poem is not about winning battles but about losing them and learning how to lose them. At a moment in time when the possibility of rational freedom seemed, to a sensitive observer, jeopardized and its uses uncertain, Vergil summoned up the strength to imagine us in our utter vulnerability and desolation, and, refusing the old impossible consolations that were being newly counterfeited, he affirmed our moral strength by insisting on our moral weakness and on the real evils that threaten the goodness we might grow towards if we could resist the belief that we have won through, that the worst was past, that evil was outside us and was real in the way that good is real. New "sensemaking," in Kermode's phrase, required of Vergil that he shape a new formulation of heroism. If Vergil's imagination had not been steeled with Lucretian discipline, his compassion might have dwindled into Gray's delicate and false antithesis:

To each his suff'rings: all are men,
Condemn'd alike to groan,
The tender for another's pain;
Th'unfeeling for his own.[144]

And had his imagination not been suffused with a Ciceronian
humanism that Christians may easily be forgiven for mistaking
for their *caritas*, his patriotism and ambition might have persuaded
him to be content with frigid reworkings of a misremembered,
misunderstood Homeric grandeur.[145]

No poet, not Dante himself, has imagined the disintegration
of justice and truth with such precision and such power, and for
this reason no poet, not Homer himself, has shown how precious
and how fragile are the formation and equilibrium of man's integrity of spirit. The multiple allegories of Vergil reveal in their
shifting configurations the reality of goodness and the unspeakable
nonbeing of evil. The poet no more condemns us to the darkness
than he promises us the light. But he shows us, in unforgettable
pictures, what the darkness means, which is, as the mystics tell
us, a way of showing the shadows of light. To minimize the intensity of Vergil's imagination of darkness is, in effect, to reject
his imagination of *to kalon*. Or, to put it another way, Vergil's
poetry can let us ponder for ourselves what society, justice, and
being mean because it has closed with and faced what their absence is and means.

His times doubtless taught him a great deal about what these
absences were and meant, but, good Epicurean that he was, he had
probably learned his hardest and best lessons about absence and
darkness from the Epicurean discipline of self-scrutiny. *Et c'est
assez, pour le poète, d'être la mauvaise conscience de son temps.*[146]
Yes and no. Aeneas, Dido, and Turnus are in us as they were in
Vergil. It is because he discovered and revealed the perennial
shape of what truly destroys us—not because he accurately reflects the grandeurs and miseries of a crucial and dynamic age (as
he does), not because he croons us gentle lullabies of culture re-
born (as he does not)—that we continue to trust him to guide us
through the dim mazes of our arrogance and fear.

NOTES

CHAPTER I

1. F. Kermode, *The Sense of an Ending: Studies in the Theory of Fiction* (Oxford, 1967), 39.

2. Ogilvie, *Greek and Roman Studies in England from 1600 to 1914* (London, 1964); R. D. Williams, in *Virgil*, ed. D. R. Dudley (London, 1969), 119–139.

3. The extent of the Homerists' triumph may be measured by the feebleness of D. Comparetti's challenge to Teuffel (*Virgil in the Middle Ages*, trans. Beneche [London, 1895], 13); by Conington's polite but chilly allusions to the arrogant victors (*Commentary* [London, 1876], 2:2 f.); by J. Henry's oblique petulance (*e.g.*, "Homer, the Paragon of Perfection," *Aeneidea* [London, 1873], 1:9); and by Mackail's wonderful refusal to notice that there was any controversy (see the introduction to his fine edition of the *Aeneid* [Oxford, 1930], *passim*). This tactic of refuting "the old German prejudice" (see M. L. Clarke's review of Pöschl in *CR* 65 [1951]:178) by ignoring it is prevalent in what now seems the rather undernourished pro-Vergilian criticism of D. L. Drew, *The Allegory of the Aeneid* (Oxford, 1927); R. S. Conway, *The Vergilian Age* (Cambridge, Mass., 1928); C. N. Cochrane, *Christianity and Classical Culture: A Study of Thought and Action from Augustus to Augustine* (Oxford, 1940, 1957); E. K. Rand, *The Building of Eternal Rome* (Cambridge, Mass., 1943); in this regard see also the remarks and bibliography by T. E. Wright in the new edition of M. Platnauer's *Fifty Years of Classical Scholarship (and Twelve)* (London, 1968), 387–415. A. Cartault ignores the controversy also, in his remarkable *L'art de Virgile dans l'Enéide* (Paris, 1926), and he can almost afford to ignore it. A. Bellessort (*Virgile* [Paris, 1920], 327–331, calls attention to what the Germans have been up to, and are up to, with futile hysteria. The "renascence" may be properly said to begin in the early thirties in Germany, Austria, and Switzwerland (see H. Opperman's introduction to his collection, *Weg zu Vergil* [Darmstadt, 1963]; and F. Klingner, "Wiederentdeckung eines Dichters," in *Römische Geisteswelt* [Wiesbaden, 1953], 177–214 for good sketches of the history of the renewal). But it is not

until these works that the renascence gets into full swing: V. Pöschl, *Die Dichtkunst Vergils* (Innsbruck, Vienna, 1950)=*The Art of Vergil*, trans. Seligson (Ann Arbor, 1962); K. Büchner, *P. Vergilius Maro* (Stuttgart, 1961=Pauly Wissowa 2.8.1021–1486); F. Klingner, 155–176, 215–235 (the second essay dates from 1930); see his sound estimate of Heinze (224–226); B. Otis, *Vergil: A Study in Civilized Poetry* (Oxford, 1964).

4. Leipzig, 1931; Munich, 1967, trans. Wheen (London, 1934). For a generous discussion of Eliot's use of Vergil, see F. Kermode's lecture, "The Classic," *University of Denver Quarterly* 9, no. 1 (Spring 1974): 1–33.

5. Pöschl (n. 3), 22 (Seligson, 176, n. 11); Büchner (n. 3), 441. See Opperman (n. 3), xii; a German translation of "What Is a Classic?" begins his collection.

6. For the antiquity and the perdurability of the political allegory, see the remarks of Comparetti (n. 3) on T. C. Donatus, 61; L. Proudfoot, *Dryden's Aeneid and Its Seventeenth Century Predecessors* (Manchester, 1960), 258 ff; G. K. Galinksy, *Aeneas, Sicily, and Rome* (Princeton, 1969), 49–54, 165–167; G. Binder, *Aeneas und Augustus: Interpretationen zum 8. Buch der Aeneis*, Beiträge zur Klassischen Philologie 38 (Meisenheim am Glan, 1971) *passim*. For excellent arguments against the centrality of political allegory, see Cartault (n. 3), 35–36; and W. S. Anderson, *The Art of the Aeneid* (Englewood Cliffs, N.J., 1969), 18–19. For the apolitical allegorical tradition, see Comparetti (n. 3), 116–118; and, on Bernardus Silvestris, W. Wetherbee, *Platonism and Poetry in the Twelfth Century* (Princeton, 1972), 105–111. Drew's book (n. 3) has been very influential in reasserting the centrality of the political allegory; see also Conway (n. 3), 145–146 and Rand (n. 3), 57–58, 197–202.

7. See Pöschl (n. 3), 39 (Seligson, 23).

8. G. Knauer, *Die Aeneis und Homer*, Hypomnemata 7 (Göttingen, 1964):345–359, and "Vergil's *Aeneid* and Homer," *GRBS* 5 (1964): 61–84. Knauer's book is immensely valuable as a reference work; his conclusions are usefully questioned by M. Wigodsky, *Vergil and Early Latin Poetry*, Hermes Einzelschriften 24 (Wiesbaden, 1972), 8 ff., and B. Otis, "The Originality of the *Aeneid*," in *Virgil*, ed. Dudley (n. 2), 28.

9. K. Quinn, for example, speaks of Homer's "old soldiers' yarns," but that sort of thing is rare in the conduct of the old debate (see Quinn's *Vergil's Aeneid: A Critical Description* [Ann Arbor, 1968], 53; for similar remarks, see 284–288).

10. I label it in this fashion because the major works that cluster about this reading of the poem were written by critics who have been associated with classics at Harvard from the late forties to the present at some time or other: Brooks, Clausen, Adam Parry, Putnam. Some of the emphases of this school are wildly adumbrated, almost as if in caricature, by F. Sforza, "The Problem of Vergil," *CR* 49 (1935):97–108.

The central works are, in order of publication: R. A. Brooks, "*Discolor Aura*: Reflections of a Golden Bough," *AJP* 74 (1953):260–280; A. Parry, "The Two Voices of Vergil's *Aeneid*," *Arion* 2.4 (1963):66–80; W. Clausen, "An Interpretation of the *Aeneid*," *HSCP* 68 (1964):139–147; M. J. Putnam, *The Poetry of the Aeneid* (Cambridge, Mass, 1965). Independent of these works, yet not alien to some of their central concerns, are the cool deliberations of L. A. MacKay, "Hero and Theme in the *Aeneid*," *TAPA* 94 (1963):157–166.

11. See J. R. Wilson, "Action and Emotion in Aeneas," *G&R* 16.1 (1969):75.

12. Berkeley and Los Angeles, 1951, 247. The European school may be correct in emphasizing once again that the *Aeneid* in some sense adumbrates the coming of Christianity, but this kind of emphasis should be so qualified as to remind us that the matrix of early Christianity is the world of the other mystery religions, the dread and the desperate hope, the failure of nerve, the intuition of the prevalence of evil, the disgust with the flesh, the world, and time—in short, an almost total and almost hysterical rejection of pagan rationalism and the pagan belief in the goodness and eternity of nature. Vergil's imagination of the dualism is the more terrifying because he does not bother with crude materialisms; the oppositions are spiritual (see R. C. Zaehner's exact formulations in *Concordant Discord* [Oxford, 1970], 389 ff.

13. Haecker (n. 4) deals with the problem of evil in this poem—that is to say, with what Juno means in it—by blaming Allecto. Eliot deals with the evils by dismissing Turnus as "a man without a destiny." (Cartault [n. 3] is specially fine in his understanding of Turnus [864–865, 893–894].) Pöschl and Otis give far more subtle solutions to this problem, but even their solutions differ in quality rather than in kind from those of Haecker and Eliot. For Pöschl (n. 3, 18–30) Juno is "the divine symbol of the demonic forces of violence" that are finally subdued and therefore necessary for the "harmonious balance of opposites" (173, 281 f.); this conquest of the demonic is the basic theme of the poem. For Otis, Juno has not even that much importance: her functions in the poem range from that of subfate or counterfate (n. 3, 82, 378) to that of one of the lesser deities (n. 8, 49). See n. 42.

14. V. Buchheit, *Vergil über die Sendung Roms*, Gymnasium 3 (Heidelberg, 1963), 11, 191. See n. 108.

15. K. Jaspers, *The Great Philosophers*, trans. R. Mannheim (New York, 1966), 2:265.

16. My text for Dante is that given by P. Fraticelli, *Il Convivio e le Epistole* (Florence, 1893); see the translation and comments by R. S. Haller, *Literary Criticism of Dante Alighieri* (Lincoln, 1973), 99–100, and the excellent discussion of allegory in his introduction, xix–xxi, xli–xliv. For the couplet by Nicholas, see J. P. McCall, "Medieval Exegesis: Some Documents for the Literary Critic," in W. F. Lynch, *Christ and Apollo* (New York, 1960), 227–267; McCall includes an explication of Nicholas by W. J. Burghardt (241–243). There is an excellent dis-

cussion of the problems of allegory in modern criticism and of the current debates by S. Manning, "Scriptural Exegesis and the Literary Critic," in *Typology and Early American Literature*, ed. Bercovitch (Amherst, Mass., 1972), 47–68. For ancient concepts of allegory, see F. A. Wolfson, *The Philosophy of the Church Fathers* (Cambridge, Mass., 1956, 1970), 30–31; and A. B. Hersman, *Studies in Greek Allegorical Interpretation* (Ph.D. diss., Chicago, 1906), Heraclitus, 21, Philo, 22; K. Schefold, *La Peinture pompéienne*, trans. Croissille (Brussels, 1972) 86–88. But for our present purposes the seminal essay is L. A. MacKay, "Three Levels of Meaning in *Aeneid* VI," *TAPA* 86 (1955):180–189. Galinsky (n. 6, 193) properly draws attention to Pöschl's rejection of the term "allegorical" in favor of the term "symbolism" with a view to stressing multiplicities of meaning (Pöschl [n. 3], 36–37=21 ff.), but Pöschl, like Galinsky, keeps stressing a positive and political signification which is nourished by the other significations in the "hierarchy" (40=24); that is why we might do better to talk of aspects of allegory rather than levels of allegory. In any case, symbolism is a term that is closely tied to a particular period and school of poetry that has, deceptively, some characteristics in common with the poetry of the *Aeneid*. Cumbersome as it is, I would prefer the terms "multiple allegories, interdependent allegories."

17. For different and important formulations of this disciplined refusal to be committed to solutions, see Conway (n. 3, 99–112) on what he calls Vergil's "antithetical or dualistic" habit of mind; and Anderson (n. 6, 101–109, in particular 106–109) on the "sophistication" and lack of bias in his poetic style as well as in his attitudes towards his materials. Sensibilities that elect polysematic fictions and multiple allegories have certain affinities with the techniques described by E. Panofsky, *Studies in Iconology: Humanistic Themes in the Art of the Renaissance* (Oxford, 1939; New York, 1972), 174–175, when he discusses *figura serpentinata* ("revolving view"), but only some; I do not mean that Vergil is a mannerist—like Michelangelo, he is not merely a mannerist, that is to say, he is much more than a mannerist (see n. 39). Given the immensity and the diversity of his subjects—myths of cosmos and chaos (historical, moral, metaphysical), the terrors and the exaltations of history, the paradoxes of theodicy, the razor's edge of morality—it is unnerving, or at least strange, that Vergil should refuse to mediate between his contraries, fashion modulations that might reconcile them, or, by redefining the terms of their conflict (see G. S. Kirk, *Myth: Its Meaning and Functions in Ancient and Other Cultures*, Sather Classical Lectures 40 [Berkeley and Los Angeles, 1970]:259), assert their real unity as against their seeming oppositions. He does not, in short, behave as we expect mythmakers to behave. And it is his refusal to invent the reconciliations that we expect and require for "binary structures" (see E. R. Leach, "Genesis as Myth," in J. Middleton's *Myth and Cosmos* [Garden City, N.Y., 1967], 1–13) that creates anxieties in us which drive us to fabricate for him the myths he had the strength to refrain from fabricating.

The refusal to engage in mythmaking also endows his poem with much of its extraordinary fascination, difficulty, honesty, and power. See also R. Barthes, *On Racine*, trans. Howard (New York, 1964) for an excellent discussion of the principle of the poetic rejection of myth; but one need not follow him to the logical absurdity of his conclusion, that the rejection of myth is itself mythic, that "tragedy is the myth of the failure of myth."

CHAPTER II

18. E. H. Gombrich, *Norm and Form* (London, 1966), 94.
19. The terms *muthos* and *praxis* occur frequently throughout my discussion. For the meanings that I assign these words I am greatly indebted to the challenging speculations of John Jones in his *On Aristotle and Greek Tragedy* (Oxford, 1962), 24 ff. and *passim*. Crudely formulated, the following definitions will suffice for our present purposes. *Muthos*: a visible (i.e., theatrical) series of events in time and space that are ordered into a unified and intelligible whole; the plot that makes clear what happens in the fiction. *Praxis*: an invisible idea that is rendered partially visible by the *muthos* and that contains within it the universal and timeless nature of a given human choice and action, together with their possible causes and consequences; the form which makes it possible for viewers to contemplate things that may happen in existence. One might be tempted here to speak of a surface story and a deep story, but one should probably resist the temptation.
20. I offer a brief apology for my Homeric nomenclature throughout this book. If I speak of things Homeric now as a separatist, now as a literal or oral unitarian, now as a believer, now as an outraged skeptic, it is because I am constrained to speak of these matters pretty humbly, *ut homunculus probabilia coniectura sequens* (*Tusculans* 1.9). For our immediate purposes it is only necessary to keep in mind that Vergil made very little use of the *Odyssey*'s unique surfaces and depths and probably did not understand them (the borrowings are limited to pure Knauerian *muthos*). What real use could Vergil have for a poem that imagined salvation with swaggering gaiety and ferocious, healthy charm? (See N. Frye, *A Natural Perspective: The Development of Shakespearean Comedy and Romance* [New York, 1963], 118 ff.) See Conington, 2: 13–14, for Aeneas and Odysseus. It is pleasant to recall that Longinus attempted to be a kind of separatist. For the dominance of "representation narrative," see R. Scholes and R. Kellogg, *The Nature of Narrative* (Oxford, 1966), 84–89, 98 ff. For an interesting connection between Homer and the nineteenth-century novel (via Lessing), see G. Lukács, *Studies in European Realism* (New York, 1964), 151 f.
21. If an artist can be said to belong to a period; it makes more sense, sometimes, to admit that the age belongs to the artist.
22. See Gombrich (n. 18), 92; and Gombrich, *Meditations upon a Hobby Horse* (London, 1963), 74, 118.

23. See A. Janik and S. Toulmin, *Wittgenstein's Vienna* (New York, 1972), 254–256, for a succinct reformulation of the problem and some stimulating suggestions; and the brilliant discussion by M. Peckham, *Man's Rage for Chaos* (New York, 1967), 116–121, 220–222.

24. See Gombrich, *Meditations* (n. 22), 9: "Wölfflin once remarked that all pictures owe more to other pictures than they do to nature. It is a point familiar to the students of pictorial traditions but which is still insufficiently understood in its psychological implications. Perhaps the reason is that, contrary to the belief of many artists, 'the innocent eye' which should see the world afresh would not see it at all. It would smart under the painful impact of a chaotic medley of forms and colors. In this sense the conventional vocabulary of basic forms is still indispensable to the artist as a starting point, as a focus of organization"; see also K. Jaspers, *Tragedy Is Not Enough*, trans. Reiche, Moore, and Deutsch (London, 1953), 25. See Stein's classic formulation of this problem in "Composition as Explanation," "What Is English Literature," and "The Gradual Making of the *Making of Americans*," in *Writing and Lectures, 1909–1945*, ed. Meyerowitz (London, 1971).

25. See H. Zerner's useful criticism of Sherman's theory of *maniera* in his essay "Observations on the Use of the Concept of Mannerism," a contribution to *The Meaning of Mannerism*, ed. F. W. Robinson and S. G. Nichols, Jr. (Hanover, N.H., 1972), 105–121.

26. Trans. Frothingham (New York, 1957).

27. See Conington 2: 2–3, for Scaliger and his aftermath; also, Sainte-Beuve, *Étude sur Virgile* (Paris, 1870), 296–300. The *locus classicus* for this piece of silliness (my Daddy can beat up your Daddy) is Quintilian *Institutes* 10.1.85.

28. Trans. Trask (New York, 1953, 1957), 19.

29. Ibid., 20.

30. Ibid., 19–20.

31. Ibid., 12.

32. Ibid., 12–17.

33. Ibid., 10, 12.

34. Ibid., 12.

35. See Quinn (n. 9). For an excellent discussion of how complex the simplicity is, see Scholes and Kellogg (n. 20), 208–210.

36. See Henry (n. 3, 1: 486–487) for a delightfully irritable attempt to defend *fidus quae tela gerebat Achates*. "Is a verse the less Virgil's because a *tibicen*? Is Virgil always perfection?" He invents unpersuasive plausibilities where there are none. A look at Apollonius' superb parody of the convention used by Homer in this scene will illumine both Homer and Vergil (*Argonautica* 4.162–186). Jason is not much less *amēchanos* than usual, and his naïveté and that of his comrades (*thambēsan de neoi mega kōas idontes*) are grand in themselves, grander when we see Odysseus and Aeneas hovering around them (as we do).

37. See G. S. Kirk, *The Songs of Homer* (Cambridge, 1962), 369.

38. This formulation of Vergilian impressionism is at least as old

as Conington ("a thousand incongruities of costume and outward circumstances" and the "unreality" which characterizes the *Aeneid* [3, 5]);
see also MacKail (n. 3) on the "deliberate confusedness" of the underworld (527). The greatest and most influential formulation of this Vergilian mode is that of Pöschl 255 f. (=Seligson, 156 f.). What neither
he nor those who use and develop his formulations will allow for is the
"salutary antagonism" (or, to put it in the current jargon, the "tension")
that exists between this *Kunstbegriff*, this musical *Stimmungskunst*, and
the dramatic and epic form and content that he has chosen. In other
words, Vergil's harmonic impressionism is a great mode, and the elucida-
tions of it by Pöschl, Putnam, Quinn, and Otis are extremely valuable,
but the mode has the defects of its virtues, even if Vergil usually turns
them to his advantage brilliantly. To write dramatic epic as though it
were lyric is a dangerous game, and it invites the kind of misreadings
that angry Homerists have been only too happy to accord the *Aeneid*.
For a good description of the antagonism, see W. Clausen's "Callimachus
and Latin Poetry," *GRBS* 5, no. 3 (1964): 192 ff. For a rather peculiar
estimate of Vergil's narrative technique, see Scholes and Kellogg (n. 20),
69–71; "the most obviously derivative of the Roman narrative artists."
They are not much better on Ovid, just as bad on Lucan (71–72); but
they are excellent on Homer, 161 ff. and *passim*.

39. For unclassical principles of exclusion, see Gombrich, *Norm* (n.
18), 89–90 and 95–98; see also my "The Problem of the Counter-
classical Sensibility and Its Critics," *CSCA* 3 (1970): 123–151; if I
had read Gombrich when I worked at this article, I would not have
abused my time so much in beating the dying horse, mannerism. Right
direction; wrong mode of transportation.

40. Well, this is overstated. Lucan consistently outdoes Vergil in this
regard; Catullus almost outdoes him in 63 and 64. A brilliant exclusion,
where surrealism is pressed into the service of a realistic mimesis, enforms
Ovid's *Met.* 6.557–560: *radix micat ultima linguae—moriens dominae
vestigia quaerit.* Lucan, of course, had the examples of Vergil and Ovid
to draw on. But Vergil was inventing his exclusions almost *ex nihilo*
both for the purpose of impressionism and for the purpose of abstraction.
And for Vergil (but for Ovid, almost never) the means sometimes get
very close to becoming ends because his goal was no longer realistic
mimesis and because the nature of his new goal (the imagination of darkness) cannot have been clear to him when he began trying to shape his
tools. See G. Watson (*The Study of Literature* [New York, 1969], 79–
80) for a good discussion of changing goals and reformulated intentions. See n. 119.

41. It is the old problem of trying to decide whether the gods are
figures (characters, actors) in ancient epics or essentially symbols. Otis
(*Virgil* [n. 2], 309) puts the matter this way: "Juno, as the opponent,
the enemy of both Aeneas and his *fatum*, provides the outer stimulus
that corresponds to and excites the inner response. . . . The physical
reality, the outer coercion, is of quite minor significance." (See W.

Kühn, *Götterszenen bei Vergil*, Bibliotek der klassischen Altertumswissenschaften, N. F., no. 2, 41 [Heidelberg, 1971]: 110 for earlier formulations of this opinion.) In a rather similar fashion (379), Otis is tempted to make the Dira "a sort of symbol of Turnus' foreboding conscience, the voice that tells him his end has come." The use of divine intervention is considerably more complex in Vergil (and in Homer and Apollonius) than Otis allows. Eros really does shoot Medea because Hera really has effected that shooting. We have seen these events. But when Medea decides against committing suicide, *Hērēs ennesiēisi metatropos* (3.818), we may have some reason for feeling that the human psychological process is rendered and explained by symbolic divine intervention. It makes some difference, too, whether a deity appears to a mortal with or without disguise, or is not recognized by the mortal. We have in fact seven possible categories for divine action in the *Aeneid*, which may be primarily distinguished by the mimetic techniques involved (my examples are illustrative, not exhaustive):

1. The gods are seen on their own ground outside the human drama. This is very frequent in the *Aeneid*. See Perret, *Polythéisme* (n. 128), 794, who argues very well against symbolism in general and is particularly good on this category.

2. The gods enter into human territory and intervene in human affairs without the human noticing their intervention or even their presence. This is the case of the Allecto-Amata scene; Mercury in Book 1; Juno as Discordia in 7; Allecto at 7, 511 ff.; Opis at 11.855 ff.; Juturna and the wounding of Aeneas; Venus healing Aeneas in 12; Jupiter and his scales in 12; and is probably the case with Juno Pronuba in 4.

3. The gods appear to mortals undisguised and are recognized, at some point, by the mortals, who are either waking or dreaming: Venus-Aeneas in Book 2 and Book 8; Iris to Turnus in 9; Tiberinus to Aeneas in 8; Cymodocea-Aeneas in Book 10; Mercury to Aeneas waking (4.259 ff.) and sleeping (4.556 ff.). See also Penates (2), Celaeno (3), Anchises (5), Faunus (7), Hector (2): but these scenes are better placed in 7 below.

4. The gods appear disguised but are recognized by mortals: Venus-Aeneas in Book 1; Iris in Book 5 (but she is recognized only by Pyrgo, so this might be listed in 5 below); Apollo-Ascanius in 9; Juturna-Turnus in 12.

5. The gods appear disguised and remain unrecognized by the mortals: Amor–Dido in Book 1; Iris-Dido (but perhaps this belongs to 2); Somnus-Palinurus in Book 5; Juturna-Rutuli (as Camers) in 12; Allecto and Turnus in 7; Dira-Turnus (here, only, in the form of beast). This and 2 are the grimmest categories, at least as Vergil makes use of the device (see n. 112).

6. The gods appear without any kind of picture of their action: see Hera-Medea above for 3.818. The closest thing in the *Aeneid* is Allecto at 7.475 ff.

7. Portents of one sort or another; see 3 above and Kühn, 50 ff. Only

in **6** (and possibly **7**) can we speak of symbolism with any strong confidence (though it must be admitted that Juturna as Camers clearly makes use of a preexisting situation). Otherwise, Perret's insistence on the reality of the gods in the *muthos* clearly represents the norm in Vergil, and probably in Homer as well. Seen in the light of the variety and complexity of divine modes of intervention, there is a fine irony in Medea's "some god or fury brought them here; *theos ē tis Erinus*," 3.776, for Medea's casual uncertainty has become a major organizing principle in the *Aeneid*. Still, the fact that the gods intervene so frequently and sometimes so obliquely does not mean that the human must respond as the gods wish. Even in Vergil, human will is as real as the stimulus that it encounters; but in Vergil, human will is weaker than it is in Homer. Guilty and not guilty: the perennial delicate balance. For a good discussion of gods as manifestations of "internal conflict," see Scholes and Kellogg (n. 20), 175–176.

42. See the excellent discussion by Otis, "Originality" (n. 8), 47–49. An extreme and crucial example of this deliberately confused and confusing impressionism is:

> Prima et Tellus et pronuba Iuno
> dant signum: fulsere ignes et conscius aether
> conubiis summoque ulularunt vertice nymphae.
> ille dies primus leti primusque malorum
> causa fuit; neque enim specie famave movetur
> nec iam furtivum Dido meditatur amorem;
> coniugium vocat, hoc praetexit nomine culpam.
>
> (4.166–172)

> Primal Earth
> and Juno, queen of marriages, together
> now give the signal: lightning fires flash,
> the upper air is witness to their mating,
> and from the highest hilltops shout the nymphs.
> That day was her first day of death and ruin.
> For neither how things seem nor how they are deemed
> moves Dido now, and she no longer thinks
> of furtive love. For Dido calls it marriage,
> and with this name she covers up her fault.

Pronuba is a grimly ironic echo of Appollonius' *Hērē te Zugiē* (4.96), but the irony goes beyond the allusion to unlucky weddings. If Juno is *pronuba*, this is a wedding; since Dido cannot marry again, Juno's decision to be a member of the wedding is ugly and sinister; since Dido probably and Aeneas certainly are not aware that there has been a wedding, *coniugium vocat, hoc praetexit nomine culpam*, a transition to Fama, is perhaps not so much an authorial intrusion as it is a reflection of Dido's dilemma and of her misguided feelings of guilt. But I doubt that we can tell what is going on here precisely. All we know is that a real wedding is pictured; that the bride and the groom cannot see what we can see; and, finally, that the image of the wedding which we have just witnessed is obliterated. Fade in, fade out. See n. 57.

43. For a sense of how the norm for representation of human

figures is eschewed by Apollonius, see J. Jones' formulation of that norm
(n. 19), 29–45. The deliberate excess of individuation begins, apparently, in Euripides (see the witty and precise observations of Emily
Vermeule in the introduction to her translation of Euripides' *Electra*
[Chicago, 1959]).

44. See Conington, 2: 15–20; B. C. Fenik, *The Influence of Euripides on Vergil's Aeneid* (Ph.D. diss., Princeton, 1960), *passim*; Quinn,
Vergil's Aeneid (n. 9), *passim*, and particularly 323–349.

45. Gombrich, *Norm* (n. 18), 96.

46. Ibid., 92.

47. E.g., symbolism, lyrical epic, monologue, landscape; mysticism,
history, pessimistic idealism. For a good statement on Vergilian symbolism, see D. West, "Multiple-Correspondence Similes in the *Aeneid*," *JRS*
59 (1969):49. Cf. the elegant description of this kind of symbolism
by M. Turnell, *The Art of French Fiction* (New York, 1959), 19–22.
For a precise description of Vergil's exclusion of dramatic modes, see
Otis' *Vergil* (n. 3), 95–96; and, in particular, "Originality," (n. 8),
42 ff. Irreplaceable for this topic remains B. Snell's mapping of the Vergilian *Zwischenland* in his *Die Entdeckung des Geistes* (Hamburg,
1948) trans. Rosenmeyer (Cambridge, Mass., 1953; New York, 1960),
233 ff.=Rosenmeyer, 281.

CHAPTER III

48. O. Mandelstam, "Talking about Dante," trans. C. Brown and R.
Hughes, *Delos* 6 (1971):67.

49. Williams (n. 2), 135.

50. See n. 38.

51. Williams, (n. 2), 136.

52. H. Wölfflin, *Principles of Art History*, trans. Hattinger (New
York, 1930, 1950), 196.

53. *Selected Letters*, ed. H. Maas (London, 1971), 423.

54. 4.308, 415, 519, 604.

55. Note, as usual, the freshness and clarity of the Apollonian model:
3.297–298.

56. For an excellent discussion of the color symbolism in the passage,
see Putnam (n. 10), 159 f.

57. See G. Sanderling, "Point of View in Virgil's Fourth *Aeneid*," *CW*
63 (1969):81–85. See a good discussion of this technique in W. W.
Bonney's "Joseph Conrad and the Discontinuous Point of View," *Journal
of Narrative Technique* 2.2 (1972):99–115. T. G. Rosenmeyer has
pointed out to me that there is an excellent adumbration of the technique
in *Iliad* 16.364 ff. See Conway (n. 3), 99–108 for a discussion of Vergil's "dualistic habit of mind."

58. He will get a brief and bitter moment of wholeness once more
(see p. 149), but even in that moment of *conscia virtus* the heroism intensifies our sense of his despair. But we do see him, for an instant,
from the outside: this angle of vision both restores our belief in his

courage and underscores the darkness that gathers against him (see Otis, *Virgil* [n. 3], 376–377).

59. The phrase is, I think, from Stephen Crane. Vergil is, of course, capable of something like the gravity and brevity that Homer frequently uses in recording a death on the battlefield, but this mode is so far from being central to his vision that it seems to be almost a kind of elegant variation when Vergil uses it. There is a bitter, almost ugly sarcasm in infusing this kind of pathos into the *Doloneia* and in elaborating this bitter mixture so extensively. For a sense of the Homeric norm for this mode, see Wolf—H. Friedrich, *Verwundung und Tod in der Iliad* (Goettingen, 1956), 64 ff.

60. 4.564; 8.21; 12.486, 655, 914–915. The word has a natural affinity for Turnus in Book 12.

61. Conington (694) *ad loc.* remarks that Iris here might be compared with Hermes in respect of her chthonian *geras*, but Etruria seems more helpful.

62. See *Iliad* 5.82–83, for *porphureos thanatos*; see also *Aeneid* 9.349, *purpuream animam* and *purpureus flos* (9.435) for similar *maniera*.

63. See Pöschl's fine discussion of the connection between Dido and Turnus, 182 ff., 226 ff. (=Seligson 109 ff., 136 ff.); Conington 2:13–14, 17–18.

64. The problem of divided *pietas* is, naturally, common in Augustan poetry, and Ovid makes it central to some of his most memorable portraits of women in love. It is also central to Apollonius' great rendering of Medea's dilemma; see in particular 3.609–719; 772–801. For Aeneas, see my "Aeneas and the Ironies of *Pietas*," *CJ* 60 (1965):360–364.

65. See nn. 67, 75, and 115. A question of delicate emphasis here. Sforza (n. 10) in his effort to redress the balance, is extremely unfair to Aeneas; Putnam, whose closing pages are especially fine, is not unfair, but he overstates his case at times. Galinsky (n. 6, 35–36) is rather unfair to Putnam. R. Hornsby (*Patterns of Action in the Aeneid* [Iowa City, 1970], 139–40) is certainly unfair to Turnus, as for the most part was Otis; but see now Otis' "Originality" (n. 8), 63. The circle is vicious. If we can somehow fuse the precision of Otis' great defense of Aeneas with Putnam's masterly defense of Turnus, we will be able to read Books 7–12 with an unusual degree of accuracy. For our present purposes, it is worth recalling Mackail's remarks on Aeneas' nobility at 11:110 f.: *pacem me exanimis et Martis sorte peremptis / oratis? equidem et vivis concedere vellem.* Noble, indeed. Yet there is, in respect of the final scene of the poem, a cruel, almost Sophoclean irony here.

66. The most useful discussion of Vergil's similes are those of D. West (see n. 47); and "Virgilian Multiple-Correspondence Similes and Their Antecedents," *Philologus* 114, no. 3/4 (1970):262–275. Also useful is Quinn (n. 9), 342 ff. For Homeric similes, see M. Coffey, "The Function of the Homeric Simile," *AJP* 78 (1955):113–132; P. Damon, *Modes of Analogy in Ancient and Medieval Verse*, U.C. Publications in Classical Philology 15 (Berkeley and Los Angeles, 1961), 261–272; R.

Hampe, *Die Gleichnisse Homers und die Bildkunst seiner Zeit* (Tübingen, 1952); G. S. Kirk, *The Songs of Homer* (Cambridge, 1962), *passim*; G. P. Shipp, *Studies in the Language of Homer* (Cambridge, 1953, 1972), 208–222. The formulation that I have relied on most for the purpose of contrasting Vergilian and Homeric similes is W. Schadewaldt's in his *Von Homers Welt und Werk* (Stuttgart, 1944, 1951), 144–151; for him the qualities of the Homeric simile that matter most are the dramatic and the "energisch." A matter, then, of action and realistic mimesis, but the concept of action and reality is subtly and precisely defined: "Was Homer in der Erscheinungen seiner Gleichnisse darstellt . . . ist gar nicht das Sichtbare an der Erscheinungen, sondern gerade jenes Unsichtbare, das *in* den Erscheinungen erscheint" (145). It is the *Unsichtbare* that matters most to us here. The clarities of Homeric pictures, in the similes as in the images of the narrative action, function to enhance the intensity and steadiness of perception, and behind this intensity and steadiness there grows a sense of a large, indefinable, and ineffable reality that the visible realities emerge from. Particularly in the disjunctive and cumulative similes the clarities and the intensities of the things seen confirm the permanence of dynamic and luminous being (for the basis of this formulation I am indebted to T. G. Rosenmeyer). This realism, which transcends "literalness," has been elegantly described by Willa Cather in her essay, "The Novel Démeublé," in *On Writing* (New York, 1949), in particular in this passage: "Whatever is felt upon the page without being specifically named there—that, one might say, is created. It is the inexplicable presence of the thing not named, of the overtone divined by the ear but not heard by it, the verbal mood, the emotional aura of the fact or the thing or the deed, that gives high quality to the novel or the drama, as well as to poetry itself" (41–42). Clarity, then, exists for intensity, as intensity exists for the *Unischtbare*; but, in Homer as in Tolstoy (on whom Cather focuses in this part of her essay), the beginnings of this dialectical unity of immanence and transcendence are to be found in visual plausibilities. For a similar conception, shaped in a different way for different ends, see Lukács (n. 20), 152–153.

67. Immediately after this passage, Aeneas says of his response to the vision and his waking, *arma amens capio* (314 ff.), which is at once humble and exact. I would like to emphasize here that Aeneas is never a bad man or a weak man or a stupid man, though he sometimes behaves in an irrational way. But, like the other characters in the poem, he has no understanding of the world he moves in. His critics have found him dull, unheroic, a kind of weird elaboration of the *amēchanos* Jason almost in exact proportion as he shows himself not to be Odysseus. But he is neither Jason nor Odysseus and was not meant to be. He acts in a world where Tiberinus tells him (8.59 ff.): *surge age, nate dea, primisque cadentibus astris / Iunoni fer rite preces iramque minasque / supplicibus supera votis*. So, in his oath at 12.178 ff. he says: *et pater omnipotens et tu Saturnia coniunx / (iam melior, iam diva, precor)*.

That is not stupidity, it is very real *pietas*. But the injunction of Tiberinus is misleading and Aeneas' optimism is groundless, for nothing that he or we have experienced in the poem gives him grounds for believing in the reasonableness—let alone the loving-kindness—of Juno towards him or any human. His final prayer to her is touched, again, with Sophoclean irony, and his dilemma and his action throughout the poem are ironic because he acts and must act as though Juno were benevolent. This tragic aspect of the poem is brilliantly executed.

68. That the stag is not saved and that Odysseus is saved heighten our sense of the lucky *peripeteia* of Odysseus' escape. Precise parallelism is not necessary: here the *Unsichtbare* is the combination of the near destruction and the astonishing glory that replaces destruction. This mysterious and invisible reality behind the phenomenon confirms and enlarges the truth and significance of the things seen.

69. See the excellent remarks of F. Mensch ("Film Sense in the *Aeneid*," *Arion* 8, no. 3 [1969]:382–387) on this passage.

70. Once again the character is ignorant of what is happening (this does not mean, of course, totally absolved from some kind of guilt), but what in fact is there to know in the poem about anything? The poet ends the poem as he began it—by asking, not rhetorically, how these things can happen: *tanton placuit concurrere motu, / Iuppiter, aeterna gentis in pace futuras?* (12.503–504). This outraged complaint and lament, phrased as a bitter question (the bitterness bursts through the mordant juxtaposition of *aeterna pace* with *gentis futuras tanto motu concurrere* —what does *futuras* mean here, and what, indeed, does *aeterna* mean?), does not attract much attention from commentators, probably because they do not want to deal with its ramifications for the poem. But to assume that it is merely an ornament to an elegant but conventional statement of *aporia-cum-recusatione* (*quis mihi nunc tot acerba deus, quis carmine caedes . . . expediat?* [500–503]) begs Vergil's questions in a spineless fashion. (What god indeed?) T. C. Donatus (*ad loc.*) sees the problem and states it very clearly: "necessaria exclamatio poetae admirantis deorum iniquitatem qui patiebantur in alternam perniciem gentis tendere in aeternam venturas perpetuamque concordiam." This kind of oxymoron (*charis biaios*, see n. 114 and 139; *felix culpa*) can, of course, affirm order in the midst of apparent disorder, but I doubt that the implied oxymoron of Vergil's question (or rather of the poet's question) accomplishes this because the elements of the oxymoron will not be unified by dramatic action in the poem. I am not suggesting that the metaphysical despair implied in the question necessarily reflects Vergil's personal attitude to this question, but I am sure that it is an essential part of the materials of his poem, and that he uses it, very effectively, as the metaphysical background of his poem. "A Man hurrying along— to what? The Creature has a purpose and his eyes are bright with it." That sudden awareness of our ignorance of what life is and our natural, but perhaps unreasonable, inference that maybe the foundations of our life are indifferent or hostile to what we think to be our purposes, that

feeling is everywhere in the *Aeneid*. For Keats and the *Aeneid*, an interesting combination, see W. J. Bate, *John Keats* (Cambridge, Mass., 1963; Oxford, 1966), 26, 32.

71. See n. 42 and n. 57 for the problem of *pronuba* and *hoc nomine culpam*. Another problem is that though Aeneas is pastor he is also *nescius* outside the simile as well as in it. But he is not entirely *nescius*. The truth is willfully obscured here as it is in another way for another reason at 393 ff.:

> at pius Aeneas, quamquam lenire dolentem
> solando cupit et dictis avertere curas,
> multa gemens magnoque animum labefactus amore,
> iussa tamen divom exsequitur classemque revisit.

These are some of the finest verses of the poem in the perfection of their construction and the compression of emotion (see R. G. Austin's edition of Book 4, *ad loc.*). They achieve their resonance by receiving the whole weight of the scene which they close. But it should be noticed that these verses replace Aeneas' answer to Dido's second speech to Aeneas. (See n. 98 and Aeneas' silence at 6.886.) In other words, Vergil deliberately allows his drama to fail. Dido's champions who feel that he is *ho pankakistos*, a rotten son-of-a-bitch, are only justified insofar as Vergil shifts from a dramatic focus back to a combination of Dido's point of view (we watch Aeneas departing, obeying orders) and the narrator's correct justification of his departure. Note, especially, the word *pius*, which is ironic because it expresses both his compassion for Dido and his patriotism, and the subordinate clause begun by *quamquam*, in which the profundity of his love and compassion for Dido finds superb expression. Powerful as these verses are in the context, because of the brevity of this passage and the failure of the dramatic confrontation to find its own conclusion, they are swallowed up in the splendid tumult and confusion that imitates both Dido and what she perceives as Book 4 plunges to its close. Radical and deliberate, this imbalance effects a distortion of things as they are that resonates throughout the poem and cannot be eradicated from our memory even when we remind ourselves that Aeneas is not heartless, callous, etc. So, we can tell ourselves again and again that Dido is not a guilty, crazed neurotic. But the pictures are as out of focus as they are artful and powerful, and we see and remember the truth of the matter in spite of them. Nothing is more haunting and deceptively persuasive than this failed lucidity.

72. For the Apollonian original (4.1479–1480), see M. Hügi, *Vergils Aeneis und die Hellenistische Dichtung* (Bern, 1951), 35.

73. A paradigm of this technique is *discolor unde auri per ramos aura refulsit* (6.204), a verse whose significance has been definitively described in Brooks' incomparable essay (n. 10); see also West (n. 47, 46) for *brattea vento*. For our immediate purposes we need only regard the way in which the Apollonian image (4.125–126) is compressed, distorted, and elaborated by the inexplicable catachresis, *discolor aura*: the breeze (not merely, the gleam) that creates *discolor* in the gold

branches becomes golden and *discolor* itself in distorting the color of the branches: fascinating, sinister, incomprehensible, like the experience that Aeneas must endure here and elsewhere.

74. For the incongruity, see the remarks of Hügi (n. 72), 36.

75. Even at the moment of what might have been a kind of personal glory (*ego poscor Olympo* [533]), Aeneas shows his characteristic compassion even for the enemy (537 ff.), which culminates in the bitter frustration of *poscant acies et foedera rumpant* (540): not so much rage at the enemy as angry despair over the incomprehensibility of things.

76. This is an almost ordinary mode in modern literature. From Conrad's *The Secret Agent*: "In that shop of shady wares fitted with deal shelves painted a dull brown, which seemed to devour the sheen of the light, the gold circlet of the wedding ring on Mrs. Verloc's left hand glittered exceedingly with the untarnished glory of a piece from some splendid treasure of jewels, dropped in a dust-bin" (chapter 9). "A tinge of wildness in her aspect was derived from the black veil hanging like a rag against her cheek, and from the fixity of her black gaze where the light of the room was absorbed and lost without the trace of a single gleam" (chapter 11). Milton, of course, rivals his master; see, for example, *P.L.* 1.592 ff. (In dim Eclips disastrous twilight sheds) and 9.625 ff. (Hovering and blazing with delusive Light).

77. See Jones (n. 19), 24–29.

78. So, though Vergil happens to share some of the qualities, both technical and "philosophical," of modern symbolist poets, he would probably be appalled by the sad, neo-pagan affirmations of transcendence that haunt their lovely desperate poems.

79. See the superb statement of J. Perret in his "Optimisme et Tragédie dans l'*Énéide*," *REL* 45 (1967): 356–357 and 362: "Ce n'est pas contre des monstres qu'Énée doit lutter, mais contre des hommes et avec l'aide d'autres hommes. Et justement, tandis qu'en la première moitié du poème Didon seule retient le regard, le poète désormais assemble pour finir, autour de son héros, une foule de figures personelles et inoubliables. En chacun d'eux et jusqu'en l'adversaire qu'il doit combattre puisse-t-il ne jamais méconnaître le frère de misère et de grandeur, pitoyable et respectable, l'homme comme lui, périssable et lié par des devoirs! Au prince qui doit conduire une cité si divisée encore, si pleine d'affreux souvenirs, proscriptions, guerres civiles, un poète peut-il offrir plus beau présent qu'une invite à méditer sur ces thèmes?" That is at once noble and accurate. And it shows, by the way, at least one way in which this remark is inaccurate: "In general the last six books are unequal to the first six" (Otis, "Originality" [n. 8], 63). The true humility and true magnanimity of the *Aeneid* shine through the splendors and miseries of the last six books.

80. For the spondaic movement of the verse, see E. Norden's edition of Book 6 (Leipzig and Berlin, 1934), 210–211.

81. For a similar sense of alien, threatening space see 7.379, 8.24–25, 12.476, 586.

82. Of the Latins, not the bees. For this confusion of the humans with their analogues, see Hügi (n. 72), 49. For the significance of the bees, see L. P. Wilkinson, *The Georgics of Virgil: A Critical Survey* (Cambridge, 1969), 100–120.

83. See A. Parry, "Have We Homer's *Iliad*?" *YCS* 20 (1966):195, n. 36.

84. Note in particular the effect achieved by the hyperbaton and catachresis of *celeris . . . umbras.*

85. Homer undoes this equilibrium with "and how then could Hector have fled the demons of death, if Apollo, for the last, for the very last time, had not come next to him . . .?" (202–205) and by the picture of Zeus' scales, which adumbrates Hector's defeat and death (208–213); see Scholes and Kellogg (n. 20), 241.

86. Note that in Vergil the Fury replaces Athena as Juturna replaces Apollo. It is an interesting replacement since, at one level, it suggests that, though without his knowledge, the Fury becomes the ally of Aeneas.

87. The fine compression of the catachresis, *avidos cursus*, stresses the frustration and the immense strain of the pursued. For a good discussion of the simile, see West "Similes and Antecedents" (n. 66), 269.

88. *Der Traum in der Aeneis*, Noctes Romanae 5 (Berlin and Stuttgart, 1952), 72–75.

89. N. 10 (=Commager 121 ff.).

90. He weeps again at 469–470; not excessive even by Anglo-Saxon standards of stolidity.

91. See G. Dumézil, *Archaic Roman Religion*, trans. Knapp (Chicago, 1970), 2:466–467 for *caput acris equi* in 1.444. The irony of *melius confidere* is brief but strong enough to illumine the rest of the poem (see n. 67 for the quality of this irony).

92. See J. M. C. Toynbee (*The Art of the Romans* [London, 1965], 115) for a good description of the styles employed here (i.e., triumphal and legendary in late second or early third styles); also, K. Schefold, *Pompejanische Malerei* (Basel, 1952), 97–111, 156–166; Conington's note on 453.

93. The *tulisset* is rather close to the cynical Tacitean pluperfect subjunctives that describe what might have been only to emphasize the horror of what is actual.

94. His Greek masters in poetry, as he knows, excelled in plausible representation: *excudent . . . spirantia mollius aera . . . vivos ducent de marmore vultus* (847–848). It is a nice irony that Greek poetry is suppressed in the list of Greek artistic and intellectual achievements.

95. Vergil did not "wish to close on a note of triumph and exultation" (here at the end of 6, and, one might add, at the end of 12): Otis (n. 3), 303 ff., 391 f. But, in order to avoid triumph and exultation, it was not necessary to add despair to tact, prudence, and humanism. The close of 6, like the close of 12, is much more complicated, is possessed of much more darkness and much more light, than Otis will allow: the

principle involved is, the darker the brighter. In any case, Vergil is fond of picturing disintegration, nonbeing, failure of potentiality; see 2.557–558: *iacet ingens litore truncus / avolsumque umeris caput et sine nomine corpus*; 4.88–89: *pendent opera interrupta minaeque / murorum ingentes aequataque machina caelo.*

96. From this we get a good sense of Parry's intuition of "man as the brilliant free agent in Homer's world" (n. 10, 121).

97. See *De senectute* 25 (n. 141).

98. Cf. G. Highet, *The Speeches in Vergil's Aeneid* (Princeton, 1972), 188: "Hector and Turnus both beg for mercy (although Hector is dying and Turnus is not). Achilles and Aeneas both refuse, and claim the death of the foe as requital for the slaying of a friend. Hector and Turnus die and their souls fly with a groan into the darkness." He ignores the second speech of Hector and its significance (see n. 71).

99. For *devotio* see *Der kleine Pauly* (1964), 1:1501; Livy 8.9.6–8; Macrobius 3.9.10–11; Dumézil (n. 91), 555; Conington's note to 11.440–442, Turnus' *devovi*, where the datives are of advantage; E. T. Salmon, *Samnia and the Samnites* (Cambridge, 1967), 146–147, 267.

100. See G. Else, *The Origin and Early Form of Greek Tragedy*, Martin Lectures 20 (Cambridge, Mass., 1965; New York, 1972), 48, 64, 67, 76; see also S. Weil, "The *Iliad* or the Poem of Force," trans. McCarthy, *Politics* (November 1945) 1 ff.; and R. Bespaloff, *On the Iliad*, trans. Broch (Princeton, 1947), 43 ff., 91 ff.

101. *Iliad* 4.5–6.

102. See V. Basanoff (*Evocatio* [Paris, 1947], in particular 69–91) for Juno's special connections with the rite and 166–182 for his discussion of possible connections of Turnus and Juturna with the rite outside Vergil's poem; see also Dumézil (n. 91), 425 ff.; 481–483.

103. See Macrobius 3.9.7–9 for the *evocatio* pronounced to Juno Caelestis by Scipio Aemilianus. See Dumézil (n. 91), 469–470; Basanoff (n. 102), 63 ff. See Servius, note to *retorsit*, 12.841: *sed constant bello Punico secundo exoratam Iunonem, tertio vero bello a Scipione sacris quibusdam etiam Romam esse translatam.* It is worth noting that Macrobius gives the texts of *devotio* and *evocatio* together (see n. 99). While Basanoff (4–5) is correct in insisting that the formulation *nulla devotio sine evocatione* is misleading, we may safely suggest that the two rites have a certain natural affinity that Macrobius rightly affirms and that Vergil makes into poetry.

104. He puts in a brief, almost perfunctory appearance at 725 with his scales. These verses are for the most part incantatory *Stimmungskraft*; they are not part of the images and drama of the action of Book 12, as is easily seen if we compare them with *Iliad* 22.211–215 where the action of Zeus *immediately* yields two results: Apollo abandons Hector to his doom, and Athena goes to Achilles to hint that the end of the duel is in sight.

105. The repetition of *olli subridens* from 1.254 is mordant. It was as easy to smile at the silly, petulant, maternal, and beautiful daughter

as it was to kiss her—she is more or less harmless, usually charming, and rather dumb. To smile at this fiend is fiendish. Nor can this Jupiter bring off this kind of smile, for he has not in him the wild bright laughter of Zeus (21.388). The image is deliberately grotesque.

106. See Conington on 830–831: one sympathizes with Heyne's attempt to read, *et germana Iovis . . . irarum tantos volvis sub pectore fluctus?* This provides Jupiter with a touch of decent anger at what she is and what she has done, and it disassociates her from him and what he stands for—or is supposed to stand for. But it does not suit *olli subridens*, nor does it suit the poem. T. E. Page's suggestion that "Jupiter humorously recognizes in 'the waves of passion' which surge in Juno's bosom the proof of her kinship to himself" takes *olli subridens* into account but adds a frisson of its own; see his note *ad loc.*, in vol. 2 of his edition of the poem (London, 1900, 1962). W. W. Fowler (*The Death of Turnus* [Oxford, 1919], 144 ff., understands the irony of the passage perfectly and shows that Jupiter's irony centers on what he means by *supra ire deos pietate videbis* (839), an irony that escapes Juno since it is precisely this virtue that she lacks utterly. But considering what lies behind his irony, Jupiter is being frivolous himself, however profound his recognition of Juno's true nature. Neither Buchheit (n. 14, 140 ff.) nor P. Boyancé (*La religion de Virgile* [Paris, 1963], 35–38) deals with these problems; nor do they interest Otis much. For a good examination of the nature and conduct of the debate, see Kühn (n. 41), 162–165. For a superb discussion of the gods in general and Jupiter in particular, see R. G. Austin's remarks on 2.604–623 in his edition of Book 2 (Oxford, 1964): *Iuno saevissima* (612), *ipse pater Danais animos viresque secundas / sufficit, ipse deos in Dardana suscitat arma* (617–618); *apparent dirae facies inimicaque Troiae / numina magna deum* (622–623). Of Venus' speech, which follows this vision, he says: "An obedient faith in divine guidance, blandly manifested after the apocalypse of devils, is more than incongruous: it is irrational" (xxi). That is not too strongly stated, and the quality that he correctly identifies in this part of the poem radiates forward to the close of the poem.

107. Without Juno's intervention it would have been a pure *devotio* on Turnus' part, and it is also unlikely that he would have lost his nerve in so dreadful a fashion; nor is it likely that Aeneas would have been angry in the way that he becomes angry—at least his anger would lack the degree of justification that it possesses. Since we are dealing with Juno here, we have a right to consider the historical "if." The breaking of the truce, at Juno's instigation, cheapens the duel and drains the actions of the poem's two heroes of much of their nobility.

108. *Mortalin decuit violari volnere divom?* (797). A neat irony on his part that, again, she does not pick up. Naughty enough to call Aeneas *divus* to her face, naughtier to play with the meaning of *mortali* in this way. It means—in collation with *divom*—*mortifero*, as Heyne saw (see Conington *ad loc.*). But Jupiter, feigning ignorance, knows that the marksman was Juturna. This fact Juno readily, if somewhat unguardedly,

admits (*non ut tela tamen, non ut contenderet arcum* [815]) when claiming that she had only suggested that Juturna go help her brother, in any way she might have to (*Iuturnam misero {fateor} succurrere fratri / suasi et pro vita maiora audere probavi* [813–814]). In other words, she prefers to plead guilty to the lesser—and indeed the more honorable—charge, of counselling *pietas* to a distraught sister. But her instructions had been more explicit at 156 ff. than she prefers to remember here:

> "non lacrimis hoc tempus," ait Saturnia Iuno.
> "accelera et fratrem, si quis modus, eripe morti,
> aut tu bella cie conceptumque excute foedus:
> auctor ego audendi."
>
> "This is no time for tears," Saturnian Juno
> cries out to her. "Be quick; snatch back your brother
> from death if there is any way, or else
> incite them all to arms and smash the treaty.
> It is myself who order you to dare."

In a sense, then, she is directly responsible for the wounding of Aeneas, and her swearing by the Styx does not deflect Jupiter's attention from the truth in these matters. In any case, the epic Queen of Heaven is not bothered by juggling with semantic niceties when taking the Stygian oath (*Iliad* 15.34–46). Page *ad loc.* (n. 106) finds that "To us the whole discussion appears rather comic, and indeed it is only in very early and simple composition that it is possible to introduce divine beings arguing, debating, and acting like mere mortals without verging on the ridiculous." Is his ideal Robespierre's Festival of the Divine Being or the President of the Immortals? Still, it is better to find the scene comic than to find it profoundly serious, etc.; but *fratzenhaft* is perhaps the word for it.

109. For et=sed, see Hale, *Latin Grammar*, 1655.

110. On *mentem retorsit* Servius says, "iste quidem hoc dicit, sed constat bello Punico secundo exoratam Iunonem," etc. (n. 103). See Dumézil (n. 91), 481–483 and Buchheit (n. 14), 58 on Horace, *Odes* 3.3. B. C. Fenik (n. 44) formulates the question accurately by emphasizing the importance of 10.11–14 (*adveniet iustum pugnae, ne arcessite, tempus*) for *mentem retorsit* (see 139, 236 ff.). See Kühn (n. 41) 132–133. It is worth noting that Jupiter is as tactful at 10.11 ff. as he is in this scene in Book 12; see T. C. Donatus on *abnueram bello Italiam concurrere Teucris:* "praedixerat enim in primo libro futurum bellum in Italia atque hoc bellum Aenean feris et indomitis adhuc gentibus inlaturum; hic dicit hanc fuisse dispositionem, ne Itali vim belli Troianis inferrent, quod revera non fieret, si Iunonis tergiversatio quievisset, quam Iuppiter oblique pulsat et quasi nescius auctorem facti perquirit." He is doubtless also aware of Dido's curse at 4.621–629. At issue is not a conflict between his foreknowledge and his power. The problem is that in Book 10 as in Book 12 he is essentially indifferent to what is going on (*oblique pulsat et quasi nescius*). This is not carelessness or clumsiness on Vergil's part; it is design, as 12.500 ff. show. He is using the irony of

Juno's multiple *evocationes* (see Basanoff, n. 102) to show that this last and crucial evocation, signaled by *mentem retorsit,* is unreal and that Jupiter knows it is unreal. This is what bothered Servius when he recalled the rites offered Juno in the second and third Punic Wars (and there is the matter of Veii as well), and it should bother us also. It is a pity that the comments of T. C. Donatus for 781–846 have been lost. For the kind of disparity we find here between the author's question and his epic narrator's random objectivity, see Scholes and Kellogg (n. 20), 52–53 and 240.

111. See Pöschl, 220 (=Seligson, 133); Kühn (n. 41), 165 f.

112. See Putnam's excellent comments on the Dira, 194 and 198 (n. 10). He neatly compares her with Somnus in 5.835 ff., and he catches the quality of horror brilliantly. Otis, *Virgil* (n. 3) is not concerned with the malignant horror of the Dira, but he is probably not far from the truth in suggesting that "it is really the Dira, not Aeneas, that defeats Turnus" (380). That is a way of saving Aeneas' reputation, perhaps, but not a very good way; if anything, it increases the nightmare; see Servius to 846: *"Tartaream Megaeram*: bene Tartaream addidit, ut ostendat esse et terrenam et aeriam Megaeram: nam, ut etiam in tertio (209) diximus, volunt periti quandam triplicem potestatem esse et in terris et apud superos, sicut est furiarum apud inferos. ideo autem . . . et latenter oriri et intolerabilem esse iram deorum." In other words, even the *periti* were puzzled by a celestial fury (see n. 113) and reached hard for a solution to their bewilderment; see Fowler (n. 106, 149 ff.) for a good description of the Etruscan coloring.

113. See, e.g., the expulsion of Ate by Zeus (*Iliad* 19.125 ff.) and Apollo's speech to the Furies in the *Eumenides,* 179–197. It is true that both of the personae who invoke this Olympian rejection of chthonian unreason do so for reasons that have little to do with the exultation of reason, but they reflect a rather disinterested tendency towards establishing reason as the ideal (see G. S. Kirk, "The Structure and Aim of the *Theogony,*" *Entretiens,* Fondation Hardt 7 [Geneva, 1960], 93–94; Kirk [n. 17], 224, 241–251; H. Lloyd-Jones, *The Justice of Zeus,* Sather Lectures 41 [Berkeley and Los Angeles, 1971], 77; R. Hinks, *Myth and Allegory in Ancient Art* [London, 1939], 22–29).

114. For Etruria, see F. De Ruyt, *Charun, démon étrusque de la morte,* Institut Historique Belge de Rome 1 (Brussels, 1934), 206, 216–217, 233. For tragedy see Jebb's note to *Oedipus Colonus* 1381: it is Justice who shares the throne with Zeus (*sunedros;* 1267); Aidos is *sunthakos.* See also *Agamemnon* 1562–1563 and *Eumenides* 229. I think that Vergil has a sense of such passages in mind when he writes, *hae Iovis ad solium.* But in this echo of the Greek struggle for theodicy, Vergil is not equating the Dira with *Dike*; on the contrary, he is showing the perversion of *Dike* in this poem. I have suggested that Juno's hideous parody of *evocatio* recalls the close of the *Eumenides,* and I suspect that the trilogy was much in Vergil's mind (whether consciously or not one cannot tell, nor does it matter) when he wrote the close of Book 12. I

am not prepared to argue whether or not the play shows in the unfolding of its *muthos-praxis* a development toward Justice; it seems to me fairly clear that the *charis biaios*, which was adumbrated so early in the trilogy (*Agamemnon* 182) and on which changes are rung throughout the trilogy, is finally made visible in the closing of the poem, a dramatic vision that arises—in a manner that is at once mysterious and natural—out of the trilogy's *muthos-praxis*. H. Lloyd-Jones (n. 113, 93) is correct in saying ". . . at the end of the play these hideous and sinister beings are extolled and honoured by Athene and, at her order, by her citizens. Far from having their traditional functions taken from them, as they have feared they will be and as some scholars, incautious in their liberalism, have supposed they are, they are given a special place of honour in Athens, which will benefit enormously from their proximity." In terms of our comparison, the point is that the Dira cannot be honored or extolled at the end of the *Aeneid* because she is in no way connected with the works of Justice; the Eumenides are finally seen as an essential aspect of *charis biaios*, and Aeschylus' shaping oxymoron succeeds in the articulations and the perfections of its architecture. There is no *charis biaios* in the *Aeneid*, and it is the Dira who shows that there cannot be any such healing renewal in this poem. (For Athena, *peithō*, and *stasis* in relation to Vergil's poem, see n. 139).

115. Aeneas kills Turnus out of frustration and anger, chiefly anger with himself, because his ideals and his actions cannot deal with the actualities that Juno shapes. See M. M. Crump, *The Growth of the Aeneid* (Oxford, 1920), 91–92, for an excellent discussion of Turnus' actions: "The killing of Pallas is not a crime but a necessity; it is exactly parallel to the killing of Lausus by Aeneas; in both cases a young, untried man is slain by a proved hero. . . . Again, Turnus does not exceed his rights in taking the belt, for Aeneas in the same way takes the armour of Mezentius." Aeneas feels guilt for Pallas' death because he had promised Evander he would take care of him; the sight of the belt triggers the uncontrollable rage he feels against himself and the world he is forced to live in. Such behavior does not make him a bad man any more than it makes Turnus a good man. It means that he, like Turnus, is a human being, and that both men are held in human bondage even though both men are authentic heroes. See also Turnus' words at 12.646–649.

116. See Putnam (n. 10, 201) for the definitive statement on this aspect of the poem.

117. See, again, Putnam (196, 200) for a slightly different emphasis on the crucial importance of comparing *Iliad* 24 with *Aeneid* 12 for a proper reading of the latter (and, perhaps, of the former). I think I need not explain why I refer so much to Putnam at the close of this section: he taught us how to read Book 12.

118. See n. 32.

119. See K. Quinn, "Did Virgil Fail?" in *Studies in Honour of H. Hunt* (Amsterdam, 1972), 206: ". . . the more Virgil appeals to our moral sense, the more that sense is outraged by a story whose fundamental

data are so out of keeping with the use Virgil seeks to make of it. . . .
We can then imagine that Virgil felt, each time he recast his poem, that
he had made it a better poem (more expressive of a mature, civilized
sensibility) and a poem which it was more impossible than before ever
to get right." This is somewhere near the truth, but why does Quinn feel
that to appeal to our moral sense by outraging our moral sense cannot
have come to be part of the uses of this poem? See Gombrich, *Norm*
(n. 18), 58: "He [Leonardo as painter] works like a sculptor modelling
in clay who never accepts any form as final but goes on creating, even
at the risk of obscuring his original intention." In short, if the *Aeneid* is
a failure in any sense of the word, who cares for success? See n. 40,
Watson.

CHAPTER IV

120. For the poetic of Catullus in this regard, see Williams (n. 2),
132; and D. O. Ross, Jr., *Style and Tradition in Catullus* (Cambridge,
Mass., 1969), 166–175; for that of Lucretius, see, *passim*, D. West, *The
Imagery and Poetry of Lucretius* (Edinburgh, 1969).

121. See Cochrane (n. 3), 120.

122. A. Baehrens, *Poetae Latini Minores* (Leipzig and Berlin, 1886),
6:360.

123. For the ups and downs of hopes and fears, see my "Propertius
and the Emotions of Patriotism," *CSCA* 6 (1973):173–180.

124. But note the nobility of Turnus in reformulating his *devotio* as
a kind of reparation for the broken treaty at 694–695. See Conington
(n. 3) *ad loc.*: *foedus luere=poenas pro foedere rupto luere*; cf. Otis
(n. 3), 373–374: "the intervention of Juturna (at Juno's behest)
clearly reflects a prior human motivation (it is the same with Iris in
5, Allecto in 7). The Latins *want* to break the *foedus*; they are ready in
their hearts for the demonic suggestion." One is pleased to find that the
suggestion is accurately characterized as being "demonic" (see n. 41).

125. See Quinn, *Vergil* (n. 9), 287–288: "Greek philosophy too
leaves its clear imprint. . . ." I suggest that this notion needs to be re-
examined carefully; the clarities have disappeared.

126. See Dodds (n. 12, 245) on the gradual failure of traditional
rationalism at this time and on the corresponding growth of "the antirationalism that spreads from below upwards, and eventually wins the day."

127. See F. Cumont, *Oriental Religions in Roman Paganism*, trans.
Showerman (New York, 1911), 38; and Schefold (n. 16), ibid.

128. See J. Perret, "Le polythéisme de Virgile," *Revue Archéologi-
que*, Mélanges Picard 31–32 (1949):800.

129. See the prayer of Iphis to Isis in Ovid's *Metamorphoses* 9.773 ff.
and the goddess' compassion, 782 ff. (the irony of *pronuba quid Iuno*
[762] is grand); see also the superb prayer of Myrrha, 10.483 ff., *o
siqua patetis / numina confessis*, after which there occurs another act
of compassion (they are rare in this poem) by a mysterious and again a

non-Olympian deity: *numen confessis aliquod patet* (488). See Kühn (n. 41), 168; see also the very persuasive discussion of Galinsky (n. 6), 224 ff. which demonstrates Cybele's authentic role in the political allegory.

130. See F. Cumont, *After Life in Roman Paganism*, trans. Irvine (New Haven, 1922), 174 ff., who makes Vergil "the interpreter of the Hellenic tradition," but immediately goes on to examine Etruscan and Near Eastern motifs that are present in Book 6 but are not present in the Hellenic tradition. See the elaborate transformation of *Iliad* 5.449–463 at *Aeneid* 10.636–665 where Juno's zombie far surpasses the wraith fashioned by Apollo. There is nothing in the Homeric model like *at primas laeta ante acies exsultat imago / inritatque virum telis et voce lacessit* (643–644), which is more Apuleian than it is Homeric. See Mackail (n. 3) 526–527 for the baffling geography of hell; and Conington (n. 3) *ad loc.* for the expansions and complications of the Homeric models. For the incongruities and difficulties in general, see Norden (n. 80), 20–48.

131. See H. H. Scullard, *The Etruscan Cities and Rome* (Ithaca, 1967), 281 f.

132. See n. 28, 46.

133. See Cumont (n. 130), 164 ff. See J. Carcopino (*La basilique pythagoricienne de la Porte Majeure* [Paris, 1927, 1953], 185–204) for a good discussion of why Pythagoreanism should have seemed attractive to some people in the first century B.C.; also, A. J. Festugière, *L'idéal religieuse des grecs et l'Évangile* (Paris, 1932), 75–81. E. R. Dodds (*Christians and Pagans in an Age of Anxiety* [Cambridge, 1965], 3–18) discusses the adumbration of gnostic notions before their great flourishing in the third and fourth centuries A.D.

134. See n. 111; and W. Hübner, *Dirae im römischen Epos,* Spudasmata 21 (Hildesheim, 1970), 36–37.

135. Note the repetition of *venenum* here, which is, of course, appropriate for the serpent but recalls the use at 1.688.

136. See De Ruyt (n. 114), 206–248; F. Poulsen, *Etruscan Tomb Paintings: Their Subjects and Significance* (Oxford, 1922), 49–59; R. Bloch, *Etruscan Art* (Greenwich, Conn., 1965), 89–91; M. Grant, *Roman Myths* (London, 1971), 162–163.

137. Scullard (n. 131, 215–216) gives a properly cautious assessment of the problem; see also Grant (n. 136), 27, 73–76. For Aeneas' affiliations with Etruria, see Galinsky (n. 6), 120 ff.

138. I am not denying that Euripides had toyed with the idea. Obviously Lyssa in the *Herakles* suggests some of Allecto, but even in the *Orestes* Euripides does not seriously consider the problem of evil—because it is not yet a problem. The illusion of evil, and the various ersatz ways of dealing with that illusion, are problems for Socrates to probe and annihilate. But evil does not become a problem until the climate of the mystery religions (see H. Cherniss, "The Sources of Evil according to Plato," *American Philosophical Society* 98 [1954]:23 ff.).

139. Note, once more, that *tantaene animis caelestibus irae?* and *tanton placuit concurrere motu?* function, among other things, as a frame for the poem (see n. 70). We have seen too that Juno replaces Ennius' Discordia in order to begin what amounts to a civil war. All of this contrasts sharply with the Aeschylean solutions to not unsimilar problems. Aeschylus' Athena closes with the forces of *ira* and composes them, *su d'eupithēs emoi* (*Eumenides* 829–831). Note that though she addresses the Furies, she is in fact primarily concerned with the problem of civil war (858 ff.; 885 ff.). *all' ei men hagnon esti soi Peithous sebas*: but if Persuasion's sanctity is in your eyes truly a holy thing (885): this is the banishing of *ira* and *discordia*. There is no trace whatever of *Peithous sebas* in the *Aeneid* (unless it is in Aeneas' desperate and futile attempts at peaceful solution); so, no trace of *charis biaios* (n. 114). It is in this void and darkness that human courage and dignity are glimpsed. Without Homer and Aeschylus to echo against, this poem could not exist: it shows, in various ways and in various places, the absence of truths and beauties that they, however, signify as present in the world to men if men struggle to approach them.

140. For an excellent description of this species of myth, see M. Eliade, *Myth and Reality*, trans. Trask (New York, 1963), 67, 134–138, 176.

141. He shows, that is to say, a loyalty to (not necessarily a belief in) the ideals of reason and freedom that were vanishing as the consensus of his fellows about their validity vanished. He shows a patriotism that it would be both heartless and stupid to ridicule, even as it is heartless and stupid to ridicule that patriotism, that grieving nostalgia, in Cicero: *nec vero dubitat agricola, quamvis sit senex, quaerenti cui serat respondere: 'dis immortalibus, qui me non accipere modo haec a maioribus voluerunt, sed etiam posteris prodere'* (*De senectute* 25); *neque me vixisse paenitet, quoniam ita vixi, ut non frustra me natum existimem, et ex vita ita discedo tamquam ex hospitio, non tamquam e domo; commorandi enim divorsorium nobis, non habitandi dedit* (84). By the time these words were written, few Romans will have failed to learn the *arcanum imperii*: "that its [*res publica*] rulers and chief beneficiaries no longer seriously believed in it. . . . A generation later it became clear that they and their sons were no longer willing to defend what their rulers had so shamelessly abandoned." Badian's elegant description of the aftermath of Sulla's victory (*Roman Imperialism in the Late Republic* [Ithaca, 1968], 80) suggests the reason for Cicero's despairing idealism and for Vergil's desperate loyalty to the lost ideals. By the time that Cicero wrote these words it was impossible, and by the time that Vergil wrote the *Aeneid* it seemed possible but unlikely that Romans could really understand—much less live by—the selflessness, the humility, the decency, and the joy that shine through these words and radiate from most of Aeneas' actions. That does not mean that the ideals were lacking in reality; they could, for instance, inspire the homage and the anxiety of Vergil.

142. In Vergil's poetry the objects of fear and the pity he feels for himself and for us in the contemplation of what endangers us are delicately veiled in the pastorals; in the *Georgics* the great dangers are only partially concealed, moving into greater and greater prominence. In the *Aeneid* (again, a good comparison is offered by the *Iliad*) the moments of respite between visions of hazard are fairly rare, and the intense epiphanies of dread, combined with the rarity of conversations and debates between the actors (which ease the sense of isolated anxiety, bad solitude, which is a Vergilian hallmark), drench the poem with apprehension.

143. See Eliade (n. 140), 132–134.

144. *Ode on a Distant Prospect of Eton College*, 91 ff.

145. Their rhetoric and diction are no longer to our taste, but Conway's pages on Vergilian *caritas* (n. 3, 109–112) are still well worth reading.

146. St.-John Perse, *Poésie.*